Affairs of the Hearth

Victorian poetry and domestic narrative

ROD EDMOND

ROUTLEDGE
LONDON AND NEW YORK

First published in 1988 by
Routledge
a division of Routledge, Chapman and Hall
11 New Fetter Lane, London EC4P 4EE

Published in the USA by
Routledge
a division of Routledge, Chapman and Hall, Inc.
29 West 35th Street, New York NY 10001

©1988 Rod Edmond

Printed in Great Britain at the University Press,
Cambridge

All rights reserved. No part of this book may be
reprinted or reproduced or utilized in any form or
by any electronic, mechanical or other means, now
known or hereafter invented, including
photocopying and recording, or in any information
storage or retrieval system, without permission in
writing from the publishers.

British Library Cataloguing in Publication Data
Edmond, Rod
Affairs of the hearth : Victorian
poetry and domestic narrative.
1. English poetry—19th century—History
and criticism
I. Title
821'.8'09   PR591

ISBN 0-415-00656-2

Library of Congress Cataloging in
Publication Data
Edmond, Rod.
Affairs of the hearth : Victorian poetry and
domestic narrative / Rod Edmond.
         p.   cm.
Bibliography: p.
Includes index.
ISBN 0-415-00656-2 (U.S.)
1. English poetry—19th century—History and
criticism. 2. Narrative poetry, English—History
and criticism. 3. Family in literature. I. Title.
PR599.N3E35 1988
821'.03'09355—dc19

*For Sarah, Cass, Daisy, and Jo,
protagonists in a contemporary
narrative*

CONTENTS

	Preface	vii
1.	Introduction	1
2.	The 'celled-up dishonour of boyhood': Clough's *The Bothie of Toper-na-Fuosich*	44
3.	'A sweet disorder in the dresse': Tennyson's *The Princess*	90
4.	'A printing woman who has lost her place': Elizabeth Barrett Browning's *Aurora Leigh*	130
5.	Who needs men? Christina Rossetti's *Goblin Market*	170
6.	'Turbid pictures': George Meredith's *Modern Love*	204
7.	Conclusion	240
	Index	251

PREFACE

This book is concerned with the ubiquity of family narratives in the Victorian period. It deals with a cluster of related themes and subjects which recur in these narratives – gender, sexuality, love, marriage, the role of women, parent–child relations, adolescence – and sees them as aspects of a more basic preoccupation with the institution and ideology of the middle-class family.

A word needs to be said about the book's organization. The opening chapter provides the context within which the following text-centred chapters are discussed. These chapters, in their turn, take up and develop aspects of the introductory chapter. Thus Chapter 2, on Clough's *The Bothie*, is concerned with adolescent male sexuality and cross-class marriage; Chapter 3, on Tennyson's *The Princess*, with gender and marriage; Chapter 4, on Barrett Browning's *Aurora Leigh*, with women, gender, and writing; Chapter 5, on Christina Rossetti's *Goblin Market*, with adolescent female sexuality, and illness; and Chapter 6, on Meredith's *Modern Love*, with the closed circle of middle-class marriage. A number of themes are common to more than one of these works. Parent–child relations, for example, are important in every text except *Modern Love*. Gender is a central issue in at least three of the main poems. Sexuality is never far from the surface of any of them. And common to each is a preoccupation with the middle-class family and domestic ideology, the large subject of this book.

The main texts discussed are all narrative poems with formal similarities to other kinds of Victorian narrative which explored family and domestic matters. I refer frequently to other writing and also painting of the period, sometimes developing more detailed and lengthy comparisons. *The Bothie* chapter, for example, encloses sections on *Tom Brown's Schooldays* and the diaries of Arthur Munby and Hannah Cullwick. Such comparisons allow me to broaden the subject under discussion, and in several chapters these dilations become mini essays. *The Princess* chapter has a section on transvestism in Victorian writing, and the *Goblin Market* chapter has one on female wasting illnesses. In other words, although the main texts are examined individually and in some detail, I have tried to situate them within a larger discourse on the family and domestic ideology which had become of central importance by the middle of the nineteenth century.

Why should it have become of such importance? There are two main kinds of answer to this question. The first concentrates on how the middle-class family became the focus of many things Victorian culture found disturbing. This emphasizes the social consequences of industrialization and urbanization, and the ideological consequences of secularization. In an age of unprecedented social tensions and antagonism the family became an image of reconciliation and transcendence, its comforting sameness offering assurance in the midst of uncertainty. There is nothing intrinsically wrong with this kind of explanation, and it is in fact an underlying assumption of this book. It is, however, too general to be of much use in any detailed study and has resulted in the *image* of the hearth-bound, complacent, and hypocritical Victorian bourgeois family being taken as an historically accurate description. My own approach is much more from within the history and sociology of the family. It tries to see behind the images of domestic sweetness and light, to trace some of the shifts, tensions, and contradictions of Victorian family life and to show how these were represented in the writing and painting of the period. In doing so I hope to show that images of family life were more complex and various than is often thought. This has involved me in the recent historiography of the family and has brought me into conflict with the work of Linda Pollock on the history of childhood (see Ch. 1) and that of Alan Macfarlane on marriage (see Ch. 6). Historians will no doubt think I have strayed into areas beyond my competence. These matters, however, seem to me too important to be left entirely to historians.

Preface

Each of the chapters, except for the opening one, has a similar structure, although this varies occasionally to meet the particular requirements of the text under discussion. The opening section has a summary of the narrative and a discussion of the poem's form. Later sections look closely at the poem itself, and then try to draw out its wider significance by developing connections with other related texts. In doing so I hope to show how *active* these poems were, in their relation to each other, to previous and subsequent writing, and to other areas of social and political practice. I am also interested in how they have been reactivated in recent years and why they are being reread today.

This book is a symptom of that renewed activity and, I hope, a contribution to the rereading of these texts. It falls, I know, between several stools, a consequence of trying to sit on more than one. For picking me up, dusting me off, and encouraging me to try again, I am grateful to Claire Buck for help with Chapter 4, and Kate McLuskie for help with Chapter 5. I would also like to thank the English Department staff–student seminar at the University of Auckland for responding so usefully to my early thoughts on these matters; Lynn Nead for suggestions and encouragement in writing about Victorian painting; and Tony Skillen, with whom I once taught a first-year course which set me thinking along these lines. My thanks to Kate, and also to Andrea, Mary, Michele, and Rita at H. & H. for all their work.

1
Introduction

I

Victorian writing is full of family tableaux. In Tennyson's poem 'Enoch Arden' (1864), Enoch is shipwrecked and marooned for more than ten years before being rescued. He returns home to discover that his wife Annie, convinced he must be dead, has married Philip, an old childhood friend and former suitor. Enoch peers in through the window of their home – his former home – and we see a snug domestic scene:

> For cups and silver on the burnished board
> Sparkled and shone; so genial was the hearth:
> And on the right hand of the hearth he saw
> Philip, the slighted suitor of old times,
> Stout, rosy, with his babe across his knees;
> And o'er her second father stoopt a girl,
> A later but a loftier Annie Lee,
> Fair-haired and tall, and from her lifted hand
> Dangled a length of ribbon and a ring
> To tempt the babe, who reared his creasy arms,
> Caught at and ever missed it, and they laughed;
> And on the left hand of the hearth he saw
> The mother glancing often toward her babe,
> But turning now and then to speak with him,
> Her son, who stood beside her tall and strong,
> And saying that which pleased him, for he smiled.
> (ll. 738–53)

Tennyson's original title for the poem was 'Idylls of the Hearth' (*Idylls of the King* had appeared in 1859). The hearth is the centrepiece of this scene, Godlike, with Philip on its right hand, Annie on its left. Around it Enoch sees his daughter, the image of his wife as he once knew her, and his former self, in the figure of his tall strong son. The scene is a piece of literary genre painting, related in composition and theme to many Victorian genre pictures.

It combines two common subjects of mid-nineteenth-century painting: family rituals, and the father returning home from work, war, or sea.[1] Frith's 'Many Happy Returns of the Day' (1856), in which the painter used members of his own family in depicting a birthday celebration, is a well-known example of the first kind. In 'returning home' paintings the wife either lovingly greets her husband or waits patiently or anxiously for him. Henry Nelson O'Neil's 'Home Again' (1858), a sequel to 'Eastward Ho! August 1857', which had shown soldiers leaving for India during the Mutiny, depicts returning soldiers disembarking and being reunited with their families. Like many other public scenes in Victorian painting, the packed canvas divides into different family groups. The main focus is on a wounded sergeant being helped ashore while his anxious young wife follows carrying his crutches; she will now be able to take over from them. In Christopher Wood's *Victorian Panorama*, Jane Maria Bowkett's 'Preparing Tea' and Joseph Clarke's 'The Labourer's Welcome' are presented as companion pieces.[2] In both paintings the wife awaits the return of her husband from work; tea is laid, and children or pets add to the welcome of the hearth. The similarities between Bowkett's middle-class drawing-room and Clarke's well scrubbed working-class cottage interior are striking. It is as if the painters had together set out to show the seamlessness of family life underlying the apparent class divisions of mid-nineteenth-century Britain.

Comparison with these paintings helps to show what is wrong with the tableau from 'Enoch Arden'. There is no welcome for Enoch; he is shut out from his own family. His wife no longer waits patiently for his return; she has remarried and he has been replaced. The happy domestic scene is extremely fragile, a cardhouse which at Enoch's reappearance would collapse. Enoch turns away from his former home. Not to do so would 'shatter all the happiness of the hearth' (1.766). To reappear would be to convict his wife of bigamy and taint the 'creasy-armed' babe with

Plate 1   Henry Nelson O'Neil, 'Home Again', 1859

illegitimacy.[3] It would destroy the scene as surely as David Copperfield and Steerforth's entrance 'instantaneously dissolved' the 'little picture' inside Mr Peggotty's house-boat on the night little Em'ly and Ham announced their engagement. Steerforth has no compunction about destroying the happy family scene; Enoch refuses to do so.[4]

There is another family tableau in Dickens's *Dombey and Son* (1848). Florence Dombey, her mother long dead, her brother Paul recently dead, and rejected by her father, spends many hours in the deserted drawing room of her own home looking across at the windows of the house opposite, observing family life of a kind she has never enjoyed. The family opposite is a saddened happy family – a father, four daughters, but no mother. Their motherless state is a point of identification for Florence, and their loving, caring father a point of identification she wishes she could make:

> When he had dined, she could see them, through the open windows, go down with their governess or nurse, and cluster round the table; and in the still summer weather, the sound of their childish voices and clear laughter would come ringing across the street, into the drooping air of the room in which she sat. Then they would climb and clamber upstairs with him, and romp about him on the sofa, or group themselves at his knee, a very nosegay of little faces, while he seemed to tell them some story. Or they would come running out into the balcony; and then Florence would hide herself quickly, lest it should check them in their joy, to see her in her black dress, sitting there alone.[5]

The method of presentation is again strongly pictorial. Florence poses no threat to this family, but like Enoch she is careful not to be observed in her watching. To see her in mourning would remind them of their own loss. Although much less vulnerable than in the previous example, the happiness observed again seems tender and fragile.

Florence is particularly interested in the eldest daughter. She watches her waiting at the drawing-room window for her father's return, occupying the same position as the waiting wife in Bowkett's 'Preparing Tea'. Florence observes her sitting up with her father after the younger children have gone to bed:

> – happy little house-keeper she was then! – and sat conversing with him, sometimes at the window, sometimes in the room, though she was some years younger than Florence; and she could be as staid and pleasantly demure, with her little book or work-box, as a woman.[6]

This is one of many examples in Dickens's writing in which family relationships are transposed. This daughter, wife to her father, is mid-way towards the later example of Amy and William Dorrit in which the daughter mothers her father. For Florence, however, the sight of this father–daughter relationship uncovers everything she most wants and is denied: 'But when the time came for the child to say "Good-night, Papa," and go to bed, Florence would sob and tremble as she raised her face to him, and could look no more.'[7] Florence's father-hunger makes the sight too painful to bear, and like Enoch she turns away, shut out from the heart's-ease of family life pictured by the 'rosy children' opposite.

My third tableau is from *Wuthering Heights*. Cathy and Heathcliff, attracted by the lights of the Grange, peer in at the Linton's drawing-room window. The immediate contrast is between the privations of their home at the Heights and the plush interior of this drawing-room. Heathcliff describes the scene to Nelly:

> – ah! it was beautiful – a splendid place carpeted with crimson, and crimson-covered chairs and tables, and a pure white ceiling bordered by gold, a shower of glass-drops hanging in silver chains from the centre, and shimmering with little soft tapers. Old Mr and Mrs Linton were not there. Edgar and his sister had it entirely to themselves; shouldn't they have been happy? We should have thought ourselves in heaven![8]

The setting is that for another tableau of domestic tranquillity, but the human reality is very different. Heathcliff fills in the picture:

> Isabella . . . lay screaming at the farther end of the room, shrieking as if witches were running red-hot needles into her. Edgar stood on the hearth weeping silently, and in the middle of the table sat a little dog shaking its paw and yelping, which, from their mutual accusations, we understood they had nearly pulled in two between them.[9]

The reality of middle-class family life is exposed. The household pet, an important prop of the domestic ideal in Clarke's 'The

Labourer's Welcome', has become the victim of a petty, malicious squabble. The scene demystifies this domestic ideal and compels agreement with Heathcliff's conclusion: 'I'd not exchange, for a thousand lives, my condition here, for Edgar Linton's at Thrushcross Grange – not if I might have the privilege of flinging Joseph off the highest gable, and painting the housefront with Hindley's blood!'[10] Heathcliff prefers his own wretched existence with Hindley to what he has seen. Whereas Enoch and Florence are at pains not to be observed in their watching, Cathy and Heathcliff's contempt for the young Lintons leads them to disrupt the scene. Their scornful laughter is heard by the children who are then taunted and terrified by more frightful noises coming from outside the window. Derision has replaced reverence.

Although this episode from *Wuthering Heights* is notably free of any sentimentalization of home and hearth, these three scenes have a number of things in common. Each is realized pictorially. There is a structural similarity in that the observer, and the reader, have their face pressed against a window, spying on a family scene unobserved. Peter Conrad has described the Victorian genre painter as a peeping Tom, spying through keyholes,[11] and writers and painters shared a fascination with what went on behind the closed doors and drawn curtains of Victorian houses. Most painters, in fact, remove a wall to show us what is happening inside. In these scenes I have been discussing the writers leave us outside the room peering in at the window. This point of view from outside is important. The observers are excluded; Enoch from returning to his own family, Florence from family life with her own father, and Heathcliff gratefully. In the case of Florence and Cathy, this exclusion is emphasized by the fact they are in mourning, Cathy for her father and Florence for her brother. Heathcliff, too, has been 'orphaned' by Mr Earnshaw's death. Finally, none of these families is orthodox, complete or entirely happy. In 'Enoch Arden' the ideal is fragile and insecure. In *Dombey and Son* the family is motherless, and this makes it vulnerable to any glimpse of Florence in her mourning dress. And in *Wuthering Heights* this friable ideal is exposed. The orphaned Cathy, and Heathcliff whose origins are unknown, both suffering from Hindley's vindictiveness, are better off than the gently raised Linton children.

These three scenes suggest something rather obvious about

Introduction

Victorian writing which is nevertheless often ignored when generalizations are made about the Victorian family and domestic ideology. There are very few durable happy families in Victorian literature. General studies of the period depict the Victorian home as a peaceful, even sacred, place, a haven in a heartless world. Walter Houghton's influential study *The Victorian Frame of Mind* is of this kind. Houghton represents Victorian writers as showing the home and family as the fount of all goodness and a storehouse of moral and spiritual values.[12] Ruskin's famous definition in *Sesame and Lilies* is quoted, and his lecture 'Of Queens' Gardens' is described as 'the most important single document ... for the characteristic idealization of love, woman, and the home in Victorian thought'.[13] But a glance at almost any Victorian novel, narrative poem, or domestic melodrama shows that this idealization is less than half the picture. Victorian writing is full of unhappy homes, appalling families, and the break-up of happy homes and families. *Mary Barton* and *The Mill on the Floss* are just two, very different kinds of novel, in which cheerful, functioning families disintegrate and are unable to be reconstituted. David Copperfield loses his father before he is born, his mother soon after, acquires wicked step-parents and runs away, passing through a series of homes which are miserable or broken. The few good families he meets are fragile. The Peggottys are destroyed by Steerforth; the Micawbers can find no home in Britain and must travel to Australia to find one. The novel's final picture of David as a happy family man is overshadowed by everything that has come before. All of Charlotte Brontë's heroines are orphans who have to go out in search of homes and create their own families, if they can. The great Victorian novel of family life is surely *Wuthering Heights*, a narrative of relentless domestic violence and conflict within and between families. There is no need to go on. The picture of family life and domestic ideology which emerges from Houghton's book – the angel in the house, rearing her family, yielding to her husband's sexual demands at decently spaced intervals, tending his soul while the family capital accumulates from his efforts in the world outside – is quite obviously contradicted by a cursory examination of a few Victorian novels.

A similar thing happens in much of the writing about Victorian painting. The proliferation of narrative paintings on domestic subjects in the nineteenth century is striking, but most art historians have stressed the complacency of this work. Raymond Lister describes it as 'an escapist art', distorting reality and providing the bourgeoisie with its comforting parables.[14] Christopher Wood claims that most of these paintings extol the joys of domestic happiness, and in so far as misfortune is admitted, it is only shown as drawing families closer together.[15] Peter Conrad accuses Victorian narrative paintings of evasion, and contrasts their truth to detail with their desertion of truth in larger matters.[16] Melvin Waldfogel sneers gently at the self-assurance with which 'the affection and tender sentiments of the Victorian family' were depicted in these paintings.[17] Yet Waldfogel also points out how frequent was the theme of the dissolution of home and family, discussing Robert Martineau's 'The Last Day in the Old Home' (1861), which is also the cover picture of Conrad's book. Paintings as early as David Wilkie's 'Distraining for Rent' (1815) and as late as W.P. Frith's narrative series 'The Road to Ruin' (1877–8) attest to this. Indeed, as Martin Meisel has argued, the sin against domesticity, in the form of prostitution or adultery, was one of the two main subjects represented in modern life narrative paintings (the other was the urban crowd). He also argues that domestic anxieties of all sorts, with partings and reunions prominent, flourished in these paintings.[18] A list of some of the favourite themes of Victorian narrative paintings – broken vows, the long engagement, marital discord, the fallen woman, emigration (Ford Madox Brown's 'The Last of England' [1855] is a domestic narrative painting) – supports Meisel's claim.

This sample of art-historical comment on the domestic painting of the period is similar to the generalizations made by Houghton and others about Victorian writing on the family. There are such stubborn preconceptions about the Victorian period that contradictory evidence simply disappears when general formulations are made about its 'frame of mind'. Christopher Wood provides a spectacular example of this, claiming that Victorian painters showed 'an unwillingness to face up to unpleasant facts, such as poverty, death, deserted children, seduction'[19] while including many paintings on these subjects among his illustrations. And the only reason Ruskin should figure so prominently in Houghton's section 'Home, Sweet Home', and Emily Brontë not at all, is the title he has chosen for the section. For too long now Ruskin has

Introduction

been taken as the representative voice on these matters.

There can be no representative voice, nor can there be a single frame of mind ('The Late-Twentieth-Century Frame of Mind' wouldn't be a promising title). One must insist on voices, on debate and argument, on the questioning of normative values, even on a lack of consensus as to what was normative. The explanatory model used by many literary and art history commentators assumes that writers and painters simply express or reflect the dominant values of their period. Such a model is incapable of explaining the complex process of cultural production. At the very least we need an analytic model able to deal with contradiction and explain the simultaneous existence of different, often conflicting, values within a society. Raymond Williams has developed a model of this kind in his discussions of the Marxist concept of hegemony.[20] Williams, following Gramsci, defines hegemony as something more than the *conscious* system of ideas and beliefs imposed on a society by a dominant, hegemonic class; it is, 'the whole lived social process as practically organized by specific and dominant meanings and values ... which ... constitutes a sense of reality for most people in the society'.[21] Hegemony is neither static nor uniform, but active, formative, and transformational. It must be alert and responsive to anything which questions its dominance; it must continually be renewed, recreated, and defended, thereby sustaining and extending its power. No hegemony, however, can be total or exclusive. It is never organic; it is always full of contradictions and unresolved conflicts. For this reason Williams develops a model which can accommodate variation and contradiction, alternatives and change.

This involves the use of three categories: dominant, residual and emergent. By *dominant*, Williams means the central system of practices, meanings, and values which constitute the sense of reality for most people in a society at a particular time. The *residual* is those meanings and values formed in the past which are still active as an effective element of the present. The examples he gives – organized religion, the ideal of rural community, and the monarchy – are predominantly residual but still active constituents of the dominant culture. The first two examples also have a certain limited alternative or oppositional potential. The ideal of rural community, for instance, has formed an important element in the critique of urban industrial capitalism. The *emergent* is those new meanings, values, practices, and relationships which are continually being created. These are often difficult to distinguish from merely novel elements which are, in fact, some new phase of the dominant culture. Alternative or oppositional elements are often neutralized or incorporated by the hegemonic culture. Nevertheless in any society, especially in its class structure, there is always a social basis for independent, effective opposition to what is dominant. This is because any dominant culture must select from, and hence exclude, the full range of human practice: 'no mode of production and therefore no dominant social order and therefore no dominant culture ever in reality includes or exhausts all human practice, human energy, and human intention'.[22] This model needs to be used flexibly, as Williams's examples of residual elements makes clear. It will be necessary to differentiate within these categories, and to be aware of how they overlap and inform each other.[23] Residual and emergent are significant in themselves, but equally in what they reveal of the dominant.

In terms of this model it becomes clear that the attitudes and values commonly attributed to 'the Victorians' by literary critics and art historians are those of a dominant, male, middle-class culture. 'The Victorians' as a term ignores differences of class and gender, and furthermore assumes that all middle-class males related comfortably to this dominant culture. In the case of the family, domestic ideology, and related questions of gender and sexuality, we need to examine the ways in which a dominant ideology and set of practices struggled to sustain and extend its hegemony, the different kinds of challenge it confronted, and the ways in which these challenges were neutralized, marginalized, incorporated, or were unable to be met. Dominant, emergent, and residual jostle against each other. In Clough's *Bothie* we shall see how a residual set of values and practices relating to the family is turned against the dominant and also the limited oppositional potential of such residual forms. Elsewhere we shall see how a century commonly thought to have been a particularly repressive one for women saw, for example, important reforms in family law which mark the first erosion of male dominance within the family. In these and other instances, careful distinctions will need to be made between different kinds of emergent practice; between those which are genuinely emergent but incorporated, those which seem emergent but are actually complicit with the dominant culture, and those which persisted as active opponents.

Although no hegemony can be total, it is nevertheless the case that as capitalist society has developed, the dominant culture has penetrated further into the whole social and cultural process than ever before. Williams gives only the briefest and most general explanation of this.[24] A most suggestive account of this process is found in the work of Michel Foucault, in particular for the purposes of this study *La Volonté de Savoir*, translated as *The History of Sexuality* (Vol. 1). Foucault's later work centred on a critique of the idea that power operates primarily through repression and prohibition. He argued that power in the west in recent centuries has been concerned to generate forces, to make them grow so that they can be ordered, rather than to impede them and make them submit. In *The History of Sexuality* he argued that the relation of power to sexuality has not been one of suppression but of incitement and proliferation. Sexuality has not been disobedient to a power which has tried to subdue it but rather of great instrumentality to power and one of its main agencies.[25]

By challenging what he calls the 'repressive hypothesis' – the idea that sexuality was suppressed and driven into hiding during the nineteenth century – Foucault has overturned the commonly accepted view of the period. Williams's metaphor of penetration to describe how a dominant culture extends its hegemony is drawn from the repository of repressive language normally used to describe this process. Foucault's characteristic metaphors are those of excitation and seduction:

> The power which thus took charge of sexuality set about contacting bodies, caressing them with its eyes, intensifying areas, electrifying surfaces, dramatizing troubled moments. It wrapped the sexual body in its embrace. There was undoubtedly an increase in effectiveness and an extension of the domain controlled; but also a sensualization of power and a gain of pleasure . . . the pleasures discovered fed back to the power that enriched it. . . . Power operated as a mechanism of attraction; it drew out those peculiarities over which it kept watch. Pleasure spread to the power that harried it; power anchored the pleasure it uncovered.[26]

It is clear from this, as Alan Sheridan has said, that Foucault has not constructed an inverted, symmetrical version of the repressive hypothesis.[27] Foucault is not saying that power in bourgeois society is more tolerant or less effective, but that it operates differently.

A principal means of what Foucault termed this 'deployment of sexuality' was the 'incitement to discourse'. He noted, as other historians have, the proliferation of writing about sex in the eighteenth and nineteenth centuries. But whereas most historians concentrate on the moralism, evasions, and scruples of such writing, thereby fitting it into a repressive framework, for Foucault the important point is that medical, educational, criminal, literary, and other discourses felt compelled to speak about sex, to overcome their hesitations, to draw sex out into the open and examine it in ever proliferating ways.[28] From this point of view, the increasing amount of pornography produced in the eighteenth and nineteenth centuries is not the underbelly of prudery and sexual repression but a further example of the discursive explosion around sex in this period. Walter, the pseudonymous author of the eleven volumes of *My Secret Life*, recounting in tumid detail the events of a life wholly dedicated to sexual activity, is therefore not aberrant but representative. William Acton's *The Functions of Disorders of the Reproductive Organs in Youth, Adult Age, and Advanced Life Considered in their Physiological, Social, and Psychological Relations* (1857) – even the title has discursively exploded – is significant less for its admonitions and eschewals than for the fact that such a book was written, widely read, and frequently reprinted. Foucault outlines the determination of the agencies of power to have everything to do with sex passed through 'the endless mill of speech' in ever accumulating detail:

> One had to speak of sex; one had to speak publicly . . . one had to speak of it as a thing to be not simply condemned or tolerated but managed. . . . Sex was not something one simply judged; it was a thing one administered . . . it had to be taken charge of by analytical discourses.[29]

The focus of this deployment of sexuality, and the anchorage point for the proliferation of discourses around sexuality, was the middle-class family, which, Foucault insists, was far more than a monogamic and conjugal cell:

it was also a network of pleasures and powers.... The separation of grown-ups and children, the polarity established between the parents' bedroom and that of the children ... the relative segregation of boys and girls, the strict instructions as to the care of nursing infants ... the attention focused on infantile sexuality, the supposed dangers of masturbation, the importance attached to puberty, the methods of surveillance suggested to parents, the exhortations, secrets, and fears, the presence – both valued and feared – of servants: all this made the family, even when brought down to its smallest dimensions, a complicated network, saturated with multiple, fragmentary, and mobile sexualities.[30]

Foucault identified four main elements in this new deployment of sexuality. These were the medicalization of female sexuality, the problematization of infant and adolescent sexuality, regulation of the birth rate, and the classification of all deviations from genital heterosexuality ('perversions'). Each of these was specified and located within the bourgeois family, whose role was not so much to restrain sexuality as to anchor it, ensure its production, and provide it with a permanent support. The family, according to Foucault, was not primarily an agency of prohibition but a major factor of sexualization, indeed its most active site. Although the end was one of control and direction, the means was that of incitement rather than repression:

from the mid-nineteenth century onward, the family engaged in searching out the slightest traces of sexuality in its midst, wrenching from itself the most difficult confessions, soliciting an audience with everyone who might know something about the matter, and opening itself unreservedly to endless examination.[31]

This process was central to the emotional intensification of family life in the eighteenth and nineteenth centuries, to the fact that since this period the family has been the place where our strongest feelings of love and affection have arisen and been fostered.

Foucault sees the deployment of sexuality as decisive in the increasing hegemony of bourgeois culture during the nineteenth century, arguing that the bourgeoisie was creating its own sexuality, and with it a specific 'class body' whereby it was able to distinguish itself from other social classes. This 'class body' was characterized by its strength, health, and vigour, by self-affirmation rather than by the enslavement of itself and other classes:

> What was formed was a political ordering of life, not through an enslavement of others, but through an affirmation of self. And this was far from being a matter of the class which . . . became hegemonic believing itself obliged to amputate from its body a sex that was useless, expensive, and dangerous as soon as it was no longer given over exclusively to reproduction . . . on the contrary . . . it provided itself with a body to be cared for, protected, cultivated, and preserved from the many dangers and contacts, to be isolated from others so that it would retain its differential value.[32]

There are many problems with Foucault's arguments, some of which I have touched on (see notes 25 and 28), but nevertheless they seem to me extremely important. I had been studying and teaching the Victorian period for fifteen years before reading *The History of Sexuality*, and it was only when I did that many of the period's puzzling aspects started to become clearer, and I began to find ways of reading its literature which contradicted conventional wisdom without making me feel I was 'misreading'. I had wondered about a culture which was notorious for its silence about sex and yet which seemed to me deeply preoccupied with it. I had wondered about a period in which the ideals of domestic harmony and conjugal bliss were said to be celebrated everywhere, yet whose literature and painting so often dramatized domestic anxieties. And even when these ideals were celebrated, I wondered why they needed to be. Why, in other words, was something which everyone valued constantly examined, scrutinized and made the subject of so much writing in so many different fields?

It is Foucault's critique of the repressive hypothesis which I have found particularly illuminating. Most writing about the nineteenth century family, historical and sociological as well as literary and art historical, is held within an interpretative framework of repression and liberation. Lawrence Stone's study *The Family, Sex and Marriage in England 1500–1800* bases its arguments on the development of the family on a pendulum swing between repression and permissiveness. The rise of 'affective individualism' produced the closed, domesticated nuclear family, which Stone describes in the eighteenth century as relatively egalitarian, individualistic and companionate. There was then a swing back towards repression in the Victorian period with the re-emergence of the patriarchal family, a decline in the status of women, renewed authoritarianism in parent–child relationships, and the sexual repression of women and children. Our own century, according to Stone, has seen these trends reversed. Edward Shorter's *The Making of the Modern Family* offers a linear rather than a pendulum interpretation, and a different chronology from Stone's, but is also structured in terms of repression and liberation. What Shorter calls the 'surge of sentiment' – the growth of intimacy, the rise of companionate marriage, new respect for children – emerged between 1750 and 1850, was the principal ingredient of nineteenth-century domesticity, and was the crucial step on the way to contemporary enlightenment which has added a more liberated attitude to sex to these ingredients. This is a more sophisticated version of Houghton's Whig account of 'the Victorians'. Both regard the past from a position of liberated superiority, but Shorter sets the beginnings of liberation back in the nineteenth century itself.[33]

Macro-historical explanations from within a repression–liberation framework tell us more about what the authors regard as liberated and repressed than anything else. In the history of childhood, for example, there are many points of agreement between Philippe Ariès and Lloyd de Mause's account of changes in the treatment of, and attitudes to, children.[34] Both agree that our concept of childhood is an invention – de Mause would probably prefer 'discovery' – of the modern period. For Ariès, this was a central element in the increasingly repressive nature of the bourgeois family; the closer interest taken in children involved a reduction of their freedom. For de Mause, these new attitudes to children are evidence of improved levels of care and greater empathy between parents and children. Very similar evidence is used to support diametrically opposed arguments.

It is also difficult for a repression–liberation model to handle contradictions. Stone's insistence that the nineteenth century saw a decline in the status of women leaves him unable to explain the 1857 divorce act and the later married women's property acts

(1870 and 1882). He can only say that they were an 'important exception to the drift of patriarchy'.[35] A number of questions follow from this. Why should Parliament, that fount and symbol of patriarchy, introduce limits on male power? How important were these exceptions? Are they important enough to modify the picture of a drift to patriarchy? None of these questions is easily answered from within the explanatory framework Stone uses. Williams's understanding of hegemony, and his categories of dominant, emergent, and residual, on the other hand, allow us to begin to interpret changes in family law in ways that take account of their complex history. This does not rule out differences of interpretation. It is possible to see these reforms as the result of a dominant system incorporating emergent elements. It is possible to see them as a result of emergent practices which managed to resist, partly at least, the attempt to incorporate them. There are further possible interpretations, but my point is that this kind of model escapes the limits of the repression–liberation one which has dogged even sophisticated studies of the Victorian period.

It also avoids the lofty, sometimes amused, condescension with which modern commentators have looked back on the Victorian era, and allows us to understand the deep continuities between the nineteenth century and our own period, as well as the superficial differences. Nineteenth-century family narratives were different in kind from those which preceded them; they are remarkably similar to our own.

There is a pervasive interest in family and domestic matters in nineteenth-century writing and painting. There is also widespread use of narrative forms in painting and poetry, as there is self-evidently in fiction and drama. My interest in this study is to explore the conjunction of these two things, primarily in narrative poetry, to a lesser extent in painting, and with fiction playing a supporting role. Some of the ground for this has been finely prepared by Martin Meisel's elegant and compendious work, *Realizations: Narrative, Pictorial, and Theatrical Arts in Nineteenth-Century England*, which did not appear in this country until my work was well advanced. Meisel's subject is the collaborative narrative-pictorial style, the formal similarities and shared expressive and narrative conventions of nineteenth-century fiction, painting, and drama. He tracks the dialogue of literary and pictorial forms, the alliance of narrative and picture, and describes

Introduction

a representational art which cut across medium and genre and constituted a common style. Poetry figures infrequently, and the narrative poems I am interested in not at all, but there is an opening acknowledgement of the connections between the long narrative poem and prose fiction.[36]

My interest is in how this narrative-pictorial style was used to explore family and domestic matters, particularly in relation to poetry. Meisel casts his net much wider and is not solely concerned with domestic narratives. Nevertheless, he not only gives full weight to the importance of the domestic strain in the common style he is exploring but also shows how ubiquitous this strain was. History painting, for example, was scaled down to domestic requirements, becoming anecdotal and familiar, a hybrid form of narrative and genre painting rather than an epic vehicle.[37] O'Neil's 'diptych', referred to earlier, is an example of this hybrid. Nautical melodrama had a strong domestic element, usually involving a threat to conjugal happiness.[38] Its dominant motif, the shipwreck, widely used as an image of psychological, social, or metaphysical disaster in the iconography of the period, was full of domestic implications. Shipwreck separated Enoch Arden from his family,[39] condemned Lucy Snowe to spinsterhood, avenged the Peggotty family, and in the form of Clarkson Stanfield's painting 'The Abandoned' (1855–6), figured on the wall of the violated home in Egg's triptych 'Past and Present' (1858). Another dominant motif of the period which Meisel notes was frequently domesticated was the prison scene.[40] The accused, imprisoned criminal, with his family waiting, wondering, or forgiving, is, Meisel suggests, the male counterpart of the Victorian fallen woman.[41] He examines configurations of the prisoner in Holman Hunt's 'Claudio and Isabella' (1850–3), Millais' 'The Order of Release, 1746' (1853) – another historical-domestic hybrid – Solomon's 'Waiting for the Verdict' (1857), and Egg's illustration for Tom Moore's 'Come, Rest in this Bosom' (1855). *Little Dorrit* (1855–7), with its contrasts and transpositions between prison and domestic settings, is overwhelmingly of this kind; *A Tale of Two Cities* (1859) is another. Meisel in fact picks out a scene from *Little Dorrit* which is another tableau of the kind I examined at the opening of this chapter. Released from the Marshelsea, and now touring Italy in grand style, William Dorrit one evening observes his brother and younger daughter. He looks in through a draped doorway and sees the framed image of a scene from which he has been displaced. His brother and his daughter are sitting together:

> ... he, with his chair drawn to the hearth, enjoying the warmth of the evening wood fire; she seated at a little table, busied with some embroidery work. Allowing for the great difference in the still-life of the picture, the figures were much the same as of old; his brother being sufficiently like himself to represent himself, for a moment, in the composition. So had he sat many a night, over a coal fire far away; so had she sat, devoted to him.[42]

Meisel's book brings out the ways in which nineteenth-century writing and painting assimilated an extraordinarily wide range of subjects to its central concern with the family.

The preoccupation with family and domestic matters extended beyond the middle classes. Martha Vicinus has shown that the family was the most common subject of dialect literature in the mid and late nineteenth century.[43] Edwin Waugh's 'Come Whoam to Thy Childer and Me' is a classic example. Printed in 1856 as a penny broadside it sold 20,000 copies within a few days and was widely reprinted on calendars, in church bulletins, temperance pamphlets, anthologies, and newspapers. It had a temperance theme but its primary emphasis was on the positive values of home. Vicinus claims that Waugh's celebration of the family was echoed everywhere in dialect literature, with its characteristic subjects of the contentments of family and hearth, happy family Sunday outings, and the family as a refuge from a harsh outside world. But she also shows that here, as elsewhere, it is not just the sentimental domestic vein which is found. There were also tough, detailed accounts of hard-won domestic security, humorous and sardonic treatments of courting and marriage, and parodies of the sentimental vein like Ben Brierley's parody of Waugh, 'Go, Tak' thi Ragg'd Childer an' Flit'. Again there is a multiplicity of voices, a lack of any single point of view. While it is true that during the nineteenth century there was a colonization of the working classes by middle-class family values, it is also true that these were often resisted. Lord Ashley's speeches on married women's employment during the factory debates of the 1840's are a rich source of evidence of this concern to organize working-class families according to middle-class norms.[44] If the sentiments and popu-

Introduction

larity of Waugh's poem suggests that middle-class values had extended to the working class, parodies such as Brierley's can perhaps be seen as indications of resistance to this process.

To summarize, the family became the focus of many things Victorian culture regarded as central and disturbing. It was the eye of the storm quite as much as it was a safe harbour. Foucault's picture of the family as a complex network of pleasures and powers, the site for the development of sexuality, and the arena within which fundamental issues were contested, opens up the subject of the Victorian middle-class family in ways I want to explore in the chapters which follow. Foucault's idea of a discursive explosion around sex and the family, and the proliferation of narratives is another emphasis I want to carry forward. In my examination of specific poems I shall also use related, overlapping, supporting and conflicting texts on family and domestic ideology as further points of reference in a whole discourse on these matters. And more generally I shall work within the broad terms of Foucault's recognition of the constant struggles within definitions of family norms, gender roles, and sexuality. As Williams's understanding of hegemony as a complex, contradiction-riven formation also helps to make clear, the attempt to categorize, organize, and control these matters simultaneously produces points of opposition and challenge. And in so far as Jeffrey Weeks and others are right in suggesting that Foucault has failed to understand the conditions of existence of these social practices in terms of concrete historical, social, economic, and ideological situations, I shall make use of the categories Williams has provided for specific social and historical analysis.[45] I don't intend to examine the poems which form the body of this work in terms of a mechanical or systematic application of these ideas and categories. Rather, I want to use this general emphasis derived from Williams and Foucault to try to read and place some highly sophisticated writing on the subject of family and domestic ideology in terms of a larger, conflictive discourse on these matters.

II

First, however, I must look more closely at what was happening to the middle-class family in the nineteenth century. For the nonspecialist the history of the family is a can of worms. My comfort is that this seems true for the specialist as well.

Michael Anderson has distinguished three main approaches to family history: the demographic, the sentiments, and the household-economics approaches.[46] The *demographic approach*, associated with the work of Peter Laslett and the Cambridge Group for the History of Population and Social Structure, has been concerned with the size and structure of households – in particular the relatively unchanging nature of a dominant nuclear household structure over many centuries – and has little relevance to this study. This approach has largely ignored those non-quantifiable aspects of family life – how it was understood and experienced, the meanings and expectations associated with it – which are my concern. As Anderson has pointed out, knowledge of the size and composition of households does not necessarily tell us a great deal about family life.[47] Association football, for example, has been played between teams of eleven members for well over a century, but the game itself – attitudes to it, values associated with it, its economic structure – has changed enormously. Nor does a focus on the household tell us much about how family behaviour related to other aspects of social life, another concern of my study.[48]

The *household-economics approach*, of which the anthropologist Jack Goody is a leading British exponent, is concerned with the social processes underlying family structure, which are seen as determining family behaviour.[49] This work has concentrated on matters such as the laws and customs of inheritance, the family economy of the peasantry, and the proletarianization of labour. Its main interest has been in the family as a productive unit, and its relation to a larger economic structure. Again, it has little relevance for my purposes. I am interested in the middle-class family at precisely the point when it was ceasing to be a production unit and becoming one in which reproduction and consumption were dominant. This is not to deny that the nineteenth-century middle-class family existed within an ultimately determining economic setting, but the relationship between this and middle-class family life was more mediated and complex than, for example, in the case of the industrial proletarian family, which was more directly affected by the changed conditions of life brought about by employment in large-scale capitalist work organization.[50]

Introduction   21

The *sentiments approach* is concerned with changes in meanings rather than structure, and in particular with the emergence of modern social and personal relationships.[51] This approach is clearly the most appropriate for my purposes. One of its leading examples, although it overlaps with that of the other two schools, is Jean-Louis Flandrin's *Families in Former Times*. Flandrin starts with changing dictionary definitions of the word 'family'. Seventeenth- and eighteenth-century dictionaries define family as either a whole household, including servants, or a whole kinship group, including non-residents. Only in the early nineteenth century are these concepts of kinship and co-residence conflated into a single definition approximating to our contemporary understanding of the primary meaning of the word.[52] In other words, the concept of the family as a father–mother–child triad, distinct from a relation with kindred or domestic staff, had not developed much before the nineteenth century. Flandrin goes on to argue that the family in earlier centuries was linked to society by many ties of solidarity based on neighbour and kin. Between the sixteenth and nineteenth centuries these ties were broken, but family solidarity survived and was strengthened, emerging as the fundamental unit in a culture where most services are bought or sold, or provided by the state.[53]

Stone gives a similar account: 'The key definition of the nuclear family is that the ties that bind its members together are stronger than those which bind any one member to outsiders, whether relatives, friends, associates or patrons'.[54] This, he argues, has been the crucial change in family life since the eighteenth century. Professional, social, and private life have become increasingly separate, and the family has become closed to relations, friends, neighbours, associates, and servants. The apparent stability of residential form – the persistence of the nuclear family – 'conceals enormous changes in the reality of human relationships'.[55]

I now want to look in more detail at some of these 'enormous changes in the reality of human relationships', beginning with the home itself, the structure of the house rather than the household. Mr Wemmick's house in *Great Expectations* is the classic nineteenth-century literary expression of the division between public and private spheres which is at heart of the development of the family in recent times. Wemmick's home is literally a castle, with turrets, a drawbridge, a separate fortress, and a gun. When at work in the City he wears a kind of character armour which only comes off when he is safely home with the drawbridge pulled up behind him. Then he can relax and 'be himself'. Wemmick is probably literature's first suburban character, an early type of the commuter.

This polarization of the public and private is something historians have noted going on within the home as well as between the home and the world outside. Stone and Flandrin both have interesting sections on the changing interior architecture of upper- and middle-class houses in the seventeenth and eighteenth centuries. The specialization of rooms for sleeping, eating, conducting business, and so on, dates from this period, and with the introduction of corridors allowed the development of privacy within the home.[56] As rooms became more specialized and numerous the family began to achieve its independence within the home from servants and visitors.[57] This was followed by further segregation within the nuclear family itself, as first parents and children, and then brothers and sisters, slept apart, no longer sharing beds or even rooms. Children in wealthier homes had separate bedrooms by the nineteenth century.[58] This increased privacy for individual members of the family was partly offset by a new emphasis on family rituals such as prayers, baptisms, and later birthdays and Christmas. There was a double emphasis, on privacy within the family but also on the family as a distinct, discrete unit, with its own patterns of collective behaviour.

The changing organization of space within the home was both cause and effect of other changes in the nature and meaning of family relationships which I shall consider next. It does however have a particular relevance to nineteenth-century writing and painting which made such frequent and varied use of domestic interiors. Some of the most resonant images in nineteenth-century writing are of figures in rooms or houses – Fanny Price in the unheated East room of Mansfield Park, Jane Eyre in the red-room, Mr Dombey and his house, Casaubon in his library. Examples are endless, as Charles Kingsley recognized when he wrote in *Alton Locke*, 'I have as yet given no description of the old eccentric's abode – an unpardonable omission, I suppose, in these days of Dutch painting and Boz'.[59] This nineteenth-century habit of using living quarters as an extension of the character who inhabits them, so that they become what Michael Irwin calls an 'outer shell of personality'[60] is more than just an inevitable consequence of realism. In Hardy's novels, for instance, the characteristic image is a figure in a landscape rather than a room. This, of course, is because of the predominantly rural, lower-class settings of Hardy's novels, where bourgeois practices and values have hardly infiltrated. The focus of life has not yet shifted indoors, with all that meant for the organization of space, differentiation of function, and privacy. Only when this has happened can writing and painting begin to use domestic interiors to suggest a symbiotic and expressive relationship between people and their homes. The separation of public and private space, corridors, doors, and keyholes, privacy and its transgression, opened up a new world to the writer and painter, a domestic continent waiting to be explored.

As the family became less open to the world around it, the marriage relationship was slowly redefined. One indicator of this is the control of marriage choice, which shifted away from parents and towards children. What this meant, broadly speaking, was that marriage became a union of individuals rather than families, with personal motives predominant. Companionate marriage slowly replaced economic or lineage marriage. There was nothing rapid or absolute about this shift. Personal choice would normally be made from within one's own class. Parental power would remain an important factor so long as parents controlled property or wealth vital to their children's future. Companionate marriage seems to have developed earlier in England and America than in Europe.[61] Eighteenth-century French observers were struck with the closeness of husbands and wives in England.[62]

A similar picture emerges from the literature of the period. Disputes between parents and children over marriage choice are more central in eighteenth- than nineteenth-century writing. There is no equivalent to *Clarissa* in the Victorian period, nor even, I think, to *Tom Jones*.[63] In *Mansfield Park* Fanny Price is under strong but not irresistible pressure to accept Henry Crawford. Her uncle, Sir Thomas Bertram, has divided feelings about his daughter's engagement to the respectable but stupid Mr Ashworth. He is concerned about Maria's happiness, but he does not want to throw away such an advantageous alliance. In the event, he sacrifices his judgement to his interests, thereby bearing some responsibilty for the ensuing family disgrace. The treatment of marriage in Austen's fiction is interestingly placed in terms of the shift from lineage to companionate marriage. Neither personal nor family motives are allowed too much dominance. The marriage of Emma and Mr Knightly is the paradigm. Here personal and social motives are finely balanced. Supporting their mutual affection and respect is the fact that Hartfield and Donwell are adjoining estates; their eldest male offspring will inherit both. In *Middlemarch*, Dorothea's preference for Casaubon to Sir James Chettam is regarded as odd, but she is left free to make up her own mind. Her garrulous uncle for once sums up rather succinctly the position as it stood by the mid-nineteenth century:

> Chettam is a good match. And our land lies together. I shall never interfere against your wishes, my dear. People should have their own way in marriage, and that sort of thing – up to a certain point, you know. I have always said that, up to a certain point.[64]

Accompanying this changing pattern of marriage choice was a sentimentalization of the marriage relationship. Expectations of domestic happiness and conjugal friendship became dominant. This is not to suggest that marriages before the eighteenth century were devoid of feeling. Affection and compatibility must always have been welcome, and were no doubt often present, but they were a bonus and their absence did not spell the end of a marriage. Flandrin has argued that only recently has there been a widespread expectation of mourning the death of one's spouse.[65] My own work has uncovered very little domestic elegiac writing before the nineteenth century and a great deal of it since.[66]

Increased expectations of marriage as an institution created a new self-consciousness about its practices and values. From at least as early as the 1830s there was extensive public discussion of the marriage habits of the middle classes, with the issue of when to marry and how much to marry on especially prominent. Domestic economy rather than evolution was the science of the day. Books like J.H. Walsh's *A Manual of Domestic Economy; Suited to Families Spending from £100 to £1000 a Year* (1857), and magazines such as Mrs Beeton's *Englishwoman's Domestic Magazine*, proliferated, and the subject became more and more elaborate.[67] In 1857 *The National Magazine* announced that its regular feature 'The Home' would in future be divided into departments and placed under the care of specialist writers:

> The MORALS and CULTURE of Home will be dealt with by a LADY. The NATURALIST ... will be intrusted to the well-known author of ... *British Song-birds*. The HEALTH-LAWS and matters directly connected with them, such as VENTILATION have been placed under the charge of a PROFESSIONAL MAN. The articles on GARDENING and RURAL ECONOMY will be from the pen of SHIRLEY HIBBERD, author of 'A Happy Family' in the present number.[68]

In all this we can see the codification of middle-class norms and aspirations, and the production of that domestic ideology which had become dominant by mid-century. A crucial aspect of this was an increasingly sharp gender differentiation, with the ideal of domestic womanhood at its centre. The domestic manuals and guide books which began appearing in the 1830s and 1840s, such as those by Mrs Sandford and Mrs Ellis, emphasized that woman's proper place was the home.[69] Ray Strachey described these works as 'poisonous little books of moral maxims'[70] and argued that they had become necessary because the duty of female submissiveness was no longer being taken entirely for granted.[71] Jeffrey Weeks also sees this new domestic ideal and the conscious articulation of its ideology as a product of social crisis, the expression of a fear of social disintegration for which the breakdown of familial and sexual order had become a dominant metaphor. But he also sees it, and there is no necessary incompatibility here, in more Foucaultian terms as the self-expression and development of an increasingly dominant class.[72] Dominant classes necessarily have their fears.

This cult of domesticity, and the resistances it provoked, are found everywhere in Victorian writing. Women were confined to the home, cut off from productive activity, and held fast by the doctrine of sexual spheres which provided an elaborate ideological justification for this sexual division of labour. Christopher Lasch has argued that this confinement within the home as moral arbiters of the family actually gave women a new power base and enabled them to reshape the family in their own interests. Demands for married women's property rights, more equitable divorce laws, greater control in regulating the frequency of intercourse and pregnancy, and wider reforms in social justice and purity, all arose, he argues, out of the wife's moral tutelage of her husband and children. He discerns a dialectical interplay between domesticity and feminism, with feminism actually taking support from the ideology it seemed to challenge.[73] Although I disagree with Lasch's larger thesis about the family in *Haven in a Heartless World* and *The Culture of Narcissism*,[74] I find his argument here an interesting one. If Lasch is right, it is a good example of how contradiction is inevitably built into any attempt to establish hegemony. Even so, his argument does beg the question of whose interests the reforms he cites really served. Feminism, both pre- and post-Victorian, developed a far more radical critique of the family and women's role within it than any of the demands Lasch labels as feminist. Furthermore, women may well have extended their control over certain areas of family life without winning real power. Nevertheless Lasch does point to something significant, which I believe must have added to the strains and conflict within the nineteenth-century family. Patriarchy did not go unchallenged, and nor did it abdicate.

Another aspect of companionate marriage was the containment of sex within conjugality. Middle- and upper-class society in earlier centuries did not have the same expectation of monogamy; as Donzelot puts it, the sexual and the familial remained relatively separate.[75] However, as the marriage relationship slowly changed, the sexual and the familial merged. This is not to deny the reality of extra-marital sex in the nineteenth century, nor the intensified double standard which operated. It is a point about norms and expectations. These, however, must have influenced attitudes towards transgression – even one's own – and, to some extent, affected behaviour. Jeffrey Weeks has also related this new emphasis on sex within conjugality to the increasing preoccupation with 'perverse' and 'aberrant' sexualities. The more that the dominant ideology emphasized heterosexual monogamy, the more important it became to classify and regulate other forms of sexuality.[76]

Parent–child relations, it has been argued, underwent a similar transformation to marriage relations. The classic account of the development of our modern concepts of childhood and parenthood is Philippe Ariès' *L'Enfant et la Vie Famille sous l'Ancien Régime*, translated into English as *Centuries of Childhood*. According to Ariès, medieval and early modern society lacked any concept of childhood as a separate stage in the human life cycle. The child, once it had outgrown infancy and the need for constant care, became a member of adult society. By the seventeenth century, attitudes to childhood were changing. Children were coming to be seen as fragile beings whose growth and development needed protection, guidance, and correction. The crucial event in this change, Ariès argues, was the development of schooling. The duration of childhood extended as the school cycle lengthened. Children were now subjected to a kind of quarantine before being allowed to enter adult life. These new feelings and attitudes towards children developed further. The relationship between parent and child came to be seen as a unique one. The new solicitude of this relationship often took severe forms, but the severity of discipline was the product of an obsessive concern with their children which came to dominate parental attitudes from the eighteenth century onwards. By this time our modern concept of childhood had more or less evolved. Children were confined within an emotionally intense, intrusive, and closed nuclear family, their health and education the main preoccupation of their parents. The family, increasingly separate from the world of work, came to specialize in child-rearing and emotional solace, and the mother's sole happiness was now assumed to be in her children. Until recently most historians have accepted the broad lines of this account while making refinements and modifications for British society. Stone sees the eighteenth century as a turning point in the recognition of childhood as a period with its own distinctive requirements.[77] Shorter, with more vigour than subtlety, has described 'the ghastly slaughter of the innocents that was traditional child-rearing'.[78] 'Good mothering', he announces, 'is an invention of modernization'.[79] The 'invention of childhood' has passed into educated consciousness and has become an idea known by many who have never read Ariès' book.

Recently, serious questions have been raised about the Ariès thesis. Alan Macfarlane and Keith Wrightson have used evidence from seventeenth-century diaries to dispute that caring parent–child relationships are of recent origin.[80] Linda Pollock has developed the work of this revisionist school in her recently published attempt to refute the work of Ariès, Stone, and most others in the history of childhood. In *Forgotten Children: Parent–*

Child Relations from 1500 to 1900, she argues that the sources upon which the received view is based are suspect, and certainly not sound enough to warrant the 'grand theories' derived from them. She also finds many aspects of the Ariès thesis, in particular that there was no concept of childhood much before the eighteenth century, completely unjustified.[81] Pollock's work is based on the study of more than 400 American and British diaries and autobiographies written between the sixteenth and twentieth centuries. Some of these diaries were written by children or begun when the diarists were children. Most of the diarists were middle class. She concludes that there was a concept of childhood in the sixteenth century; that there were very few changes in parental care and child life in the home between the sixteenth and nineteenth centuries; that most children were not subjected to brutality; that parent–child relations were not formal and distant but close and intimate. She concedes a few changes – a slightly increased emphasis on the abstract nature of childhood and parental care, more parental self-consciousness about different modes of child care and rearing, and stronger parental demands for obedience and conformity in the early nineteenth century – but maintains that changes in attitude to children made very little difference to how they were actually treated. She concludes:

> ... there is no dramatic transformation in child-rearing practices in the 18th century. It is a myth brought about by over-hasty reading, a burning desire to find material to support the thesis and a wilful misinterpretation of evidence. Our method of child care ... appears to be an enduring one. Instead of trying to explain the supposed changes in the parent–child relationship, historians would do well to ponder just why parental care is a variable so curiously resistant to change.[82]

Pollock's study establishes less than she claims, which is hardly surprising given the extent of those claims and her scorn for almost everyone who has worked in this field. It is not at all clear that her own sources are any more convincing than those of the historians she attacks. The self-consciousness implicit in the writing of a diary or an autobiography makes it unsurprising that her diarists should reveal a degree of self-consciousness about relations with their parents or children. She has not established that they are representative. Her reading of these sources, and the use she makes of her own categories, is very literal and sometimes naïve. For example, her long chapter on discipline and control is almost entirely about corporal punishment. This is too narrow. She also takes no account of what is missing from these diaries. Role differentiation is ignored, presumably because the diaries don't mention it, and yet we know that boys and girls were treated differently and that this intensified during the nineteenth century. I am certain there must be material on this in the diaries even if it is not explicit. The questions Pollock asks are too narrowly defined by her sources, and she never attempts to explore what the diarists themselves took for granted. Sexuality is also ignored by Pollock. Should we conclude therefore that a concern with sexuality was entirely absent from parent–child relations? Sources which suggest otherwise are of the kind that Pollock tends to dismiss as concerned with attitudes rather than behaviour. But we know, for example, that the proliferating literature about masturbation from the mid-eighteenth century onwards did affect parents' behaviour. Alex Comfort's account of mechanical devices designed to set bells ringing throughout the house whenever little hands strayed, is lurid evidence of this.[83] Pollock's failure to consider sexuality is another example of the way she reports on her sources rather than interpreting them.

I am also suspicious of any historical account running over a number of centuries which concludes that virtually nothing has changed. This is surely an odd conclusion for an historian to come to – why should parent–child relations be immune from a process which has affected every other area of social life? This is the final question she flings at her opponents, but the onus is really on her to provide the answer.

Pollock's opening chapters on the historiography of childhood are most useful in bringing order to a field which has become overgrown. Many of her specific criticisms of other historians are valid and helpful. But her own, rather insistent case of 'no change' (itself a 'grand theory'), although correcting many of the excesses of the 'child abuse' school of childhood history, has not fundamentally shaken the argument that attitudes and behaviour to children changed as the nature of the family altered. This is the heart of Ariès' thesis. Whether or not one agrees with his diagnosis of the modern nuclear family, the history of its emergence as he and others have described it and the slow transformation of parent–child as well as husband–wife relations, remains intact.

There is no doubt that from around the beginning of the nineteenth century the child and childhood figured prominently in literature for the first time. 'Frost at Midnight', in which Coleridge addresses his sleeping baby, is a new kind of poem. (Indeed, the 'conversation poems' as a group treat and celebrate domesticity in a new way.) Many of Wordsworth's poems in *Lyrical Ballads* are the expression of a belief in the special nature of childhood, its unique view of experience and its moral authority. *The Prelude* rests on this. Other landmarks in this discovery and use of childhood in nineteenth-century literature are well known: *The Old Curiosity Shop*; the opening books of *David Copperfield* and *The Mill on the Floss; Alice in Wonderland* and *What Maisie Knew*. Literary 'evidence' is one thing; actual social behaviour another. But attitudes and behaviour are more complexly related than Pollock allows. The prominence given to childhood in nineteenth-century writing, to say nothing of the new, non-didactic forms of writing for children which developed during the century, is in tune with the general account of childhood given by Ariès and others.

To summarize, the Victorian middle-class family was, as Stone puts it, the first in history to be long-lasting and intimate.[84] Declining mortality rates and the difficulty of divorce meant that marriages lasted longer than before or since. When Dorothea Brooke returns to Lowick Manor after her honeymoon, the wintery view from the window of her boudoir is an image of the life that now stretches before her: '. . . she saw the long avenue of limes lifting their trunks from a white earth, and spreading white branches against the Sun and motionless sky. The distant flat shrank in uniform whiteness and low-hanging uniformity of cloud'.[85] Gwendolen Harleth, becalmed 'in well-bred silence' on the Mediterranean with the husband she is tempted to murder, is similarly placed.[86] Only the premature deaths of their husbands release Eliot's heroines from a living death.

In the nineteenth century fewer marriages ended prematurely by death than ever before. Children survived more often than they had in earlier centuries and were sent away from home less often. The nuclear family had become the focus for the emotional lives of all its members, and was increasingly self-conscious about its values and practices. By the middle of the nineteenth century it was engaged in deep self-examination and constantly writing narratives about itself.

III

In this century Victorian poetry has been rather squeezed out between Romanticism and Modernism, the main poetic revolutions of the last 200 years. In its own day it came to be overshadowed by the Victorian novel. Although there has been renewed academic interest in Victorian poetry over the last thirty years, the attitude of non-specialists and students is still close to that of early Modernism, itself part of a wider Edwardian reaction against Victorian culture. The legacy of Pound and Eliot is still with us.

For Pound, the nineteenth century had been 'a rather blurry, messy sort of period':[87] 'Thought was churned up by Darwin, by science, by industrial machines, Nietzsche made a temporary commotion, but these things are extraneous to our subject, which is the *art of getting meaning into words*'.[88] Nineteenth-century culture was inimical to poetry as Palgrave's *Golden Treasury* (1861) and the work of Tennyson illustrated: 'The British public liked, has liked, likes and always will like all art, music, poetry, literature, glass engraving, sculpture etc. in just such measure as it approaches the Tennysonian tone'.[89] Tennyson was the litmus test which a philistine English culture applied to all its art works. Browning was the only major Victorian poet, but he had spoiled even his best work by the intrusion of thought and ideas, by 'ratiocination and ... purely intellectual comment'.[90]

Eliot was less iconoclastic, but his general attitude was similar. The Victorian period was 'the epoch ... of *The Golden Treasury*, birthday albums and calendars with a poetical quotation for each day'.[91] He was more sympathetic to individual writers. Tennyson was treated as a major poet rather than a public monument to be derided. Arnold engaged his attention and divided his sympathies. But, like Pound, he felt there was something fundamentally wrong with English poetry, and that Victorian poetry was the culmination of centuries of bad habits.[92]

Despite their different preferences and emphases, Pound and Eliot were in general agreement about Victorian poetry. It had paid too much attention to meaning, and not enough to language and form. It was weighed down with opinion and moralizing. It was too discursive and imprecise, too soaked in public and social life, too conformist and official. It was also too insular – the dead end of a narrow tradition. All this, and more, they aimed to set right in their own poetry. These opinions have died hard. In 1950 Hardin Craig drew up a charge sheet of the main criticisms of Victorian poetry compiled from some of the most influential inter- and immediate postwar critics (Richards, Blackmur, Winters, Tate, Leavis, Brooks, etc.). Victorian poetry was discursive and expository. Emotions and attitudes were stated rather than incarnated in the formal imaginative structure of the poem. Its language was denotative rather than connotative, and meaning was conveyed directly with a verbal notation common to prose as well as verse. It had too little sense of contradiction, paradox, ambiguity and irony. Lacking compactness and close-knit texture, it became dispersed, obvious, and often platitudinous, providing 'a minimum of surprise and discovery'.[93] None of this goes much beyond Pound; the judgements have simply been tidied up and lent academic sonority.

Specialist opinion has shifted in the second half of this century, and it might seem that I'm flogging a dead horse. Modernism's reductive account of Victorian poetry has been corrected, and a recent book, Carol Christ's *Victorian and Modern Poetics*, has argued that the central elements in Modernist poetics actually came from the Victorians. But news of this change has not travelled very far. Among academic colleagues, even in my own department, I remain faintly embarrassed at owning up to being at work on a book on Victorian poetry. At the University of Kent we have no courses on Victorian poetry at present, although our nineteenth-century fiction course attracts more students than any other. English graduates from my university would regard Victorian poetry rather as Pound and Eliot did.

This is part of a more general persistence of neo-Edwardianism which I have touched on earlier in this chapter. Generations of social historians have not entirely undone the work of Lytton Strachey. Undergraduate essays still dwell on how 'the Victorians' covered the legs of their chairs because they could not bear the sight of naked wood. Traces of this persist in most detailed studies of the period, including, no doubt, my own. 'Victorianism' has been constructed as our polar opposite – our 'other'. It remains difficult to write about the period in a way which entirely escapes this binary opposition and which sees our culture as a development and intensification of tendencies in the Victorian period rather than a progressive elimination of them.

This kind of difficulty seems to me more acute in Victorian poetry than in most other areas of nineteenth-century studies. Victorian fiction never had its obituary written. James and Lawrence were respectful children, and the sons and daughters of Modernism have gone on rereading nineteenth-century novels. Critics in the 1980s find them receptive to the most recent developments in critical theory and method. Victorian poetry, on the other hand, was disowned by its heirs, and the reinstatement of the last thirty years has occurred within the academy, indeed within specialist journals and studies. The scholarship and criticism responsible for this reinstatement has been detailed, thorough, sound, necessary, and rather conservative. Victorian poetry has not been opened up in the way that its prose counterparts have been, and the absence of reasonably priced complete editions of all but the most major Victorian poets have reinforced this 'ghettoization'. I have not, therefore, felt free to assume that the Modernist case against Victorian poetry has been answered.

I now want to go on and consider the debate about the nature and function of poetry in the mid-nineteenth century and examine the way in which the narrative poem of contemporary life emerged at this time as a special kind of mixed-form response to both literary and social pressures. In *Victorian Scrutinies*, a study of Victorian periodical reviews of poetry between 1830 and 1870, Isobel Armstrong has demonstrated the the lack of consensus about the function and nature of poetry in this period. Poets and critics faced a rapidly changing social and cultural environment which seemed hostile to the very idea of poetry.[94] Macaulay's dictum 'as civilization advances, poetry almost necessarily declines' , in his essay on Milton (1825), had been anticipated in Peacock's *Four Ages of Poetry* (1820) and gained currency in the following decades. In 1845 a writer in the *British Quarterly Review* remarked that most of the functions of poetry were being taken over by prose.[95] The reviewer of Arnold's *Poems* (1853) in *Fraser's Magazine* thought that poetry 'has ceased to be the natural expression of the deepest currents of man's thought'.[96] Both

Elizabeth Barrett Browning and Clough, as we shall see in later chapters, feared these remarks were true. The consequences of industrialization and urbanization, the influence of utilitarian thought, and the slow but palpable democratization of reading and writing were major reasons for Arnold's complaint to Clough that the age was 'unpoetical'.[97]

Many poets and critics, however, were concerned to resist the declining significance of poetry and to develop new forms which would establish its function and significance in the world's first industrial capitalist society. Sterling's essay on Tennyson in the *Quarterly Review* (1842) called on poets to seize the energies at work in contemporary existence and produce a 'creative survey of modern life' in all its aspects.[98] Elizabeth Barrett Browning was quickly alert to such a call and by the late 1840s Clough and Tennyson had responded as well. By the time of Arnold's Preface (1853), in which the contemporary world was dismissed as incapable of providing material for poetry, a number of poets were engaged in trying to prove him wrong.

This feeling that poetry should have a closer relation with the age also raised the question of its relation to other forms of writing which had made the age their business. Primarily this meant the novel, but it also included the discursive prose of a writer such as Carlyle, who had established most of the terms on which the cultural debate about the character of early Victorian society was conducted, and whose influence on fiction and poetry was profound. But it was the newly dominant form of the novel which was the most challenging. Between 1847 and 1850 Dickens published *Dombey and Son* (1848) and *David Copperfield* (1849–50); Thackeray published *Vanity Fair* (1847–8) and *Pendennis* (1848–50); Emily Brontë brought out *Wuthering Heights* (1847), and Charlotte, *Jane Eyre* (1847) and *Shirley* (1849); Elizabeth Gaskell published *Mary Barton* (1848), and Kingsley, *Yeast* (1848) and *Alton Locke* (1850); Trollope's earliest novels appeared. The English novel had truly risen. It was an unparalleled couple of years, and it is no surprise that poets and reviewers of poetry were concerned at the power of this newly dominant form. It was at this moment that the narrative poem of contemporary life emerged.

That is putting it too baldly. Romantic poetry had extended the traditional boundaries of narrative verse, but even here original and contemporary narratives were rare. Legend and history remained the most common source of the narrative poem, and this tradition persisted in the Victorian period in the narrative poems of Arnold, Morris, and Tennyson's *Idylls of the King*. There were two major early nineteenth-century exceptions to this, however: Wordsworth and Crabbe. Crabbe was the more important influence on the narrative poems I shall be considering. Several critics have noted the parallels between 'Enoch Arden' and Crabbe's tale *The Parting Hour*. Crabbe was also an influence on Tennyson's tales of country life, and his work was one of the few models available to Elizabeth Barrett Browning when she began to contemplate writing a long poem of contemporary life.[99]

There was no agreed name for this new kind of narrative poem which emerged in the 1840s. Elizabeth Barrett Browning called it first the 'poetical novel', and later the 'novel-poem' or 'verse-novel'. Any of these will do. The texts I have chosen are all narrative poems with common or overlapping themes, but they cannot be grouped together under a single genre classification. This is really what they have in common and why they interest me. They are all mixed-genre works. Meisel has argued that the idea of genre as fixed and immutable finally dissolved in the nineteenth century,[100] and in different ways each of these texts is an example and product of that dissolution. *Aurora Leigh* is most obviously a novel-poem; *Goblin Market* least obviously so. *The Bothie*, *The Princess*, and *Modern Love* all have something in common with nineteenth-century fiction but can hardly be called verse-novels. The subtitle of the *The Princess* – 'A Medley' – advertises its mixed form in which no single element clearly predominates. Although subtitled 'A Long-Vacation Pastoral', *The Bothie* is also a medley. In *Modern Love*, which revives the traditional poetic form of the sonnet sequence, the Elizabethan sonneteer and the Victorian novelist come face to face.

These texts were not isolated examples of mixed-genre narrative poems of contemporary life in mid-century writing. All the main poets I am looking at wrote other work of this kind, and I shall consider some of this in later chapters. There were also other poets attempting similar experiments in form in the 1840s, 1850s and early 1860s.

In 1844 Bulwer Lytton's narrative poem *Eva, or the Unhappy Marriage* (1842) was one of the few examples Elizabeth Barrett Browning could find of 'the poetical novel, with modern manners inclusive' she hoped to write.[101] Two decades later she would have had many more examples to choose from. The Spasmodic poets produced a number of very long dramatic poems, at least one of which, Alexander Smith's *A Life Drama* (1853) is closely related to the poems I shall discuss. Clough obviously recognized a kinship between Smith's poem and his own work and enlisted *A Life Drama* in his criticisms of Arnold's poetry.[102] The antecedents of *A Life Drama*, Clough thought, were to be found in *The Princess* and in parts of Mrs Browning's work.[103] Thomas Woolner's *My Beautiful Lady*, which appeared in *The Germ* in 1850 and was revised and republished with great success in the 1860s, is another contemporary narrative poem of this time.[104] Better known, and now notorious, is Coventry Patmore's *The Angel in the House*, the archetypal domestic verse-novel. This appeared in two parts in 1854 and 1856, and its later parts, eventually grouped together under the title *The Victories of Love*, were published in 1860 and 1863. Bulwer Lytton's son, writing under the pseudonym Owen Meredith, published a contemporary verse-novel, *Lucile*, in 1860, around the same time as William Allingham was writing his novel-poem *Laurence Bloomfield in Ireland*, which Turgenev admired. Subtitled 'A Modern Poem' and described by its author as a 'poem on every-day Irish affairs', this was an interesting attempt to extend the range of the novel-poem beyond the domestic. *Laurence Bloomfield in Ireland* deals with conflict between landlords and tenants and is an attempt to move into territory occupied by the social novel. Wilfrid Scawen Blunt's sonnet sequence *Esther*, published in 1892, was initially a blank-verse narrative poem begun in the 1860s. Its subject, a young man's sexual awakening, is a Cloughian one, and the form it eventually took was that which Meredith had reworked in *Modern Love*.[105] And in 1860 Browning purchased a book of documents in a second-hand market in Florence which was the genesis of what he called his 'great venture, the murder-poem' – *The Ring and the Book*, eventually published in 1868–9.

Many of these works are no longer names to be reckoned with. They are casualties of literary history and are unlikely to be revived. But it would be wrong to dismiss this mixed-genre writing as a futile rearguard action against the overwhelming power of the novel. New forms of writing were being developed to deal with matters of pressing importance. This experimentation was partly a result of the lack of consensus about the nature and function of poetry. It was not just the novel which had broken traditional notions of literary genre but also poetry which, in the nineteenth century, was following a parallel and sometimes intersecting course. Like a great deal of Victorian poetry, these narrative poems (-novels) were experimental, turbulent, and imperfect in form. Geoffrey Tillotson's comment on *The Ring and the Book*, that it 'has the imperfection we associate with plenitude',[106] can be extended to many other long Victorian poems. W.P. Ker remarked that 'many narrative poems are all the better for being roomy and wandering' and, like the novel, 'require and enjoy liberty'.[107] 'Roomy and wandering' recalls Henry James's description of Victorian novels as 'baggy monsters', and it was the freedom of the novel, with its lack of canons and ground rules, that these contemporary narrative poems were trying to emulate. Yet these works were not novels. Although deeply affected by realism, they were also trying to hold it at bay. The freedom of the novel had its limits, and the narrative poems of Tennyson and Christina Rossetti, Clough, and Elizabeth Barrett Browning, were also attempts to retain space within narrative form for other kinds of writing – lyric, meditative, didactic – which the realist novel was beginning to exclude. They wanted to use the privileges of the novel without succumbing to its limitations; hence the importance of Tillotson's word 'plenitude'.

Of course, plenitude is one thing, indigestion another. To try to read Sydney Dobell's *Balder*, or indeed, for me, *The Angel in the House*, is to suffer the latter. Many of these experiments were manifest failures. But to judge the mixed-form writing of the mid-nineteenth century by its best and most interesting examples is to recognize that here, as elsewhere, the Modernist tradition of criticism has got Victorian poetry very wrong. These, like many other Victorian poems, are not perfectly crafted self-referring verbal icons but large, loose, open, and various works. A similarly open and various critical language is necessary to discuss them. They are experimental in form, in language, and in subject. They are in tension with the dominant values of their age. And in the case of *Aurora Leigh* and *Goblin Market* they are at the head of an alternative tradition of women's writing, only now being properly recognized, which connects them with some of the most interesting developments in late-twentieth-century writing.

NOTES

1. On this latter subject see Helene E. Roberts, 'Marriage, redundancy or sin: the painter's view of women in the first twenty-five years of Victoria's reign', in Martha Vicinus (ed.) *Suffer and be Still: Women in the Victorian Age* (London: Indiana University Press, 1980), p. 51.
2. Christopher Wood, *Victorian Panorama: Paintings of Victorian Life* (London: Faber & Faber, 1976), p. 60.
3. There is an interesting discussion of this issue in P.G. Scott, *Tennyson's Enoch Arden: A Victorian Best-Seller* (Lincoln: Tennyson Society Monograph, 1970). Scott shows there were many sources and analogues for the bigamous marriage theme in nineteenth-century writing, particularly in the late 1850s and early 1860s; e.g. Trollope, *Castle Richmond* (1861); Elizabeth Braddon, *Lady Audley's Secret* (1862); Elizabeth Gaskell, *Sylvia's Lovers* (1863). Scott argues that in most versions of the bigamous marriage story the hero returns openly and has no compunction about breaking up the wife's second marriage. Some reviewers were troubled by Enoch's failure to do so, and a debate about this question went on in the periodical press.
4. *David Copperfield* (Harmondsworth: Penguin, 1976) Ch. 21, p. 369 and facing illustration. There is a good discussion of this tableau from *David Copperfield* by Stephen Lutman, 'Reading illustrations: pictures in *David Copperfield*', in Ian Gregor (ed.) *Reading the Victorian Novel: Detail into Form* (London: Vision Press, 1980).
5. *Dombey and Son* (Harmondsworth: Penguin, 1975), Ch. 18, p. 319.
6. ibid., Ch. 18, p. 319.
7. ibid.
8. *Wuthering Heights* (Harmondsworth: Penguin, 1975), Ch. 6, p. 89.
9. ibid., p. 89.
10. ibid.
11. Peter Conrad, *The Victorian Treasure-House* (London: Collins, 1973), p. 57.
12. Walter E. Houghton, *The Victorian Frame of Mind, 1830–1870* (New Haven and London: Yale University Press, 1973), pp. 341–8.
13. ibid., p. 343.
14. Raymond Lister, *Victorian Narrative Paintings* (London: Museum Press, 1966), pp. 10–11.
15. Wood, pp. 59–60.
16. Conrad, pp. 63, 120.
17. Melvin Waldfogel, 'Narrative painting', in Josef L. Altholz (ed.) *The Mind and Art of Victorian England* (Minneapolis: University of Minnesota Press, 1976), p. 161.
18. Martin Meisel, *Realizations: Narrative, Pictorial, and Theatrical Arts in*

Nineteenth-Century England (Princeton, NJ: Princeton University Press, 1983), p. 379.
19. Wood, p. 17.
20. See Raymond Williams, 'Base and superstructure in Marxist cultural theory', *New Left Review* 82 (Nov.-Dec. 1973), and *Marxism and Literature* (Oxford: Oxford University Press, 1977), pp. 108–35.
21. Williams, *Marxism and Literature*, pp. 109–10.
22. ibid., p. 125.
23. Williams suggests refinements such as residual incorporated and not incorporated, emergent incorporated and not incorporated. He also makes repeated use of a distinction between the merely alternative and the truly oppositional.
24. Williams, *Marxism and Literature*, pp. 125–6.
25. Alan Sheridan, *Michel Foucault: The Will to Truth* (London and New York: Tavistock, 1980), pp. 183–5 has a useful discussion of what Foucault means by 'power'. He does not mean it in the sense of a unified state apparatus, nor even primarily as a system of domination exerted by one group over another. Power is not found in some primary, central point but is exercised from innumerable points (families, places of work, institutions, etc.) in unequal but shifting power relationships. Foucault has been criticized for under-emphasizing the role of the state, its legal apparatus, and the relations between the kinds of power he is interested in and the juridical framework of social life; see Jeffrey Weeks, *Sex, Politics and Society* (London and New York: Longman, 1981), pp. 8–9, and 'Foucault for Historians', *History Workshop* 14 (autumn 1982), 114–16. Foucault's failure to theorize adequately the relation between different kinds of power is a serious omission but not necessarily a damaging criticism of his arguments as they stand. There is no obvious reason why Foucault's emphases cannot be brought into relation with a more developed theory of the state. Hegemony, in the Gramsci–Williams sense, would be an important mediating concept.
26. Michel Foucault, *The History of Sexuality*, Vol. 1: An Introduction, trans. Robert Hurley (London: Allen Lane, 1979), pp. 44–5.
27. Sheridan, p. 169.
28. Sheridan, p. 186, has pointed out that for Foucault discourse follows the same principle of distribution as power. It is not uniform or stable. There is not an accepted and an excluded discourse, nor a discourse of the dominant and of the dominated. It is made up of many intersecting elements which are instruments and effects of power but also points of resistance. Discourse produces and reinforces power; it also undermines and exposes it. Weeks, 'Foucault for Historians', p. 14, has criticized Foucault's failure to elaborate the actual relationship between discourse and social formation. This is closely related to

his criticism of Foucault's understanding of power.
29. Foucault, p. 24.
30. ibid., p. 46.
31. ibid., p. 111.
32. ibid., p. 123.
33. Weeks, *Sex, Politics and Society*, p. 2, has also noted Stone's 'essentialist' view of sexuality. Sex is regarded as a driving, instinctual force which shapes social as well as personal life and which must find expression or, if blocked, produce neuroses and perversion. Shorter is more crudely essentialist than Stone. Against this, Foucault, Weeks, and others understand sexuality as an historical construct with specific conditions of existence.
34. Philippe Ariès, *Centuries of Childhood*, trans. Robert Baldick (London: Jonathan Cape, 1962). Lloyd de Mause, 'The Evolution of Childhood', in de Mause (ed.) *The History of Childhood* (London: Souvenir Press, 1976).
35. Lawrence Stone, *The Family, Sex and Marriage in England 1500–1800* (London: Weidenfeld & Nicolson, 1977), pp. 668–9.
36. Meisel, p. 3.
37. ibid., pp. 229–31.
38. ibid., pp. 190ff.
39. One of the stage adaptations of 'Enoch Arden', made by J.S. Coyne in 1869, was entitled *The Home Wreck*; Scott, p. 36, n. 103.
40. Meisel, pp. 283–301.
41. ibid., p. 292.
42. *Little Dorrit* (London: Dent, 1969), II, xix, p. 607.
43. Martha Vicinus, *The Industrial Muse: A Study of Nineteenth-Century British Working-Class Literature* (London: Croom Helm, 1974), Ch. 5.
44. See Margaret Hewitt, *Wives and Mothers in Victorian Industry* (1958; rpt Westport, Connecticut: Greenwood Press, 1975), especially pp. 10, 49, 183. Foucault, pp. 121–2, argues that although the working class at first escaped the deployment of sexuality, the organization of the conventional family came to be regarded as an indispensable element of control and regulation of the urban proletariat. It was then that campaigns for the moralization of the poor began.
45. See Weeks, *Sex, Politics and Society*, pp. 10–11.
46. Michael Anderson, *Approaches to the History of the Western Family 1500–1914* (London: Macmillan, 1985).
47. ibid., p. 36.
48. See Anderson, pp. 27–38, for a detailed summary of the strengths and weaknesses of the demographic approach.
49. ibid., pp. 65–6.
50. Inheritance is so prominent in nineteenth-century writing, even to

the point of becoming a type of plot, that literary critics might well be able to use some of the work done within this approach. As far as I know there has not been a detailed study of inheritance in nineteenth-century writing.
51. Anderson, p. 39.
52. Jean-Louis Flandrin, *Families in Former Times: Kinship, Household and Sexuality*, trans. Richard Southern (Cambridge: Cambridge University Press, 1979), pp. 4–10.
53. ibid., especially pp. 49, 216.
54. Stone, p. 26.
55. ibid., p. 26. Edward Shorter, *The Making of the Modern Family* (London: Fontana/Collins, 1977), p. 204, gives an identical picture. 'What really distinguishes the nuclear family . . . is a special sense of solidarity that separates the domestic unit from the surrounding community.' There is no agreement between Flandrin, Stone, and Shorter as to why this development came about, nor is there complete agreement about its chronology. All, however, agree that this discrete conjugal family had emerged as the dominant middle-class form by the mid-nineteenth century.
56. Stone, pp. 254–5, argues that this occurred earlier in England than in France. Anderson, pp. 46–7, notes that the segregation of servants from the dining rooms and sleeping quarters of the family was widely discussed in the eighteenth century.
57. Flandrin, p. 93.
58. Anderson, pp. 48, 9.
59. Quoted in Michael Irwin, *Picturing: Description and Illusion in the Nineteenth Century Novel* (London: Allen & Unwin, 1979), p. 109. This has an interesting chapter on 'Rooms and Houses', although written entirely from the point of view of realist technique.
60. ibid., p. 121.
61. Stone, p. 324; Flandrin, pp. 130–40.
62. Flandrin, p. 169.
63. Tennyson's arranged marriage poems are an exception; see Chapter 3, below.
64. *Middlemarch* (Harmondsworth: Penguin, 1965), Bk I, Ch. 4, p. 63.
65. Flandrin, p. 115.
66. Rod Edmond, 'Death Sequences: Patmore, Hardy, and the New Domestic Elegy', *Victorian Poetry* 19 (2).
67. See, in particular, J.A. Banks, *Prosperity and Parenthood: A Study of Family Planning among the Victorian Middle Classes* (London: Routledge & Kegan Paul, 1954), Chs. 2, 3, 4.
68. *The National Magazine*, Vol. 1, 1857, p. 63.
69. J.A. and Olive Banks, *Feminism and Family Planning in Victorian England* (Liverpool: Liverpool University Press, 1965), pp. 22–3.

70. Ray Strachey, *The Cause: A Short History of the Women's Movement in Great Britain* (London: G. Bell & Sons, 1928), p. 78.
71. ibid., p. 44.
72. Weeks, p. 27.
73. Christopher Lasch, 'Life in the Therapeutic State', *New York Review of Books* 27 (10).
74. There is a convincing critique of these works by Michele Barrett and Mary McIntosh in 'Narcissism and the family', *New Left Review* 135 (Sept.–Oct. 1982).
75. Jacques Donzelot, *The Policing of Families* (London: Hutchinson, 1979), p. 24.
76. Weeks, p. 32.
77. Stone, p. 410.
78. Shorter, p. 203.
79. ibid., p. 170.
80. Alan Macfarlane, *The Family Life of Ralph Josselin* (Cambridge University Press, 1970); Keith Wrightson, *English Society 1580–1680* (London: Hutchinson, 1982).
81. Linda Pollock, *Forgotten Children: Parent–Child Relations from 1500 to 1900* (Cambridge: Cambridge University Press, 1983), p. 52.
82. Pollock, p. 271. There is a helpful summary of Pollock's conclusions at the end of her book, pp. 262–71.
83. Alex Comfort, *The Anxiety Makers* (London: Panther Books, 1968).
84. Stone, p. 679.
85. *Middlemarch*, Bk III, Ch. 28, p. 306.
86. *Daniel Deronda* (Harmondsworth: Penguin, 1974), Bk 7, Ch. 54, p. 733.
87. 'A Retrospect', *Literary Essays of Ezra Pound* (London: Faber, 1968), p. 11.
88. 'How to Read', ibid., p. 32.
89. 'The Rev. G. Crabbe, LL.B', ibid., p. 276.
90. 'T.S. Eliot', ibid., p. 420.
91. 'Matthew Arnold', *The Use of Poetry and the Use of Criticism* (London: Faber, 1970), p. 110.
92. Eliot outlined these ideas in his essay 'The Metaphysical Poets', 1921.
93. Hardin Craig, *A History of English Literature* (New York: Oxford University Press, 1950), pp. 467, 578.
94. Isobel Armstrong, *Victorian Scrutinies* (London: Athlone Press, 1972), pp. 3–4.
95. ibid., p. 30.
96. Geoffrey Tillotson, *Criticism and the Nineteenth Century* (London: Athlone Press, 1951), p. 193.
97. See Ch. 2 below.
98. Armstrong, p. 29.

99. See Ch. 4 below.
100. Meisel, p. 141.
101. See Ch. 4 below.
102. See Ch. 2 below.
103. Clough was reviewing Arnold, Smith, and other poets in the *North American Review*, July 1853; see Armstrong, p. 154.
104. Woolner, better known as a sculptor, is perhaps best known for having provided Tennyson with the story on which 'Enoch Arden' was based.
105. For the evolution of Blunt's *Esther*, see Willing T. Going, 'Blunt's *Esther*: the making of a sonnet sequence', *Victorian Poetry* 20 (1).
106. Tillotson, p. 208.
107. W.P. Ker, *Form and Style in Poetry* (London: Macmillan, 1966), p. 265.

2
The 'celled-up dishonour of boyhood': Clough's *The Bothie of Toper-na-Fuosich*

I

Clough made an embarrassing mistake in his choice of title for this poem. Toper-na-Fuosich was the name of a cottage on Loch Ericht where Clough had stayed, and he understood it to mean 'the baird's well'. (A bothie is a hut or small cottage.) In fact, it meant 'the bearded well' and was an indecent Gaelic toast. Clough only discovered this after the poem's publication and it was not until the collected edition of his works in 1862 that he was able to clean up the title and substitute the made-up name of Tober-na-Vuolich.[1] It is now commonly referred to as *The Bothie*.

The poem was written, revised, and published within a period of two months towards the end of 1848. As a poem about an Oxford reading party its success in that university was assured, but it was more than a local triumph. Reviewers on both sides of the Atlantic praised it. Robert and Elizabeth Barrett Browning were enthusiastic.[2] Thackeray wrote to Clough:

> I have been reading the *Bothy* [sic] all the morning and am charmed with it . . . I have been going over some of the same ground [of youth] in this present number of Pendennis; which I fear will be considered rather warm by the Puritans: but I think you'll understand it.[3]

The coolest response came in a letter to Clough from Matthew Arnold :

> 'I have been in Oxford the last two days and hearing Sellar and the rest of that clique ... rave about your poem gave me a strong almost bitter feeling with respect to them, the age, the poem, even you. Yes I said to myself something tells me I can, if need be, at last dispense with them all, even with him: better that, than be sucked for an hour even into the Time Stream in which they and he plunge and bellow. I ... took up Obermann, and refuged myself with him in his forest against your Zeit Geist'.[4]

This letter was part of a continuing argument between the two friends about the nature and function of poetry which became public when Clough reviewed Arnold's collections of 1849 and 1852 and Arnold published his famous Preface to his 1853 *Poems*. Even before *The Bothie* appeared Arnold had criticized 'the deficiency of the beautiful' in Clough's poetry and declared his opposition to all that was 'JARRING'.[5] This was developed in later letters along with Arnold's sense that the age was inimical to poetry: 'how deeply *unpoetical* the age and all one's surroundings are. Not unprofound, not ungrand, not unmoving: – but *unpoetical*'.[6] This was the heart of the difference between Clough and Arnold. In his 1853 review of collections by Arnold and Alexander Smith, Clough asked why people now prefer *Vanity Fair* and *Bleak House* to poems after classical models or from Oriental sources. His answer is that novelists deal with the actual, palpable things of everyday life: 'The novelist does try to build us a real house to be lived in; and this ... is more to our purpose than the student of ancient art who proposes to lodge us under an Ionic portico'. The true haunts of the poetic powers in the mid-nineteenth century, he continues, are not 'by "clear spring or shady grove" ... [but] in the blank and desolate streets, and upon the solitary bridges of the midnight city ... there walks the discrowned Apollo, with unstrung lyre'. Alexander Smith's long narrative poem *A Life Drama*, for all its faults, deals with such material; it is 'substantive and lifelike, immediate and firsthand'. Arnold's poems, for all their strengths, turn their back on such a world.[7]

Clough consulted Arnold about this review and Arnold had certainly read it before completing his Preface.[8] Review and

Preface need each other to be fully intelligible, although Arnold is replying to other critics as well. In his Preface, Arnold challenges and dismisses what he describes as the current orthodoxy that 'the Poet who would really fix the public attention must leave the exhausted past, and draw his subjects from matters of present import, and *therefore* both of interest and novelty'.[9] Instead, poetry should appeal to 'the great primary human affections . . . which subsist permanently in the race, and which are independent of time'. Arnold compares Achilles and Prometheus with 'the domestic epic dealing with the details of modern life', and contends that 'poetical works conceived in the spirit of the passing time . . . [will] partake of its transitoriness'. Poets must resist the claims of the contemporary world:

> their business is not to praise their age, but to afford to the men who live in it the highest pleasure which they are capable of feeling. If asked to afford this by means of subjects drawn from the age itself, they ask what special fitness the present age has for supplying them: they are told that it is an era of progress, an age commissioned to carry out the great ideas of industrial development and social amelioration. They reply that with all this they can do nothing; that the elements they need for the exercise of their art are great actions, calculated powerfully and delightfully to affect what is permanent in the human soul; that so far as the present age can supply such actions, they will gladly make use of them; but that an age wanting in moral grandeur can with difficulty supply such, and an age of spiritual discomfort with difficulty be powerfully and delightfully affected by them.

Modern poets should also look to the past for their style as well as their subject-matter. The classical virtues of austerity, simplicity, directness, accurate construction, and decorum have been lost. This last point is particularly important. Arnold develops an argument he has rehearsed in letters to Clough about the need to subordinate expression to that which it is designed to express. Modern neglect of this principle has lead to a preoccupation with striking local effects which overwhelm any coherent sense of what Arnold calls 'total-impression'. As a result, 'details alone are valuable, the composition worthless'. This argument became the main burden of Arnold's short additional Preface to the 1854 edition of his poems. The modern intellect characteristically manifests itself in 'incredible vagaries'; it is *'fantastic*, and wants *sanity'*. The ancients are the only possible corrective to modern 'caprice and eccentricity'.

The differences with Clough ran deep. Arnold rejected Clough's concern with present things in his poetry, and also his formal experimentation with different modes and styles. This latter point is worth emphasizing. Arnold's Preface is sometimes welcomed as a corrective to a naïve poetics which wanted to place railways and sewers at the centre of poetry and which lacked any appreciation of poetic form. It was also, however, a deeply conservative response to the formal experimentation which characterized so much mid-nineteenth-century poetry. Clough wasn't on strong ground in seeming to prefer Alexander Smith to Matthew Arnold, but Arnold's rejection of almost everything that was interesting in the poetry of this time has not worn well either. Tennyson's *Maud*, which Arnold felt was in the same manner as *The Bothie*, was even more summarily dismissed.[10]

This debate between Clough and Arnold, central and interesting as it was, can be misleading if applied too literally to their own poetry. One of Arnold's targets in his Preface was the modern taste for morbidly introspective poetry, yet his own work has frequently been criticized for just this. As Isobel Armstrong has remarked, 'there is something flagrant about the graceful ease with which Arnold joins forces with his critics here'.[11] In fairness to Arnold it should be added that he omitted 'Empedocles on Etna' from the 1853 collection for precisely this reason. In the same way, Clough's *Bothie* is less 'realist' and more 'poetic', even in an Arnoldian sense, than contemporary reactions and reviews suggest.

Its narrative is simple enough. An Oxford reading party is in the Scottish Highlands. The protagonist is one of their number, Philip Hewson, a young radical with a dislike of landlords and bourgeois gentility and a warm admiration for working women. His opinions provoke banter from his fellow students but disturb the tutor of the reading party, Adam. Several of the students, including Hewson, set off on a walking tour leaving Adam and the others to continue their reading. We learn by report and letter of Hewson's journey. He passes through a series of houses. At the first of these he has a brief infatuation with Katie, a farmer's daughter. He then sets off on his own, full of guilt and remorse at what could have happened; nothing has. We next hear of him staying with Lady Maria, where he tastes the pleasures of aristocratic life and briefly recants his radicalism. Finally, he reaches the Bothie of Toper-na-fuosich, home of David Mackaye, a widely travelled man of yeoman stock, and his daughter Elspie. Hewson has already met Mackaye at a clansmen's dinner described in the first book and has had a mysterious encounter with Elspie in Book 4 which has precipitated his abrupt departure from Katie. Hewson and Elspie are attracted to each other but the courtship proceeds cautiously. Adam arrives, summoned by Hewson, and under his watchful, caring eye the couple decide to marry. Hewson, however, first returns to Oxford and takes his degree. The poem ends with Hewson and Elspie's marriage. Hewson has been instructed in the ways of farming by David Mackaye, and the newly married couple are preparing to emigrate to New Zealand where they will establish a new Bothie of Toper-na-fuosich.

Clough subtitled *The Bothie* 'A Long-Vacation Pastoral' and in his letters normally referred to it as 'my pastoral'. Geoffrey Tillotson has argued that the poem is mock-epic as much as pastoral.[12] In story and theme it resembles the mid-nineteenth-century novel. Its use of letters recalls the epistolary novel. It has elements of fairy tale, legend, and parable. The voice of the Victorian social critics is frequently heard in Hewson's letters and monologues. In other words, *The Bothie* is a medley, a poem of mixed modes. How well do these modes mix? Patrick Scott has argued for the poem's overall coherence in terms of its 'developing mode'. He argues that the poem develops from narrative representation in the early books through psychological representation to a symbolic conclusion. In generic terms he describes this as a movement from mock-epic through confession to pastoral. In terms of tone he notes the development from satire and self-irony to a more conventionally poetic high seriousness. Clough, he concludes, 'writes into the detail of his poem a closely controlled development. The whole mode of the poem changes as the story proceeds'. Scott admits a stylistic duality in the concluding books between 'colloquial realism' and 'pastoral idyll', but sees this duality as welded, an expression of the poem's insistence that the ideal and the prosaic are inescapably mixed.[13] This argument exaggerates the harmony of the poem's mixed modes and the ease of transition from one to another. The implied metaphor of natural growth is misleading. The different modes are there from the beginning and much of the poem's success depends on tension between them. In so far as the poem does develop into a single dominant mode, that of pastoral, in the concluding books, it is correspondingly weakened. I shall return to this point at the end of the chapter.

Unity of a kind is provided by the poem's hexameters. Even here, however, the irregularity of Clough's metre contrasts with the smoothness and monotony of a contemporary narrative poem in hexameters, Longfellow's 'Evangeline' (1847), which Clough had read aloud to his mother and sister shortly before writing *The Bothie*. In a prefatory note to his poem Clough had warned his readers 'to expect every kind of irregularity in these modern hexameters', and pointed out they were accentual, not quantitative, based on stresses rather than syllables.[14] These 'anglo-savage' hexameters, as Clough called them, sustain the narrative and provide the variety and flexibility necessary in a poem of such different modes. They accommodate a wide range of language, modulating from the stark, plain, and colloquial to the solemn, dignified and high poetic.

Clough's choice of metre was topical. Hexameters had recently come into prominence as a vehicle for translating Homer, and the possibility of reproducing classical metres in English had become a much debated question.[15] It was one that Arnold addressed in *On Translating Homer* (1861) where he argued that hexameters offered the translator of Homer the best chance of preserving his general effect, and referred to *The Bothie* as the most interesting modern example of their use.[16] But *The Bothie* is a very different kind of work from the *Iliad* and the example of Clough was only half-useful for Arnold's argument. Furthermore he deplored the roughness of Clough's hexameters. In fact, Clough's use of this metre in such an idiosyncratic poem muddied rather than cleared the hexameter debate. It is typical of his experimentalism in *The Bothie* that he should have used a metre which was the subject of debate among classical scholars and adapted it so radically for his own very contemporary poem.

Arnold described *The Bothie* as a 'serio-comic poem', a term which recalls Fielding's description of his novel *Joseph Andrews* as a 'comic epic poem in prose'. A 'comic epic novel in verse' would be an appropriate generic description of *The Bothie*. But Fielding's epic claim was serious, intended to dignify the kind of new thing he was writing. Clough's epic framework is mocking. Fielding's irony was steady; Clough's is less certain. George Eliot measured her narrative difficulties against Fielding in *Middlemarch* when she described how he would

> bring his arm-chair to the proscenium and chat with us in all the lusty ease of his fine English. But Fielding lived when the days were longer ... We belated historians must not linger after his example; and if we did so, it is probable that our chat would be thin and eager, as if delivered from a camp-stool in a parrot-house.
>
> (Ch. 15, p. 170)

Clough is another belated historian, and *The Bothie* is an exploratory narrative drawing on a range of different modes which are used seriously and comically, confidently and hesitantly. There is no single unifying mode, although the pastoral dominates the conclusion.

For all his reservations about the poem, Arnold's last word was approving:

> his composition produces a sense in the reader which Homer's composition also produces, and which Homer's translator ought to *re*produce, – the sense of having, within short limits of time, a large portion of human life presented to him, instead of a small portion.[17]

Clough, like other mid-century writers, was conscious that a single literary mode no longer seemed capable of presenting a large portion of human life. The narrative method of *The Bothie* is therefore self-conscious and exploratory. Its form has the uneveness of 'a real house to be lived in' rather than the symmetry of 'an Ionic portico'.

II

The Bothie, like many narratives of the 1840s and 1850s, traces the passage of its hero from adolescence to maturity and ends at that point where the family of origin has been left behind and a new family established. Here, as elsewhere, this passage is made without the help of a guiding or controlling family. As Florence Nightingale shrewdly observed, the main reason for the popularity of contemporary novels among women readers was that they presented life without family interference: 'the heroine has *generally* no family ties (almost *invariably* no mother), or, if she has, these do not interfere with her entire independence'.[18] Becky Sharp and Lucy Snowe have this in common, if nothing else. The absence of family was experienced as a condition of freedom. It was also, however, one of danger. Families may be repressive but to live without them is to be adrift, isolated, and vulnerable. The path towards a new family which many mid-century narratives follow is therefore scattered with surrogate families and parent figures. Some of these are false and must be rejected. Others, usually uncompromised by blood ties, are able to offer help and guidance. Jane Eyre and David Copperfield pass through a succession of such houses until finding or founding a home. Philip Hewson, *The Bothie*'s protagonist, has neither father nor mother. He has surrogates, in particular his tutor Adam who plays an important guiding and advising role without having the parental sanctions to enforce his advice. In considering this question of Hewson's surrogate family I shall develop a comparison with *Tom Brown's Schooldays*, a work that makes comparable use of parent surrogates and which, like *The Bothie*, is preoccupied with the growth and development of Victorian boys and adolescents towards manhood.

Hewson's quest ends with his arrival at the Bothie. His marriage to Elspie closes the narrative and signals his emergence into full maturity. A new home has been founded. In this case however, and there are other mid-century narratives of this kind, the marriage is cross-class; the hero has chosen to marry 'down'. In dealing with this aspect of *The Bothie* I shall develop an extended comparison with the diaries of Arthur Munby and Hannah Cullwick, which record in unparalleled detail the history of an actual cross-class Victorian marriage.

The Bothie, however, is distinctive as well as typical, and in making these comparisons I am not suggesting these texts are mere reflections of each other. Nowhere is this more true than in *The Bothie*'s explicit concern with the awakening of sexuality in its young hero, and his difficult, guilt-riven negotiation of adolescence. It is here that I shall begin. Hewson talks of this in a long monologue towards the beginning of Book 2:

> Never, believe me, revealed itself to me the sexual glory,
> Till in some village fields in holidays now getting stupid,
> One day sauntering 'long and listless,' as Tennyson has it,
> Long and listless strolling, ungainly in hobbadiboyhood,
> Chanced it my eye fell aside on a capless, bonnetless maiden,
> Bending with three-pronged fork in a garden uprooting potatoes.
>
> (Bk 2, ll. 41–6)[19]

The echo of Tennyson's 'The Miller's Daughter', in which the son of a squire marries the daughter of a miller, anticipates Hewson's eventual marriage to Elspie, but at this moment the focus is on sexual awakening and the awkward knowledge this brings:

> Shyly I shambled away, stopping oft, but afraid of returning,
> Shambled obliquely away, with furtive occasional sidelook,
> Long, though listless no more, in my awkward hobbadiboyhood.
> Still, though a new thing was in me, though vernal emotion, the secret,
> Yes, amid prurient talk, the unimparted mysterious secret
> Long, the growing distress, and celled-up dishonour of boyhood,
> Recognised now took its place, a relation, oh bliss! unto others;
>
> (Bk 2, ll. 55–61)[20]

This Wordsworthian encounter has a most unWordsworthian charge, and Tennyson's audially appropriate 'listless' is given a specific sexual denotation.

Hewson has discovered an object for desires which hitherto have been 'celled-up', but he has not been able to align these desires with women of his own class. He is full of scorn for the false gentility and refined uselessness of middle-class women:

> Better a crust of black bread than a mountain of paper-confections,
> Better a daisy in earth than a dahlia cut and gathered,

The Bothie of Toper-na-Fuosich 53

> Better a cowslip with root than a prize carnation without it.
> (Bk 2, ll. 80–2)

These urges and convictions make the Scottish Highlands dangerous territory for Hewson, and when he leaves the reading party for his walking tour he is setting out on a journey of sexual discovery. It is a kind of Victorian equivalent to the Grand Tour which, among other things, had been expected to provide young noblemen with sexual experience.[21] In Hewson's case sexuality is not so much in search of experience as a life partner.

His first stop is a farm in Rannoch where he falls for 'golden-haired Katie, the youngest and comeliest daughter' (Bk 3, l. 198) of the farmer. Hewson's companions report to Adam how he is working with Katie, fetching peat, reaping, 'drying clothes, making fires, making love' (Bk 3, l. 223), living out his ideal of love and labour. But Hewson's lovemaking is timid and after a mysterious encounter with a girl, later revealed as Elspie, he leaves Rannoch abruptly. In Book 4, now travelling alone, Hewson writes to Adam of his remorse and guilt about Katie. In particular, he describes a dream in which he is pacing the streets of 'the dissolute city':

> Where dressy girls slithering-by upon pavements give sign
>   for accosting,
> Paint on their beautiless cheeks, and hunger and shame
>   in their bosoms;
> Hunger by drink and by that which they shudder yet burn for,
>   appeasing, –
> Hiding their shame – ah God, in the glare of the public gas
>   lights?
> (Bk 4, ll. 176–9)

This dream derives from the widespread contemporary belief that seduction was the most common cause of a woman's fall from virtue into prostitution.[22] The lurid, overwrought language dramatizes Hewson's paranoia:

> Oh, who saws through the trunk, though he leave the tree
>   up in the forest,
> When the next wind casts it down, – is *his* not the hand
>   that smote it?
> (Bk 4, ll. 198–9)

Hewson hasn't laid a finger on Katie but he feels so guilty that mental seduction is seen as precipitating an actual fall. The poem confirms that his reaction is excessive by showing Katie dancing happily at Rannoch with another of the reading party immediately before his confessional letter to Adam.

By the end of Book 4, however, Hewson has continued his journey and we learn of him in the castle at Balloch with Lady Maria. She is Katie's antithesis, and while at Balloch Hewson writes a further letter to Adam in which he praises the aristocracy and argues that the social order is divinely ordained. This is a reaction to his flight from Katie and the collapse of his idealized vision of working women into horrified sexual guilt. The complacent hedonism of this letter is short-lived. Journeying on he finds his way to the Bothie of Toper-na-fuosich, home of Elspie Mackaye and her father David:

> the needle
> Which in the shaken compass flew hither and thither,
>   at last, long
> Quivering, poises to north. I think so. But I am cautious;
>   (Bk 6, l. 51–3)

Twice bitten, therefore shy, but the image of the compass and the following image of a railway train speeding to its destination while the occupants sleep is emphatic. Journey's end has been reached. (Railways seemed to quicken Clough's imagination. One of his best and wittiest poems, 'Natura Naturans', involves a sexual fantasy in a second-class railway carriage.)

It is only now that Hewson's sexuality begins to find expression. First, however, Elspie assuages Hewson's guilt about Katie and reveals herself as the one whose glance had turned him away from Rannoch. The compass image is repeated, emphasizing that true north points steadily to home. The poem's metaphoric language then develops the idea of home into one of marriage, in Elspie's image of two sides of a bridge closing together and united by the key stone, thus forming a single arch. The sexual aspect of this image is unmistakable:

> There I feel the great key stone coming in, and through it
> Feel the other part – all the other stones of the archway,
> Joined into mine with a queer happy sense of completeness,
>   tingling

> All the way up from the other side's basement-stones in the
>   water,
> Through the very grains of mine:
>
> (Bk 7, ll. 71–5)

What is also interesting about this image is the sense of the difficulty of growth and development it expresses. Elspie insists they must be patient for fear of damaging what they have worked for – 'our painful up-building' (Bk 7, l. 112). Her own development is similarly described in terms of effort and difficulty:

> – this long time slowly with trouble
> I have been building myself, up, up, and toilfully raising,
> Just like as if the bridge were to do it itself without masons,
> Painfully getting myself upraised one stone on another
>
> (Bk 7, ll. 61–4)

The sexual element in the bridge image becomes dominant in the next image the poem develops, that of the sea and the burn. Elspie likens Philip to the sea:

> Which *will* come, through the straights and all between
>   the mountains,
> Forcing its great strong tide into every nook and inlet,
> Getting far in, up the quiet stream of sweet inland water,
> Sucking it up, and stopping it, turning it, driving it backward,
> Quite preventing its own quiet running: And then, soon after,
> Back it goes off, leaving weeds on the shore, and wrack
>   and uncleanness:
> And the poor burn in the glen tries again its peaceful running,
> But it is brackish and tainted, and all its banks disordered.
> That was what I dreamt all last night. I was the burnie,
> Trying to get along through the tyrannous brine, and
>   could not;
> I was confined and squeezed in the coils of the great salt
>   tide, that
> Would mix-in itself with me, and change me; I felt
>   myself changing;
> And I struggled, and screamed, I believe, in my dream.
>   It was dreadful.
>
> (Bk 7, ll. 125–37)

This startling picture of Elspie's fear of being mastered and dominated, and the graphic image of sexual despoliation as the polluted burn, connect these lines with previous images of fear and guilt expressed by Philip. Briefly, Elspie pictures herself as Philip has pictured Katie after he has left her. But this is amended as the image is developed in terms which push aside Elspie's fears. The tide now recedes:

> That great water withdrawn, receding here and passive,
> Felt she in myriad springs, her sources, far in the mountains,
> Stirring, collecting, rising, upheaving, forth-out-flowing,
> Taking and joining, right welcome, that delicate rill in the valley,
> Filling it, making it strong, and still descending, seeking,
> With a blind forefeeling descending, evermore seeking,
> With a delicious forefeeling, the great still sea before it;
> There deep into it, far, to carry, and lose in its bosom,
> Waters that still from their sources exhaustless are fain to be added.
>
> (Bk 7, ll. 161–9)

The image is no longer one of domination but reciprocity. Elspie is not just the burn but also its inland sources which are constantly replenishing, and the burn itself has become active and seeking. There has been a controlled development of these main images in Book 7 from that of the compass (home) to the bridge (marriage) and finally the sea and the burn (consummation). Sexuality has discovered the context in which it is permitted full expression.

Book 7 is entirely the lovers', but they are not unwatched. Adam has come to Toper-na-fuosich in Book 6, summoned by Hewson, and having approved Elspie has stayed. He and David Mackaye have overseen the developing love of Philip and Elspie, and they are needed to help that love define itself socially and deal with the problems of class, education, and culture which the proposed marriage raises. Free of the handicap of actually being a parent, Adam is able to play that role to both Philip and Elspie. She finds it easier to speak to Adam than to her own father (Bk 8, l. 57). As Philip and Elspie complete the difficult journey to maturity, passing from one family to another, the unobtrusive guiding hand of Adam, the parent surrogate, is there to help them safely home.

III

In the opening chapter, I argued that our conception of childhood and adolescence as distinct and crucial stages in the journey to adulthood is of recent origin. By the nineteenth century, however, the idea of the distinctiveness of childhood had become axiomatic, and as the age of marriage rose and the age of puberty fell, thus lengthening the interval between sexual maturation and marriage, further intermediate stages were discovered within an increasingly complex developmental process. With their discovery came new problems peculiar to those stages. Our own concept of adolescence emerged during this period and so too did that indisputably Victorian idea of boyhood. Both these concepts were class and gender specific. The increased duration of dependence on home and school for children was peculiar to the middle classes, and the concept of adolescence was elaborated in primarily masculine terms. Boyhood is self-evidently gender specific, and the accompanying idea of girlhood was more shadowy and defined entirely in relation to boyhood as its opposite. The state of boyhood was an important part of that categorization along lines of gender which became so marked during the nineteenth century. Within each life-stage the primary definition was male, with the female defined as its opposite and denied independent definition.

Bruce Haley has described *Tom Brown's Schooldays* (1857) as the text which discovered and chartered the world of boyhood as a 'separate and definable stage of life different from childhood and adolescence, distinct in its outlines, unique in its perils and promises'.[23] The emphasis on perils is important. As the stages of development proliferated, the dangers besetting each stage heightened, and the journey to maturity became increasingly perilous. Clough's line, 'the growing distress, and celled-up dishonour of boyhood' gives a particular emphasis to Dr Arnold's more general conviction that he could only hope to make Christian men, not Christian boys. For the headmaster of Rugby, boyhood and adolescence were 'times of trial, the successful endurance of which was the cultivation of a healthy manhood'.[24] Tom Brown, listening to his first sermon from the Doctor, learns for the first time the meaning of his life:

it was no fool's or sluggard's paradise into which he had

wandered by chance, but a battle-field ordained from of old, where there are no spectators, but the youngest must take his side, and the stakes are life and death.[25]

Tom is deeply impressed but it will take more than Dr Arnold's sermons to bring him through to safety. The problem is the all but fallen state of boyhood, a stage of life 'before any steady purpose or principle has developed' (Pt 1, Ch. 7, p. 117). Matthew Arnold diagnosed boyhood in similar terms:

> Those who with half-open eyes
> Tread the border-land dim
> Twixt vice and virtue
>   ('Rugby Chapel', ll. 53–5)

The Doctor's task is more than the salvation of Rugby, the establishment of order and the defeat of the 'monstrous licence and misrule' which prevailed before his arrival. He must also attempt the more difficult task of combating licence and creating order within each of his boys. In fact, *Tom Brown's Schooldays* is not as tense as this suggests. The author's sturdy optimism leaves us in little doubt that his hero will pull it off. Some, however, don't reach the safety of the shore and continue to live without 'compass and purpose ... drifting helplessly on rocks and quicksands' (Pt 2, Ch. 8, p. 263).

Tom Brown's Schooldays is worth a closer look. At the beginning of Chapter 2 the narrator remarks that as the child is father to the man, so he must also be father to the boy. Tom's childhood is dealt with in detail uncommon in the school story genre which developed out of this book. Village life with the local lads is more important as Tom's prep school than the private institution he attends before starting Rugby. It is in the village that Tom learns many of the skills and values which enable him to survive and win through at public school. A wrestling throw, learnt from one of the village lads, enables Tom to secure an honourable draw in his famous fight at Rugby with Slogger Williams. Village life also teaches Tom to respect a man for what he is rather than who he is, an egalitarian principle whose application to Tom's life becomes increasingly remote as he leaves the village for Rugby with Oxford beckoning in the distance. The pastoralized rural setting of Tom's childhood is firmly established in the opening chapters and is

The Bothie of Toper-na-Fuosich 59

closely associated with the sanctified family life Tom has enjoyed. When Tom leaves home for the first time the narrator focuses on the parting of mother and son:

> Their love was as fair and whole as human love can be, perfect self-sacrifice on the one side, meeting a young and true heart on the other. It is not within the scope of my book, however, to speak of family relations, or I should have much to say on the subject of English mothers – aye, and of English fathers, and sisters, and brothers too.
>
> (Pt 1, Ch. 3, p. 57)

The book actually says a great deal more about family relations than this passage acknowledges. With the advantage of this happy and principled home life Tom is sent off to Rugby bearing the hopes and fears of his loving parents. As their influence recedes, Tom's life at Rugby starts to drift. Surrogates are available but it is a long time before Tom can fully accept them. On his first disciplinary visit to the Doctor the door opens on a happy family scene. The Doctor is making a sailing boat for one of his boys; his other children are gathered around him; the fire is glowing: 'All looked so kindly, and homely, and comfortable' (Pt 1, Ch. 7, pp. 124–5). There is a parallel scene in the opening chapter of Part 2 when Tom is invited to tea with Mrs Arnold. She presides in her drawing room but her influence radiates outwards:

> Aye, many is the brave heart now doing its work and bearing its load in county curacies, London chambers, under the Indian sun, and in Australian towns and clearings, which looks back with fond and grateful memory to that School-house drawing room, and dates much of its highest and best training to the lessons learnt there.
>
> (Pt 2, Ch. 1, p. 172)

Mrs Arnold is, of course, the book's dedicatee.

The lesson of these scenes is resisted by Tom, and it is not until his last day at Rugby that he learns from the young master how the Doctor has set up and watched over his rescue. His improvement and success, which Tom had thought entirely his own work, are revealed as due to the invisible guiding hand of the Doctor. The young master tells Tom, 'Ah! not one of you boys will ever know the anxiety you have given him, or the care with which he has watched over every step in your school lives' (Pt 2, Ch. 8, p. 279). Until this moment 'Tom had never wholly given in to, or understood the Doctor'. Now, however, 'the Doctor's victory was complete . . . there wasn't a corner of him left which didn't believe in the Doctor'. Only at the end of his school life, just as he must leave it behind, is the full paternal role of the Doctor understood. Tom's own family has long since disappeared from sight.

Not only does Tom have to leave Rugby (reluctantly – he wishes the Doctor would let him stay on until he is 20) but he also loses his surrogate father. In the final chapter Tom is vacationing in Scotland with Oxford friends when he learns of the Doctor's death and rushes 'home' to Rugby. The book leaves him sitting in Rugby Chapel. Tom's apprenticeship to life is now all but complete:

> And let us not be hard on him, if at that moment his soul is fuller of the tomb and him who lies there, than of the altar and Him of whom it speaks. Such stages have to be gone through, I believe, by all young and brave souls, who must win their way through hero-worship, to the worship of Him who is the King and Lord of heroes.
>
> (Pt 2, Ch. 9, p. 288)

On the verge of self-sufficient independent manhood Tom now only has need of the one true Father. Boyhood and adolescence have been traversed, and Tom is ready to enter adulthood and begin his long journey towards God. Heaven, it is intimated, will be a Rugby reunion.

Tom Brown's Schooldays has an archetypal structure. The initial promise of its hero is threatened and undermined but eventually redeemed and consolidated.[26] However, this archetype bears a strong mid-nineteenth-century imprint. The hero is given the best possible preparation for the dangers he will meet, and throughout his trials loving spectators hover anxiously ready to help where they can. It is less compelling than *David Copperfield*, *Pendennis*, or *Jane Eyre*, where the hero/ine is orphaned, or at least fatherless (*Pendennis*), expelled, and forced to go in search of surrogates, many of whom prove to be unreliable. It nevertheless shares the same anxious fascination with the journey through boyhood/ girlhood and adolescence to maturity. In each of these texts the spectacle is agitating, for family and school in the case of Tom

Brown, and for the reader in those narratives where parents and guardians are absent. The intensified emotional investment in children, the increased duration of dependence for the middle-class child, and the sentimentalization of the idea of home, all contributed to make entry into the world seem threatening and hazardous.[27] All of these texts are within this nexus of concern, although the more interesting narratives are those where family supports have been removed and there is no heavenly Doctor doing his utmost to ensure safe passage.

IV

Clough and Hughes were both products of Arnold's Rugby. *The Bothie* and *Tom Brown's Schooldays* have a broadly similar pattern of promise tempted, struggling and finally redeemed, anxiously observed by a father figure – Adam in Clough's poem and Dr Arnold in Hughes's work. Both texts are deeply concerned with the difficulties, indeed the perils, of growing up. *The Bothie*, as we have seen, discovers and charts a later stage in the journey to adulthood, focusing on the progress of awakened sexuality towards the safe harbour of marriage. *Tom Brown's Schooldays* is concerned with an earlier stage of development and hardly at all with sexuality.[28] The kinship between these two texts is interesting and lends support to Jeffrey Weeks's claim that the forcing ground for the social and psychological qualities of boyhood and male adolescence, as these stages came to be understood during the Victorian period, was the public school.[29]

However *The Bothie* is a more complex text, as we have already seen in its treatment of sexuality, and this is also true of its use of surrogate parents and families. It is not until the beginning of Book 8 that we learn Philip has neither father nor mother (but does have a portion of £1,000). This is important information as the narrative moves towards the social realignment of its concluding cross-class marriage. Before this, family relations have been absent from the poem. As Scott has remarked, the reading party must have been a way of escaping the constraints of family life during the long summer vacation.[30] But the reading party itself is seen as a family, within which some remain and from which others depart and later return. Its hermetic language of slang and nicknames, also a feature of *Tom Brown's Schooldays*, constitutes a kind of patois characteristic of large family groups.[31] This is reinforced by descriptions of the party as a 'household' (Bk 3, l. 85). The pitfalls of Hewson's journey are contrasted with the peace and security of life with the reading party, as, for example, in the opening section of Book 5. Adam is father and mother to the party while Hewson is his prodigal and favourite.

The relationship between Adam and Hewson has a peculiar intensity. When Adam tries to restrain Hewson's radical ideas in Book 2 he is hurt by Philip's dismissal of his argument about the moderating effects of experience. He shows 'a moisture about the eyelids' (l. 204) and reproaches Philip – 'Thus to upbraid me with years, chill years that are thick'ning to forty' (l. 206).[32] Adam is greatly agitated when he hears of Hewson's infatuation with Katie:

'But the Tutor enquired, who had bit his lip to bleeding,
How far off is the place? who will guide me there to-morrow?
                    (Bk 3, ll. 243–4)

Adam's concern shadows Philip's travels and is fed and rewarded by Philip's long confessional letters to his tutor in Books 4 and 5, letters which Adams ponders 'long with emotion' (Bk 4, l. 201) before replying to at length. Finally, he is summoned to the Bothie of Toper-na-fuosich. Hewson having left 'home' to undertake his grand tour now urges his tutor-parent to come and sanction his new family. The love between Philip and Elspie can now ripen under the benevolent supervision of Adam and David Mackaye.

Adam seems to combine the roles of the middle-class father and mother: guidance and caring. His position is also analogous to that of Dr Arnold who on becoming headmaster of Rugby assumed the duties of chaplain as well, combining two hitherto separate roles.[33] But he is neither parent nor headmaster, and his surrogate role involves significant modifications to these authority models. He is guiding but not sovereign, caring but not controlling, available but not intrusive. He lacks the ultimate sanctions available to Dr Arnold and the Victorian middle-class father: expulsion and disinheritance.

Hewson dismisses the middle-class family life of his own background as 'the old solemn gentility stage-play' (Bk 8, l. 151). He resolves to show Elspie the rest of his family, but only in order 'to leave it with all the more satisfaction' (Bk 8, l. 152). It is only from his surrogate family that Hewson gets any benefit. His confessional letters to Adam, which are less frank in the 1862 edition, involve an openness of relationship impossible within the contemporary middle-class family, where confessions were likely to be extorted rather than voluntary. Samuel Butler was a particularly jaundiced observer, but his picture of Christina Pontifex practising the 'domestic confidence trick' with her son Ernest dramatizes the minute detailed examination of the inner life of Victorian middle-class children by their parents, and the lack of personal space in those capacious family homes:

> Whenever his mother wanted what she called a confidential talk with him she always selected the sofa as the most suitable ground on which to open her campaign.... 'You know, my darling, that it would be as much our pleasure as our duty to watch over the development of your moral and spiritual nature, but alas! you will not let us see your moral and spiritual nature.... Of your inner life, my dear, we know nothing beyond such scraps as we can glean in spite of you, from little things which escape you almost before you know that you have said them....' Ernest... was still so moved by the siren's voice as to yearn to sail towards her, and fling himself into her arms, but it would not do... the mangled bones of too many murdered confessions were lying whitening round the skirts of his mother's dress, to allow him any possibility to trust her further. So he hung his head and looked sheepish, but kept his own counsel.[34]

Like other orphaned protagonists in Victorian writing, Hewson is free of this kind of struggle.

In the later books David Mackaye becomes an important role model for Philip. The brief history of his travels and his return to Scotland where:

> on his pittance of soil he lived, and raised potatoes,
> Barley, and oats, in the bothie where lived his father
>   before him
>
> (Bk 6, ll. 17–18)

'father and mother' to his daughters (Bk 6, l. 26) whose education he undertakes himself, provides an alternative model of the family and its social and productive relationships against which contemporary bourgeois family life is judged. Zaretsky's contrast between the early bourgeois family which encouraged individualism and private productive property, and the bourgeois family under industrial capitalism shorn of its productive function and reduced to the transmission and preservation of property is helpful.[35] This contrast is highly schematic, but Zaretsky's description of the self-contained productive family unit of early bourgeois society is similar to Mackaye's Bothie and the picture of Philip and Elspie's family in New Zealand in the concluding lines of the poem:

> There hath he farmstead and land, and fields of corn and
>   flax fields;
> And the Antipodes too have a Bothie of Toper-na-fuosic.
>   (Bk 9, ll. 228–9)

In other words, the poem's critique of the Victorian middle-class family is made in terms of an earlier concept of family which its hero recreates by marrying outside his class and emigrating to a world which is depicted as hardly emerged from nature, still waiting to receive the imprint of social structures. David Mackaye is therefore Philip's last tutor-father, teaching him 'to handle the hoe and the hatchet' (Bk 9, l. 141) and preparing him for the task of establishing his 'new' family in the fresh soil of New Zealand.

V

The brunt of the poem's attack on 'the old solemn gentility stageplay', however, is directed at middle-class femininity. It is in this context that we need to understand the cross-class marriage which closes the narrative, and also, I think, some other examples of cross-class marriage in Victorian culture. Throughout the poem Hewson upbraids young women of his class for their frivolous, superfluous lives:

> Oh, if our high-born girls knew only the grace, the attraction,
> Labour, and labour alone, can add to the beauty of women,
> Truly the milliner's trade would quickly, I think, be at
>   discount,

All the waste and loss in silk and satin be saved us,
Saved for purposes truly and widely productive –
(Bk 2, ll. 26–30)

Hewson's idealization of working women needs to be understood in this context, and although his encounter with Katie challenges this idealization, he is still writing in similar vein in the final book:

– Ye unhappy statuettes, ye miserable trinkets,
Poor alabaster chimney-piece ornaments under glass cases,
Come, in God's name, come down ! the very French clock
  by you
Puts you to shame with ticking; the fire-irons deride you.
Break your glasses, ye can ! come down, ye are not really
  plaster,
Come, in God's name, come down ! do anything, be
  but something !
(Bk 9, ll. 38–43)

Although this takes no account of how feminine norms are constructed, it is not just male ranting. Many women's texts of this period attack the repressive and distorting effects of the claims of social life on middle-class women.

However, the work which this aspect of *The Bothie* most closely resembles are the diaries of Arthur Munby.[36] These diaries record the history of the relationship between Munby, a Cambridge educated barrister, civil servant, and poet, and Hannah Cullwick, a maid-of-all-work. They met on a London street in 1854 and the relationship lasted until their deaths, Hannah's in 1909 and Munby's the following year. Until their secret marriage in 1873 Munby lived on his own in rooms in the Inner Temple and Hannah lived and worked as a servant in many different residences. After their marriage Hannah moved into Munby's rooms but as his servant, not his wife. This arrangement broke down after four years and Hannah returned to her family in Shropshire, where she lived in a cottage provided for her by Munby. He visited her regularly and was accepted by her family and friends. None of Munby's family and only two of his friends ever knew of his relationship with Hannah.

Munby's diaries are more than a record of his relationship with Hannah. They are full of detailed accounts of different kinds of women's work he has discovered in London and elsewhere, and constitute a remarkable record of the sorts of work done by working-class women in the mid-Victorian period. Munby began his diaries in 1859, but his interest in working women went back at least as far as his undergraduate days in the late 1840s, where it was the subject of much of his early poetry. The interest also expressed itself in private philanthropic work and in his close association with the Working Women's College. His bachelor life in London in the 1850s and 1860s was not spent entirely in pursuit of this interest, however. He also moved in Bayswater and Kensington society, which regarded him as highly eligible, but Munby found little to interest him in the conventional young ladies of his class. Dining with a family whose daughter was known to be interested in him, Munby's eye was drawn instead to the maid: 'all these young ladies, white bosomed, fairylike with muslin and flowers, found a foil for their elegance in a pretty but coarsemade rustic & redhanded waiting maid'.[37]

We have already seen Hewson's impatience with the women and social practices of his own class, and it is no surprise that *The Bothie* was a particular favourite of Munby's. 'Few books', he wrote, 'are more precious to me than this. My theories of women, my love of college reminiscences, of scenic description, of hexameters, are all satisfied by it to the utmost'.[38] He once introduced a debate at the Working Women's College on the subject 'The beauty of manual labour, and the weakness of being ashamed of it', by reading a passage from *The Bothie*.[39] But although Munby moved in Christian Socialist circles, he was not, as Hewson is described in *The Bothie*, a 'radical hot'. Nor was he, however, simply an oddity. His interest in working women was obsessive and clearly had a psychological dimension, but his reluctance or inability to marry a conventionally eligible young lady of his own class is socially as well as psychologically explicable.

Munby and Hannah's relationship was unusual, but its only unique aspect was Hannah's insistence on remaining a servant and her refusal to become a lady. There are many examples of Victorian gentlemen marrying and 'raising' working-class women. Not surprisingly, Munby noted several in his diaries. F.J. Furnivall, a distinguished philologist and one of the founders of the Working Men's College, married a lady's maid, sister of one of his students at the College. Munby records visiting them in 1862.[40]

There are several references in his diary for the following year to the case of Lord Robert Montagu, a widower with four children who married a housemaid. It was Hannah who first told Munby of this spectacular cross-class marriage,[41] and Hannah's own diaries record that this marriage had been discussed among the servants where she worked.[42] Munby later records an uncomfortable discussion about this marriage and others of its kind during the Eton and Harrow cricket match at Lords.[43]

The Pre-Raphaelite predilection for 'discovering' young working-class women to use as models and then 'raising' them to the status of lovers and, often, wives, is a further point of reference for cross-class relationships and marriage in the mid-nineteenth century. There seems to be a clear pattern in this group of examples. The men, though not always wealthy, were certainly gentlemen. The women were working class, beautiful ('stunners'), uneducated, and often ill. The men 'discovered' them, painted them and often attempted to 'raise' them. Artistic and sexual motives mixed with those of 'rescue' and 'improvement'. *The Bothie* neatly expresses this mixture of motives behind the attraction to working women when Hewson recounts his meeting with the maiden digging potatoes:

> But a new thing was in me; and longing delicious
>   possessed me,
> Longing to take her and lift her, and put her away from
>   her slaving:
> Was it to clasp her in lifting, or was it to lift her by
>   clasping,
> Was it embracing or aiding was most in my mind; hard
>   question!
>
> (Bk 2, ll. 48–51)

Of course, painters needed models and working-class women needed money. Middle-class women were less likely to agree to sit and certainly wouldn't do so for money. Elizabeth Barrett Browning refused to sit for Rossetti, writing to her sister that she had no wish to be 'perpetuated in sublime ugliness by the head of the Pre-Raphaelite school'.[44] Elizabeth Siddall and Fanny Cornforth could not afford such scruples. Clearly, however, there is more to this pattern than the strictly artistic and economic.

Several commentators have seen these models-lovers-wives as

Pre-Raphaelite creations and argued that the rescue and improvement impulse was fed by a desire to create grateful and devoted wives.[45] Although the case of Munby and Hannah seems the reverse of this, confirming Hannah's lowliness rather than rescuing her from it, this emphasis on the woman as the man's creation is central to Leonore Davidoff's analysis of their relationship. Her argument would also seem applicable to the Pre-Raphaelites. She notes middle-class fascination with the forbidden world of the working class, and the sexualization of the working classes by middle-class observers. She also argues that the power to create and transform another human being was one of the ways in which middle-class masculine identity was affirmed, and sees this power as one of the attractions of rescue work.[46] There seems to be a broad consensus that in these cross-class relationships the lower-class woman was dominated by, in a sense created by, the upper-class man. In these terms Munby's penchant for photographing Hannah in a variety of guises (as servant, slave, peasant, gentleman, and lady) can perhaps be seen as the equivalent of Rossetti's transformations of Elizabeth Siddall and Jane Burden into Beatrice and Prosperine.

There is, however, a different angle from which these cross-class relationships and their renderings in writing, painting, and photography can be viewed. From the point of view of the woman, there was undoubtedly exploitation. This, however, was not peculiar to inter-class relationships. From that of the man, however, the attraction of working-class women and their representation in literary and artistic discourse can be seen as a reaction against the dominant 'angel in the house' image to which middle-class women were expected to conform. Carol Christ has argued that nineteenth-century images of womanhood tell us at least as much about Victorian men as Victorian women. The idealization of woman's passivity, asexuality, and withdrawal from the world which she finds in Patmore, more complexly in Tennyson, and also in Ruskin and Dickens, is an expression of values they themselves would like to possess. Faced with a society that valued and rewarded male aggressiveness, and yet uneasy about its value, they idealized certain feminine qualities to escape the tensions of their own situation. The angel in the house offered freedom or salvation from man's conflicting desires. In other words, this discourse on women is actually a displaced articulation of problems of masculinity.[47] But, as Christ argues, this attempt to solve one set of problems created another, leaving these writers unable to deal with sexuality except as a kind of depraved energy.[48] The good man – Frederick Graham in *The Angel in the House*, David Copperfield, John Jarndyce, Ruskin's ideal of the gentleman – is desexualized. Christ also points out that those writers who have least difficulty in dealing with male sexuality also have less difficulty in treating female sexuality. She names Thackeray and Browning; Clough is another.

Clough, the Pre-Raphaelite painters, and the diarist Munby were producing texts intimately but complexly related to their lives, which were within an alternative discourse on masculinity expressed through a very different image of woman. Instead of the angel in the house, they constructed a resexualized image in non-middle-class terms. However, there was commonly a further twist to these cross-class relationships. This was the subsequent desire of the male to embourgeois the woman he had initially been attracted to because of her difference from middle-class norms, and it is observable in all the examples under discussion. I shall return to this point when dealing with Munby's attempt after his marriage to transform Hannah into a lady. But for the first twenty years of their relationship Munby and Hannah did not conform to this pattern. Hannah had no wish to be 'raised', and Munby was attracted by her independent spirit as well as her lowliness. Davidoff's rather belated concession of this point, and the fact that after their marriage Hannah refused to cooperate with Munby and become a lady, weakens her main argument that Hannah was Munby's creation and shows the inadequacy of understanding these cross-class relationships solely in terms of exploitation. If Munby had simply wanted a relationship in which he wielded power, he could have had this within a conventional middle-class marriage.

Liz Stanley's recent edition of Hannah's diaries has allowed her to speak for herself, and the voice we hear is one of stubborn independence. Stanley challenges Davidoff's view of Hannah as Munby's creation. She argues that Hannah was never powerless within their master and servant relationship, and that her abasement and the rituals of lowliness she went through was partly a way of using Munby's needs and obsessions to construct power for herself. Certainly, she is right to emphasize the

Plate 2 'At Margate a maid of all work', 1864

Plate 3 Hannah in evening dress, 1857

Plate 4 Hannah in peasant dress, 1872

Plate 5 Hannah dressed as a man, 1857

complexity of their relationship and that Hannah liked being lower class and working hard.[50] Her diaries, which of all the texts discussed in this book are domestic narratives par excellence, make this clear. They were, of course, written for Munby at his insistence, and Davidoff sees them as an important factor in Munby's dominance, being another of the ways in which he created her life.[51] But the diaries have more autonomy than this allows, and their descriptions of dirty work hardly suggest that Hannah was an unwilling victim of Munby's obsessions.[52] Hannah had no desire to be raised above her station. On one occasion she recorded her relief at escaping from a drawing-room where she had been interviewed for a position:

> When I got outside and in the park I actually jump'd for joy and felt as if I was let out o' prison. The feeling is dreadful – that being stuck in a drawing room & having a fussy fine lady talking to you. I'd leifer work for £8 a year with comfort[53]

That passage was not written solely to please Munby. Hannah was also convinced that if she were more socially elevated she would be unable to think herself humble enough in the sight of God. Her understanding of Christianity that salvation came through humility and service was deeply felt, and accorded with, rather than was created by, Munby's ideas and obsessions.[54] She disliked her one position as an upper servant and much preferred to be a maid-of-all-work. Munby had persuaded her to take this position, but he could not persuade her to keep it.

It is impossible to know how widely Hannah's view of the constricted lives led by middle-class women was shared by others of her class, but it was certainly expressed by middle-class women writers who interrogated contemporary definitions of femininity. In *Cassandra* Florence Nightingale used the image of Chinese women with their bound feet to express the stunting and deforming effects of these norms,[55] and images of constriction, particularly in terms of clothing, recur in *Aurora Leigh* and in Charlotte Bronte's novels. Hannah's resistance to wearing gloves was a major source of conflict with Munby in his attempts after their marriage to transform her into a lady.[56] This recalls Jane Eyre's refusal to be dressed up by Mr Rochester and the tenacity with which she clings to her grey dresses.

Munby himself, despite his later attempt to embourgeois

Hannah, was privately contemptuous of the over-refinement of middle-class femininity. His diaries are full of loaded contrasts between brawny milkwomen and novel-reading charmers, grimy dustwomen and languid belles, and his glorification of the muscular working woman is inseparable from his dislike of middle-class insipidness. I suspect this kind of analysis could be extended to the Pre-Raphaelites and their interest in working-class women. Their power to control or 'create' their wives and mistresses would not have been any less if these women had been middle class. Like Munby, like Clough's Hewson, indeed like some middle-class women, they must have found conventional middle-class women and the lives they were forced to lead dull and sexless.

This also highlights the freedom with which middle-class men were able to range up and down the class structure in their search for personally rewarding relationships. Women had no such freedom and any discussion of cross-class relationships is necessarily concerned entirely with upper-class men and working-class women. I am not aware of any examples of reversed cross-class relationships. In other words, the problem of sex and class which *The Bothie* explores, and which Munby could never resolve, was primarily a masculine one. Again, we come back to the point that what really seems to be at issue in this discourse is masculinity rather than femininity. This is not to ignore the fact of exploitation and the added vulnerability of working-class women given their lack of social status and economic independence. There was also another economic factor at work; a middle-class wife would have required a larger and more expensive establishment than a working-class one. But it should be possible to admit all this without denying that the attraction to working-class women was partly a reaction against norms of femininity which were proving unsatisfactory for some men as well as crippling for many middle-class women. In the cases I am discussing, this took the form, initially at least, of an aversion to bourgeois marriage.

Hannah's reluctance to marry Munby and her refusal to become a lady was the most striking aspect of their extraordinary relationship. As she wrote in her diary, 'But tho' I'm never so happy as when I'm with him or working for *him*, yet I want to be still a servant & working so as to be independent & get my own living'.[57] Munby, too, had his hesitations, and although his reluctance was obviously less singular and more timid than Hannah's, we should be careful not to give a reductive account of his ambivalence. There were obvious class and family reasons why Munby should hesitate before marrying Hannah, even secretly, but he also had an aversion to the whole idea of marriage. He was always depressed by his friends' weddings and once, after acting as best man, put his feelings into verse:

> When I come thus to pay my heart's full fee
> To that true maid who lives and works for me,
> No gauzy dames I'll have, no gorgeous Swells,
> No loud acclaim of mercenary bells.[58]

Munby was in retreat from the pattern of relationships and many of the values of his own class, and this added to his hesitations about marriage.

Hannah represented many things for Munby. After an evening of unsettling religious discussion with some friends, prompted by hearing a lecture from Ruskin on his religious doubts, Munby turned to Hannah as 'a cooling sedative. . . . How all intellectual conflicts fade out of hearing when I take her face between my palms, and see its loving intelligent simplicity! A refuge, this; homely, but as far as it goes, certain, divine'.[59] He used the same metaphor on another occasion when turning to Hannah as a refuge from contemporary doubts and problems; 'the sight of such a maiden (and the hearing too) in her peasant's garb, is like a cold plunge in summer'.[60] She represented permanence and stability in a world in which Munby, despite his diarist's eye for change, felt out of place.

Hannah's country origins were central to Munby's image of her. This is apparent in his recollected description of her when they first met:

> A country girl, she was . . . for she had worked in the fields, and had been pot girl at a village inn . . . her bare arms and hands were large and strong, and ruddy from the shoulder to the finger tips. . . . A robust hardworking peasant lass, with the marks of labour and servitude upon her everywhere: yet endowed with a grace and beauty, an obvious intelligence, that would have become a lady of the highest.[61]

He frequently referred to her as 'my English country lass', and he encouraged her to dress in a rural manner.[62] Munby also had a series of studio photos taken of Hannah in Shropshire peasant dress against a Pre-Raphaelite looking rural backcloth.[63]

Munby had a decided preference for peasant girls and 'country wenches' to urban working women whose aspirations to ladyhood he deplored.[64] The working women he most admired – fishergirls, colliergirls, Shropshire serving maids – came from an earlier, now vanishing social order. Future Hannahs will have been city born and bred. Although Munby was an observant recorder of his own time, the diaries have an underlying sense of decline and a sadness for things passing which is both social and personal. The period as a whole is notable for 'that decay of the English character, that dissolution of belief and of honour, which is rapidly going on around us'.[65] Munby doesn't often fulminate, but his diaries quietly register a sense of alienation from the rapidly developing industrial capitalist society in which he lived. I shall return to this, and in particular the pastoralization of Hannah, when discussing the rather different treatment of this structure of feeling in *The Bothie*.

One aspect of this alienation was Munby's deep sense of his own uselessness. This was particularly strong in the years before 1860 when he was trying to establish himself at the Bar. He hated the law, indeed all the emerging professions,[66] and his serious ambitions as a writer were early disappointed. When he received a small sum for the pulped unbound copies of his first collection of poems, *Benoni* (1852), he wrote in his diary, 'Amusing and instructive incident! It disposes satisfactorily of the amiable delusion that one has "a work to do" in the world: God having put his veto on *that* kind of work, & I being fit for no other'.[67] This note became muted after Munby secured his post at the Ecclesiastical Commissioners in 1860, but it never entirely disappeared. This post provided a steady income and guaranteed independence and social respect, but it never satisfied his sense of vocation. Hannah, and working women in general, filled this need, and his admiration for their physical strength and the utility of their labour was partly a compensation for his own failure to find satisfying and productive work. Guilt and low self-esteem fed Munby's obsessions and can be seen as a further aspect of this alternative discourse on masculinity. In the *Bothie* Hewson is in search of a vocation as well as a life-partner.

Elspie satisfies both needs, just as Hannah did for Munby.

Hudson has described Hannah as a personification of Munby's admiring sympathy for working women, and his relationship with her as a social experiment as much as a love affair.[68] This phenomenon of love as social experiment is found in other mid-nineteenth-century narratives which resolve their tensions by an inter-class marriage. *The Bothie* is one of these, and Disraeli's *Sybil* (1845) is another. *Aurora Leigh* is an interesting variant. Here the inter-class marriage is proposed but not contracted, and the middle-class philanthropist Romney is abandoned at the church by the working-class woman he is to marry. And in *Aurora Leigh* the inter-class marriage is to be the centre-piece and not the conclusion. In this way, and unusually, marriage as both an image of class reconciliation and a means of narrative closure, is resisted.

Cross-class marriage wasn't a cure-all, and in the case of Munby and Hannah it led to separation, though not of a conventional kind. Even before their marriage Munby had conducted tentative experiments with the relationship. He sat with Hannah in the gallery of the Haymarket Theatre among the ' "roughs" '.[69] On at least three occasions he showed Hannah's photograph to friends without revealing who she was, and each time recorded that she was assumed to be a lady.[70] One of these friends was Rossetti, who described Hannah's face as 'beautiful' and 'remarkable' and said he 'should like to know that lady'. Munby repeated and underlined 'that lady'.[71] After their marriage these experiments became more frequent and venturesome, and involved taking Hannah, dressed as a lady, into the respectable world. On holiday in a Surrey village Munby persuaded Hannah to accompany him on a visit to the local Rectory. This wasn't a success: 'though her behaviour was charmingly naïve and graceful, she was too much out of place (as she fancied) and too much in awe of the gentlefolks, to talk'.[72] Munby's parenthetical remark registers his demurral from any suggestion that Hannah was 'out of place', but the episode confirms that she was. And why not? She had no desire to live in that way, and for many years Munby had valued her because of her lack of drawing-room skills. But after their marriage he began to want to transform Hannah into a lady, and this seems to have been the most important cause of their separation in 1877. Munby explained Hannah's resistance to being 'raised' in terms of having learnt too well his lessons of the dignity of lowliness. This accords with the view that Hannah was Munby's creation but is disputed by the evidence of Hannah's diaries. She had her own good reasons for not wanting to be 'raised' and must have regarded these later experiments as a betrayal of their relationship. Eventually, the problem of class proved intractable. Hannah returned to Shropshire, and Munby was caught between his authentic love for a maid-of-all-work, and his need to have her ratified as a member of his own class.

After Hannah's departure from London the relationship returned to something like its former pattern. Hannah and Munby lived apart but remained committed to each other. Munby regularly stayed with Hannah in Shropshire and seems to have lived easily in working-class surroundings for the duration of these visits. This has lead Derek Hudson to suggest that if Munby could have abdicated his gentility, he might have lived happily with Hannah in a workman's cottage.[73] But neither Munby nor Hannah wanted this inverted fairy-tale ending, and it would not have resolved the issue of class. The marriage would have remained cross-class in every sense even if Munby had moved into a labourer's cottage. Munby and Hannah were not radical critics of prevailing class relations, and even if they had been, the issue of class was too complex for any one couple to solve.

Davidoff's argument that cross-class relationships were based ultimately on power and exploitation augmented by the rights traditionally due to the man within heterosexual relations is true, but it leaves out a great deal. These cross-class relations can also be seen as an expression of discontent with existing class and gender relations, particularly in connection with marriage. By the middle of the nineteenth century the changing character of bourgeois marriage and the family, with sharpened gender distinctions at its centre, was making it increasingly difficult for some men and women to reconcile their personal needs with the demands of family and class. From a male point of view the inter-class marriage and the phenomenon of love as social experiment can be understood as a response to this difficulty. This is not to deny the fact of exploitation within these marriages and relationships. Exploitation existed in all heterosexual relations, and nowhere more so than within middle-class marriage. But the differences between middle- and cross-class marriages are at least as important as the similarities. Each of the cross-class examples considered in this section has its own special character, but taken together they can be seen as an attempted realignment of the relation between the personal and the social which contemporary marriage practice was rendering unsatisfactory. In Munby's case the personal and the social remained stubbornly apart. Eventually, he wished to 'raise' Hannah, but she resisted the characteristic assimilation of the working-class woman to middle-class values and practices. In *The Bothie* the issue is resolved somewhat differently. Hewson cannot live across two worlds; instead he sets out to create a new one.

VI

At this point my earlier remark about the dominance of pastoral at the end of *The Bothie* needs to be recalled. There is an important conjunction between the domestic and the rural in nineteenth-century writing. Davidoff, L'Esperance and Newby have attempted to theorize this, arguing that the idea of the home as the ideal setting for women's lives, and the village community as the ideal setting for social relationships, constituted a dominant ideology of home and community which can be understood as a response to the need to impose order in a changing and alienating world. The rural world and its social order was seen as settled and permanent. The family – the domestic community – was similarly naturalized, and again seen as an upholder of moral and social order in a troubling world.[74]

These twin ideals were often fused. In 1852 the *Art Journal* noted the popularity of paintings of cottage domesticity and remarked that 'a cottage-interior mania seems to have set in'.[75] There is an idiosyncratic example of this taste for rural idyll in *Little Dorrit* (1855–7). As a resident of Bleeding Heart Yard, Mrs Plornish is unable to afford even a print, but she has had the whole of one wall of her parlour painted to represent the exterior of a thatched cottage. The door into her parlour doubles as the front door of the painted cottage, and when shut is seen to have the inscription 'Happy Cottage'. When Mrs Plornish hears her father singing from inside the 'cottage' it is 'a perfect Pastoral ... the Golden Age revived'. The opening chapters of *Tom Brown's Schooldays*, which describe the rural setting of Tom's childhood, rest snugly within this ideology of home and community. Their mode is pastoral, looking back from the restless, fretted present to a period of innocence and stability. They describe an idealized feudal community in which village life mitigates differences of rank. Tom and his brothers play with the village boys 'without the idea of equality or inequality ever entering their heads'. His sisters and the village girls are presumably at home getting accustomed to their ideal setting. Family relations and village community are the foundation of social order and coherence.

Munby's diaries were written from within this same structure of feeling, but its expression is more difficult. His idealization of rural working women was personally necessary but socially defensive, and had to co-exist somehow with the urban industrial world in which he lived. He was able to pastoralize Hannah in his diaries, his photographs, and in the manner he encouraged her to dress, but this construction was always to collide with the reality of her existence as a maid-of-all-work. And in his own life he experienced differences of class in a most extreme form and in a way which ensured that the rural and domestic ideals remained stubbornly apart. Munby remained shut out from the domestic.[76] *The Bothie* is a more complex and ambiguous variant of this home and community ideology. It has neither the complacent conservatism of *Tom Brown's Schooldays* nor the wistful strained conservatism of Munby's diaries. Clough's poem attempts to make more radical use of this ideology and its associated literary mode of pastoral, by turning it against contemporary bourgeois society. Not content with mourning what has been lost, *The Bothie* tries to re-establish it.

However, there are problems with this, both in the social vision itself and in its mode of presentation. The problems with the poem's backward-looking radicalism are fairly obvious. A pre-industrial family structure can hardly take root in mid-nineteenth-century Britain, and so Hewson and Elspie must emigrate to find virgin territory in which the domestic and rural can flourish together. Emigration was another common form of narrative closure in writing of the 1840s and 1850s. Carlyle had invited this on the last page of *Chartism* (1839) with a picture of Canada, its unfelled forests and untilled plains and prairies crying out 'Come and till me, come and reap me!' Gaskell responded in *Mary Barton*, which closes with Mary and Jem peacefully domiciled in their long, low wooden house in the Canadian countryside. All but one of the primeval trees have been felled; it alone remains to shade the gable-end of their cottage. This soft-focus presentation of life in a colonial outpost relaxes the earlier tensions of class, poverty, and gender in a similar way to the end of *The Bothie*.

More interesting, perhaps, is the relation between this social vision of the pre-industrial family and its pastoral mode of presentation. Pastoral can be an effective way of expressing a sense of things lost, but it is also inherently simplifying and softening. In the earlier books of *The Bothie*, pastoral has a dramatic and psychological function. It is, for example, a means of expressing the naïve, untested nature of Hewson's radicalism, as Elspie's early judgement of him makes clear:

> – Yes there he is still in his fancy,
> Doesn't yet see we have here just the things he is
>   used-to elsewhere,
> And that the things he likes here, elsewhere he wouldn't
>   have looked at,
> People here too are people, and not as fairy-land creatures;
> He is in a trance, and possessed
>
>   (Bk 4, ll. 155–9)

In the middle sections of the poem, pastoral is held in tension with other modes which modify its effects. Book 6, in which Hewson reaches the Bothie, has an epigraph from Virgil's *Eclogues* – 'Bring him home from the city, my spells, bring Daphis home' – whose associations are swiftly undercut by the determinedly prosaic description which follows:

>   it is no sweet seclusion;
> Blank hill sides slope down to a salt sea loch at their
>   bases,
> Scored by runnels, that fringe ere they end with rowan and
>   alder;
> Cottages here and there out-standing bare on the mountain,
> Peat-roofed, windowless, white; the road underneath by the
>   water.
> There on the blank hill side, looking down through the loch
>   to the ocean,

> There with a runnel beside, and pine trees twain before it,
> There with the road underneath, and in sight of coaches
>   and steamers,
> Dwelling of David Mackaye and his daughters Elspie and
>   Bella,
> Sends up a column of smoke the Bothie of Toper-na-fuosich.
>   (Bk 6, ll. 6–15)

Hewson's destination, the end of his quest, is presented in antipastoral terms which qualify and criticize pastoral modes of thought and description.

This tension between different modes also features in the presentation of Hewson and Elspie's courtship in Books 7 and 8. Hewson continues to see Elspie through a pastoral haze. He regrets that Elspie once spent a year in England and therefore is not virgin Scottish, like a sweater. He patronizingly rejects Elspie's wish to read his books:

> Weary and sick of our books we come to repose in
>   your eye-sight,
> As to the woodland and water, the freshness and
>   beauty of Nature,
> Lo, you will talk, forsooth, of the things we are
>   sick to death of.
>   (Bk 8, ll. 117–19)

Elspie will have none of this, and refuses his equally patronizing concession that he will read them to her: 'I will read to myself, when I choose it' (Bk 8, l. 124). Although their projected marriage is presented as a radical alternative to bourgeois marriage, Hewson still has much to learn. Both these emphases, however, are muted by the final book, where pastoral has become dominant.

At the end of the poem their marriage has almost become an alternative to social action rather than a manifestation of it. Hewson accepts Adam's repeated advice – 'Let us to Providence trust, and abide and work in our stations' (Bk 9, l. 72) – which he has resisted throughout the poem:

> Yes, you are right, I dare say, you always were and will be,
> And in default of a fight I will put up with peace and
>   Elspie.
>   (Bk 9, ll. 99–100)

Hewson soon reports the return of his 'old democratic fervour' (Bk 9, l. 110), but his radicalism is now muted and ambiguous, and it isn't finally clear whether it is carried into the new family created by his marriage or neutralized by it. That the poem can, uneasily, suggest both is because of the difficulty of accommodating Hewson's politics within its predominantly pastoral conclusion. This dominance of the pastoral means that love becomes an alternative to politics, and that the previously radical terms of Hewson's proposed re-entry into family are seriously qualified.

The most striking example of the way in which pastoral softens and simplifies the poem's conclusion is the 27-line simile of dawn in the city which becomes the emblem of Hewson and Elspie's love. This passage recalls Hewson's guilty dream of the dissolute city (Bk 4, ll. 175–82) and dissolves it as the light of day replaces the glare of gas-lamps and their shameful associations:

> He that goes forth to his walk, while speeding to the suburb,
> Sees sights only peaceful and pure; as, labourers settling
> Slowly to work, in their limbs the lingering sweetness of slumber;
> Humble market-carts, coming-in, bringing-in, not only
> Flower, fruit, farm-store, but sounds and sights of the country
> Dwelling yet on the sense of the dreamy drivers
> (Bk 9, ll. 118–23)

The country enters the city with the market carts, cleansing and transforming it until;

> the whole great wicked artifical civilised fabric, –
> All its unfinished houses, lots for sale, and railway outworks, –
> Seems reaccepted, resumed to Primal Nature and Beauty: –
> – Such – in me, and to me, and on me the love of Elspie!
> (Bk 9, ll. 134–7)

The city of dreadful night is absorbed by the country, the social is transformed by the natural, which then becomes an image of Hewson and Elspie's love. There is no longer any other perspective to modify the pastoral one. Hewson's pastoral vision has become that of the poem, which seems to have forgotten what he had still to learn. Clough was still several years away from his insistence that contemporary poetry should explore 'the blank and desolate streets' rather than relax 'by "clear spring or shady grove"'.

At the end of *The Bothie* the pastoral attempts to excise the social, cancelling rather than resolving tensions and suppressing or redefining 'the old democratic fervour' which would otherwise disturb the calm surface of the poem's conclusion. This is even more pronounced in the revisions Clough made for the 1862 edition, which shifted the poem further towards pastoral and idyll. As Patrick Scott has written, 'It was the revised *Bothie* which evoked the vague late Victorian nostalgia for the blissful dawn of undergraduate life because there was less in it to disturb such attitude to the poem'.[77] The text of 1848 responds sympathetically to some of the hopes of that revolutionary year. The text of 1862 is similarly affected by the more settled politics of its time. As pastoral becomes dominant there is no longer any place in the poem for those energies released by its other modes. These are neutralized or dissipated and the poem's tensions are relaxed. Pastoral blurs and softens the picture as an exploratory narrative employing different modes, ends in the closure of a single one.

'AMOURS DE VOYAGE': A NOTE

Although it was not published until 1858, the earliest sections of this poem date from Clough's visit to Rome during the spring and summer of 1849. It was reworked over the next nine years, but in its origins the poem came immediately after *The Bothie*, which had been completed in the autumn of 1848.

Amours de Voyage, like *The Bothie*, is written in hexameters and, apart from an elegiac prologue and epilogue to each canto, is entirely in letters. This basic epistolary form eliminates the authorial voice-over of *The Bothie's* narrative and allows for more dramatic rendering, shifting perspectives and oblique presentation. Nevertheless, it uses a narrative form to explore many of the same issues treated in *The Bothie*. It confronts more directly and rejects more thoroughly the socialization of love through bourgeois marriage. The only marriage in the poem is that between the silly, troublesome Georgina and Claude's little-valued acquaintance George Vernon. The reductive coupling of their forenames is just one example of how these two offer a model of marriage and family which the poem unequivocally rejects. Claude, the poem's main protagonist, is unable to translate his deep, complex feelings about Mary into an offer of marriage. This is not primarily because of sexual timidity but because of the terms on which love is incorporated into marriage. Georgina voices these in a letter to a friend:

> Mr Claude, you must know, is behaving a little bit better;
> He and Papa are great friends, but he really is too *shilly-shally*,
> So unlike George; yet I hope that the matter is going on fairly.
> I shall, however, get George, before he goes, to say something.
> Dearest Louise, how delightful, to bring young people together!
> (Canto 2, Letter 15, ll. 334–8)

As John Goode has written, it isn't sex that Claude fears 'but the factitious rhetoric of institutionalized love'.[78]

In both poems love and politics shadow each other. This note on *Amours de Voyage* considers the poem solely in relation to *The Bothie*, and there isn't space to do justice to the complexity of its political theme and its relation with those of love and culture. Unlike *The Bothie*, *Amours de Voyage* is a thoroughly sceptical poem. Claude's last letter, 'Politics farewell, however!' (Canto 5, Letter 10, l. 188), and the note struck in the concluding elegiac, 'Feeble and restless youths born to inglorious days' (Canto 5, l. 222) are similar in mood to lines from the final book of *The Bothie*:

> Neither battle I see, nor arraying, nor King in Israel,
> Only infinite jumble and mess and dislocation
> (Bk 9, ll. 93–4)

But Hewson at least has an alternative – 'And in default of a fight I will put up with peace and Elspie'. In *Amours de Voyage* love neither complements politics nor replaces it, and the rejection of family is uncompromising.

An important aspect of this rejection is the different function of pastoral in the poem. Patrick Scott has shown how the vision of Alba, the pastoral retreat of the classical poets, haunts Claude from the closing elegiacs of Canto 1,[79] and this vision becomes associated with his love for Mary:

> Ah, that I were, far away from the crowd and the streets of the city,
> Under the vine-trellis laid, O my beloved, with thee!
> (Canto 3, Prologue, 15–16)

Yet when Claude leaves Rome in pursuit of Mary, Alba remains unvisited ('Therefore farewell, far seen, ye peaks of the mythic Albano' Canto 3, Epilogue, l. 295) and Mary is not found. Pastoral has become simply a yearning, excluded from the epistolary narrative and relegated to the elegiacs, from which it has also disappeared by the final canto. Marriage and pastoral are rejected together in a poem where quest is no longer charmed but seems hopeless from the start.

NOTES

1. I am using the original text of 1848 edited by Patrick Scott, (St Lucia: University of Queensland Press, 1976). Scott's edition has further details about Clough's mistake over the title; pp. 23, 27–8.
2. Michael Thorpe (ed.), *Clough: The Critical Heritage* (London: Routledge & Kegan Paul, 1972), p. 53.
3. ibid., p. 30.
4. H.F. Lowry (ed.), *The Letters of Matthew Arnold to Arthur Hugh Clough* (New York: Russell & Russell, 1968), p. 95.
5. ibid., p. 66.
6. ibid., p. 99.
7. *North American Review*, July 1853, in Isobel Armstrong, *Victorian Scrutinies* (London: Athlone Press, 1972), pp. 154–6.
8. Lowry, pp. 123–4, 144.
9. All references to both Prefaces are from C.B. Tinker and H.F. Lowry (eds) *The Poetical Works of Matthew Arnold* (London: Oxford University Press, 1963).
10. Lowry, p. 147.
11. Armstrong, p. 38.
12. 'Clough's Bothie', Geoffrey and Kathleen Tillotson, *Mid-Victorian Studies* (London: Athlone Press, 1965), pp. 124–31.
13. Scott, pp. 12–13, 17, 18.

14. F.L. Mulhauser (ed.) *The Poems of Arthur Hugh Clough*, 2nd edn (Oxford: Clarendon Press, 1974), pp. xvii-xx, and 'Letters of Parepidemus, No. 2', pp. 554-9.
15. See Geoffrey and Kathleen Tillotson, pp. 123-4; Scott, p. 6.
16. R.H. Super (ed.) *Matthew Arnold on the Classical Tradition* (Ann Arbor: University of Michigan Press, 1960), pp. 148-51.
17. ibid., p. 151.
18. *Cassandra*, in Ray Strachey, *The Cause: A Short History of the Women's Movement in Great Britain* (London: G. Bell & Sons, 1928), p. 397.
19. In the 1862 edition Clough revised l. 41 as 'Never, believe me, I knew of the feelings between men and women'.
20. These lines were cancelled in the 1862 edition.
21. Lawrence Stone, *The Family, Sex and Marriage in England 1500-1800* (London: Weidenfeld & Nicolson, 1977), p. 518.
22. See Lynda Nead, 'Seduction, prostitution, suicide: "On the Brink" by Alfred Elmore', *Art History* 5(3). For an account of voluntary prostitution leading to wealth and respectability, see Derek Hudson (ed.) *Munby; Man of Two Worlds: The Life and Diaries of Arthur J. Munby 1828-1910* (London: John Murray, 1972), pp. 40-1.
23. Bruce Haley, *The Healthy Body and Victorian Culture* (Boston: Harvard University Press, 1978), p. 146.
24. ibid., p. 144.
25. Thomas Hughes, *Tom Brown's Schooldays* (Harmondsworth: Puffin Books, 1983), Pt 1, Ch. 7, p. 116.
26. This redemptive pattern becomes clear in Part 2. At the end of Part 1 Tom's character and therefore his future is in the balance. In Part 2 'the tide turns' and the redemption theme becomes insistent, including not only Tom's rescue but also Arthur's delivery from death and East's confirmation.
27. Jeffrey Weeks, *Sex, Politics and Society* (London and New York: Longman, 1981), pp. 48-50.
28. We do learn of 'the miserable little pretty white-handed curly-headed boys, petted and pampered by some of the big fellows, who wrote their verses for them, taught them to drink and use bad language, and did all they could to spoil them for everything in this world and the next'. Part 2, Ch. 2, p. 182. The language of this passage and the dire consequences of their unspoken sins makes the implication of these lines perfectly clear. The narrator underlines their significance by footnoting a defence of this so-called 'small friend system' by an old Rugbeian, and then commenting darkly, 'I can't strike out the passage; many boys will know why it is left in'.
29. Weeks, p. 49.
30. Scott, p. 11.

31. There is an excellent discussion of 'small-group vocabularies' in *The Bothie* in Scott, pp. 13–15.
32. Both these lines were cancelled in the 1862 edition.
33. Haley, p. 141.
34. Samuel Butler, *The Way Of All Flesh* (Harmondsworth: Penguin, 1976), pp. 197, 198, 200.
35. Eli Zaretsky, *Capitalism, The Family and Personal Life* (London: Pluto Press, 1976), Chs. 2–3.
36. Hudson (ed.).
37. ibid., p. 83.
38. ibid., p. 114.
39. ibid., p. 237. Munby met Clough at a dinner in 1859 in the company of Louis Blanc. Thomas Hughes, already known to Munby through their association with the Working Men's College, was also present; ibid., p. 27.
40. ibid., pp. 123–4.
41. ibid., pp. 145.
42. Liz Stanley (ed.) *The Diaries of Hannah Cullwick: Victorian Maidservant* (London: Virago Press, 1984), p. 115.
43. Hudson, pp. 167–8.
44. Rosalie Glynn Grylls, *Portrait of Rossetti* (London: Macdonald, 1964), pp. 48–9.
45. Grylls, p. 70. Jan Marsh, 'Pre-Raphaelite women', *New Society*, 23 February 1984. This kind of argument typically fails to distinguish between the women themselves and their image in Pre-Raphaelite painting and writing. For a detailed discussion of this and related points, see Deborah Cherry and Griselda Pollock, 'Woman as sign in Pre-Raphaelite literature: a study of the representation of Elizabeth Siddall', *Art History* 7(2). They make a fundamental distinction between the artistic-literary construction 'Siddal', the mis-spelling of her name initiated by D.G. Rossetti, and the historical individual Siddall (the correct spelling of her name), who has been all but lost in the conflation of model, pictorial image, and tragic life which the Pre-Raphaelite historians have perpetuated.
46. Leonore Davidoff, 'Class and gender in Victorian England', in J.L. Newton, M.P. Ryan and J.R. Walkowitz (eds) *Sex and Class in Women's History* (London: Routledge & Kegan Paul, 1983), esp. pp. 26, 45–6.
47. Carol Christ, 'Victorian masculinity and the angel in the house', in Martha Vicinus (ed.) *A Widening Sphere: Changing Roles of Victorian Women* (Bloomington and London: Indiana University Press, 1980). See also Cherry and Pollock, n. 59, p. 227.
48. See, for example, Shirley Keeldar on how men misunderstand

women: 'they misapprehend them, both for good and evil; their good woman is a queer thing, half doll, half angel; their bad woman almost always a fiend'. Charlotte Brontë, *Shirley* (London: Dent, 1970), Ch. 20, p. 278.
49. Christ, pp. 60–1.
50. ibid., p. 14.
51. Davidoff, p. 35.
52. See in particular Hannah's description of cleaning the hole under the stairs (Stanley, p. 119), and going up the chimney naked except for boots and head cover, (p. 139). Even 'those strange trials' which Munby referred to in his diary (Hudson, p. 324), and which certainly included rituals of abasement such as boot-licking, seem to have been initiated by Hannah; see Hudson, p. 424, and Stanley, n. 7, p. 314.
53. Stanley, p. 74.
54. ibid., p. 17; also p. 137.
55. Strachey, p. 407.
56. Stanley, p. 266; Hudson, p. 371.
57. Stanley, p. 193; see also pp. 170, 233–4, and Hannah's cool reaction to Munby producing a marriage licence, p. 253.
58. Hudson, p. 190. The Tennysonian echo of 'mercenary bells' was provoked by the bell-ringers at the ceremony asking for more than Munby felt was their proper fee. If they had been women, Munby would have doubled the fee and made a different kind of entry in his diary. Hannah also disliked weddings; Stanley, p. 233.
59. Hudson, p. 142.
60. ibid., pp. 79–80.
61. ibid., pp. 15.
62. See Stanley, pp. 223, 247, 276, 281. Munby particularly liked an old-fashioned print dress which had previously belonged to a farmer's daughter and which Hannah thought must be sixty years old.
63. For two of these photos, see Davidoff, p. 51, and Stanley, facing pp. 152, 153. Hannah's account of these photos is in Stanley, pp. 230–1.
64. Hudson, p. 79.
65. ibid., p. 252.
66. ibid., pp. 28, 54, 56.
67. ibid., p. 21.
68. ibid., p. 70.
69. ibid., pp. 54–5.
70. ibid., pp. 73, 127, 223.
71. ibid., p. 127.
72. ibid., p. 373.

73. ibid., pp. 383–4.
74. L. Davidoff, J. L'Esperance and H. Newby, 'Landscape with figures: home and community in English society', in Oakley and Mitchell (eds) *The Rights and Wrongs of Women* (Harmondsworth: Penguin, 1983), esp. pp. 140–3, 146–60.
75. Helene E. Roberts, 'Marriage, redundancy or sin: the painter's view of women in the first twenty-five years of Victoria's reign', in Martha Vicinus (ed.) *Suffer and be Still: Women in the Victorian Age* (London: Indiana University Press, 1980), p. 55.
76. Of course Munby's attitude to women and work differed sharply from this domestic ideal. Although his attitude to work for middle-class women was more ambivalent, he never held the view that a woman's place was in the home.
77. Scott, p. 24.
78. John Goode, '*Amours de Voyage:* The Aqueous Poem', in Isobel Armstrong (ed.), *The Major Victorian Poets: Reconsiderations* (London: Routledge & Kegan Paul, 1969), p. 288.
79. Patrick Scott (ed.) *Amours de Voyage* (St Lucia: University of Queensland Press, 1974), p. 13.

3

'A sweet disorder in the dresse': Tennyson's *The Princess*

I

The Princess tells not one story but several; nor does it have a single mode or voice for its narratives.[1] Its frame narrator is a guest at Sir Walter Vivian's ancestral home, along with other college friends of Sir Walter's son. He is shown a medieval chronicle which tells of a noble lady turned warrior who fought and defeated a 'wild King'. The narrator is fascinated by this story and takes the chronicle with him into the park which has been thrown open for the day to 'the people' (tenant families and members of the local Mechanics Institute) to enjoy sporting and scientific activities. He joins his friends and the ladies in the ruins of a Gothic abbey elsewhere in the grounds. One of the women, Aunt Elizabeth, talks fervently of 'an universal culture', using the day and the crowd as her 'text', but the students gossip and recount college japes. This clash of serious and mocking modes is to recur throughout the poem.

Lilia, Sir Walter's daughter, has draped an orange scarf around the statue of a medieval warrior, Sir Ralph, an ancestor of the Vivian's, whose chronicle the narrator is carrying. The sight of this 'feudal warrior lady-clad' reminds the narrator of the story of the lady warrior and he entertains the company by recounting it. Lilia is stung by her brother's question – ' "Where . . . lives there such a woman now?" ' (Prologue, ll. 124–6) – replying that women are held down by convention and conditioning, and expressing her

The Princess

dream of being 'some great princess' and establishing a college where women could learn 'all that men are taught'. This provokes the story of 'The Princess', a serial narrative told by each of the seven undergraduates in turn. Aunt Elizabeth wants an heroic tale, but this is laughed aside and the 'mock-solemn' seems to be established as the basic narrative mode. Lilia, who is consistently described in terms of diminutives – 'The little hearth-flower Lilia' – is the mock-heroine:

> 'Take Lilia, then, for heroine' clamoured he,
> 'And make her some great Princess, six feet high,
> Grand, epic, homicidal . . . '
> (Prologue, ll. 217–19)

The male narrative is to be interspersed with female song;

> So I began,
> And the rest followed: and the women sang
> Between the rougher voices of the men,
> Like linnets in the pauses of the wind:
> And here I give the story and the songs.
> (Prologue, ll. 235–9)

The poem raises the questions of gender and genre in the very structure of its narrative.

The story of 'The Princess' proceeds on these principles until the end of Section 4, when Lilia breaks into the narrative with a song which is clearly her own, unlike the earlier intercalated songs which have been anonymous and collective. Lilia's song is heroic rather than elegiac, and sung with 'fury' (undercut by the epithet 'warbling') provoked by the 'raillery, or grotesque, or false sublime' of the male narrative (Sect. 4, ll. 10–12). The by-play between Lilia and the next narrator which follows this song qualifies but does not entirely cancel Lilia's call for a narrative which would 'make us all we would be, great and good' (Sect. 4, l. 23). Lilia's fervour is mocked by the sheer farce of a scene which immediately follows in which the Prince appears before his father and the soldiers in woman's dress – 'disprinced from head to heel' – but the mood and mode does change in the final sections, so that by the Conclusion the mock and the solemn are in equal contention, leaving the narrator with a problem:

> Yet how to bind the scattered scheme of seven
> Together in one sheaf? What style could suit?
> The men required that I should give throughout
> The sort of mock-heroic gigantesque,
> With which we bantered little Lilia first:
> The women – and perhaps they felt their power,
> For something in the ballads which they sang,
> Or in their silent influence as they sat,
> Had ever seemed to wrestle with burlesque,
> And drove us, last, to quite a solemn close –
> They hated banter, wished for something real,
> A gallant fight, a noble princess – why
> Not make her true-heroic – true-sublime?
> Or all, they said, as earnest as the close?
> Which yet with such a framework scarce could be.
> Then rose a little feud betwixt the two,
> Betwixt the mockers and the realists:
> And I, betwixt them both, to please them both,
> And yet to give the story as it rose,
> I moved as in a strange diagonal,
> And maybe neither pleased myself nor them.
>
> (Conclusion, ll. 8–28)

The women's resistance to mock-epic and their desire for something serious and heroic in some ways anticipates *Aurora Leigh*. As we shall see in the following chapter, Barrett Browning claims epic status for her story, refashioning for her own ends the ancient form most suitable for high subjects. This appropriation of an exclusively male genre occurred at a point when it no longer seemed possible for male writers to use such a mode. Unlike Clough's *Bothie*, *Aurora Leigh* avoids the serio-comic altogether and is completely without self-consciousness in its use of an epic voice. In *The Princess*, male mock-heroics are challenged and modified by female 'heroinism' (the term is Ellen Moers's) as the twin problems of gender and genre are explored. These are first raised in the Prologue by the story of the lady warrior, by Lilia's defence of women and desire for an heroic tale, and later by her dramatic interruption of the narrative at the end of Section 4. Their reappearance in the Conclusion, however, is significantly different. Lilia has been silenced and is now outside the feud between male mockers and female realists:

> But Lilia pleased me, for she took no part
> In our dispute: the sequel of the tale
> Had touched her; and she sat, she plucked the grass,
> She flung it from her, thinking: last, she fixt
> A showery glance upon her aunt, and said,
> 'You – tell us what we are' who might have told,
> For she was crammed with theories out of books.
>   (Conclusion, ll. 29–35)

This challenge to her maiden aunt indicates the disturbance caused Lilia by the narrative of 'The Princess' and is endorsed by the narrator's pleasure at her change of heart.

Prologue and Conclusion provide a frame-story (which itself encloses the story of the lady warrior) for the narrative of 'The Princess', which I must now summarize. A northern prince, betrothed since childhood to a southern princess, travels to the southern kingdom with two companions, Florian and Cyril, to claim his bride. However, the princess, Ida, with two companions Lady Blanche and Lady Psyche, has left her father's palace and established a closely guarded university for women with the inscription on its gate – 'Let no man enter in on pain of death'. The prince and his companions disguise themselves as women and enter the college. There they observe Ida's feminist principles at work, and learn she scorns marriage and utterly rejects her betrothal to the prince because it was made without her consent. Eventually, the men are discovered and forced to flee. War between the northern and southern kings over the broken betrothal is averted by a tournament between the prince and Ida's brother, each supported by fifty of their men. The prince and his followers are defeated and badly wounded, but are nursed back to health by Ida and some of her women. The college is disbanded. Ida recants the 'harder' elements of her feminism and expels Lady Blanche, who is held responsible for its 'distortions'. Florian marries Blanche's daughter, Cyril marries Lady Psyche (who is Florian's sister), and Ida marries the prince. The 'acceptable' elements of her feminism are assimilated to a companionate marriage – 'The two-celled heart beating, with one full stroke' (Sect. 7, l. 289).

Tennyson used frame-stories in other narrative poems concerned with frustrated marriage hopes (lamely in 'Locksley Hall', more subtly in 'Edwin Morris'), but this technique is most highly developed in *The Princess*, where it allows the narrative counterpointing which is central to the poem's structure. Lilia is the main point of connection between the narratives and is responsible for the single irruption of one into the other. She is the princess of the frame-story, and her withdrawal from the gender feud in the Conclusion echoes Ida's recantation. Narrative counterpoint also pairs Aunt Elizabeth with Lady Blanche. Blanche has been Ida's 'second mother'; Aunt Elizabeth is Lilia's chaperone. Blanche is physically unattractive, a man-hater, dogmatic, twisted, and unfeeling. Aunt Elizabeth is treated more gently, but the epithet 'maiden' places her; she is cerebral and humourless. Ida's rejection of Blanche anticipates Lilia's final challenge to her aunt. The opposition of mockers and realists is also common to both the main narratives. Male mockery, condescension, and chauvinism are partly subdued by female fervour and idealism, just as feminism is mocked and persuaded back into femininity.

II

Most socially orientated readings of *The Princess* concentrate on the poem's obvious theme of feminism, and the challenge this poses to marriage.[2] Much less attention has been paid to the poem's examination of the determinants of marriage, in particular gender, sexuality, and the family, and the way these are related to the feminist theme. I want to examine this question, looking first at the poem's treatment of gender – what is masculine? what is feminine? what are the consequences of gender uncertainty for marriage, the family and the social order? – and second, the disturbance of family within the poem and its eventual reconstitution.

There is a marked strain of androgyny in *The Princess*, often expressed in terms of transvestism. The lady warrior, the statue of Sir Ralph draped with Lilia's orange scarf, and the prince and his companions disguised in 'maiden plumes' are, of course, treated lightly. Yet the lady warrior obviously suggests both Lilia and Ida; the serious, peaceful concluding lines of the poem have Lilia disrobing Sir Ralph in a spirit very different from the sportive one in which she has robed him; and if the prince's disguise provokes scenes of sheer farce, not only when exposed to his father and the soldiers but also when he is forced to sing 'O Swallow, Swallow' in a croaking falsetto, it also points up his discomfort with traditional male roles and contributes to the vision of androgyny at the end of the poem:

> Yet in the long years liker must they grow;
> The man be more of woman, she of man
> (Sect. 7, ll. 263–4)

Androgyny lies at the heart of *The Princess* in the opposition of a 'feminine' prince and a 'masculine' princess. The prince is described as 'blue-eyed, and fair in face/Of temper amorous, as the first of May/With lengths of yellow ringlet, like a girl' (Sect. 1, ll. 1–3). Ida is strikingly beautiful, but presented as someone who has denied her essential femininity by appropriating male roles. The prince's father is prototypically masculine – 'Man is the hunter, woman is his game'. Ida's father is a 'spindling King' with 'dwarfish loins' who panics at the prospect of the tournament – ' "Boys!" shrieked the old king, but vainlier than a hen/To her false daughters in the pool' (Sect. 5, ll. 318–19). In terms of the poem, neither offers a sound model of fatherhood; one is brutish, the other weak. The northern king's understanding of gender difference is stark and crude, but the southern king seems to have lost all sense of such difference. Both extremes must be rejected.

If the fathers seem too fixed in their respective characters, too much themselves, their children are uncertain and incomplete, searching for their other half. Prince and princess temporarily find this in their friendships with Florian and Psyche, who are, of course, brother and sister. Florian is described by the prince as 'my other heart/And almost my half-self, for still we moved/Together, twinned as horse's ear and eye' (Sect. 1, ll. 54–6); Ida says of her friendship with Psyche, 'now should men see/Two women faster welded in one love/Than pairs of wedlock' (Sect. 6, ll. 235–7). These unions can, however, only be transitory, and they loosen or fall apart as the narrative moves towards the 'mature' heterosexual marriages of the poem's conclusion. Ida and the prince discover themselves in each other, as do the other couples.

In Freudian terms it is as if the younger characters have been frozen in some bisexual stage from which the narrative eventually releases them. When it does so, the gender confusion disappears, and with it the recurring transvestite motif. This motif has been a way of dramatizing the conflict between self and role which both prince and princess have experienced. This is obviously true in the case of the prince. He is unable to accept the idea of masculinity embodied by his father and therefore remains half-gendered and incomplete until he marries Ida and discovers a more liberal concept of manhood. But it is also true in Ida's case. The poem sets out to demonstrate that her apparent completeness is illusory, and eventually has Ida admit that she was 'but a girl . . . a Queen of farce!' (Sect. 7, ll. 227–8), thereby conceding the mockers' case, the male point of view. Significantly, the return of her femininity is imaged in terms of disrobing – 'and all/Her falser self slipt from her like a robe/And left her woman' (Sect. 7, ll. 145–7) and occurs before the very eyes of the prince. As the disguise falls away, Ida is revealed as 'herself' and the uncertain sexuality of hero and heroine is resolved. This revelation, which draws on the conventions of fairy tale and masque, anticipates Lilia's disrobing of Sir Ralph, whose chronicle has contained the story of the lady warrior.

These gender reversals which characterize much of the narrative, are reminiscent of the ritual sexual inversion that traditionally accompanied festive misrule. The point of such enactments of gender disorder was, it has been argued, to dramatize the need for a stratified sexual order in which the male was dominant and the female submissive. The disorder of temporary female ascendancy was followed by the restoration of gender and social order.[3] The narrative of *The Princess* seems to enact a drama of this kind. There is, however, a significant difference. The marriage of princess and prince is based on their discovery of reformed roles for women and men. Ida must soften her feminism and '"Come down . . . from yonder mountain height"', but not to lose herself in the 'soft and milky rabble of womankind' (Sect. 6, l. 290). The prince must steer a course between the extremes represented by the two kings. Unlike the southern king, he does respond to war-music, feeling 'the blind wildbeast of force,/Whose home is in the sinews of a man' (Sect. 5, ll. 256–7), but he avoids the rampant male chauvinism of his father.

In each case the influence of the mother is crucial. Ida's mother is long dead, and she was brought up by Lady Blanche, a false mother figure who is blamed for the 'excesses' of Ida's feminism. It is a memory of her mother which begins Ida's softening (Sect. 6, ll. 95–8) and this process is hastened when her father rebukes her in the name of her mother (Sect. 6, ll. 215–20). When she finally relents and opens the doors of the college to the wounded soldiers she does so in the name of her mother (Sect. 6, ll. 314–17). Blanche's authority is lost as Ida's memory of her mother becomes clearer and its influence stronger. When the prince and his father argue about the nature of women, it is the prince's mother who is the focus of their disagreement (Sect. 5, ll. 144–97). The prince's image of true marriage as the 'two-celled heart beating, with one full stroke' derives from his mother, from whose example 'faith in womankind/Beats with his blood' (Sect. 7, ll. 309–10). His description of her – 'Not learned, save in gracious household ways . . . Interpreter between the Gods and men,/Who looked all native to her place, and yet/On tiptoe seemed to touch upon a sphere/Too gross to tread' (Sect. 7, 299–306) – is much closer to an idealized version of the northern king's position ('A lusty brace/Of twins may weed her of her folly' Sect. 5, ll. 453–4) than the poem and many of its commentators would have us believe. Nevertheless, it does highlight the importance of both mothers. Each tempers the undesirable elements of gender difference, brutish masculinity on the one hand and separatist feminism on the other. Both show the way to the humane companionate marriage based on the modification of gender roles which the poem so clearly endorses. Gender order is recovered from transvestite confusion, but it is re-established on a reformed basis.

III

Before turning to the question of the disturbance and reconstitution of family within the poem, I want to look in more detail at some other examples of tranvestism in nineteenth-century writing and culture, and explore the significance of this recurring motif. Although there is a long literary tradition of transvestism, its ubiquity in Victorian culture indicates a pressing contemporary significance. Clothes, like domestic interiors, are important in many Victorian narratives – prose, poetry and painting – and were, of course, socially as well as personally expressive.

As manliness and femininity were redefined, cultural and symbolic representations of sexual difference took on particular significance. Male clothing changed dramatically during the first half of the nineteenth century.[4] Most finery, and all signs of foppery went. Knee-breeches and stockings, which showed off the limbs, were replaced by trousers which hid physical shape. Most colour was eliminated, and silk and satin became mainly feminine materials. By mid-century the standard male appearance expressed perfectly those qualities of dignity, sobriety, and restraint which were held to be inherently masculine.

Changes in women's clothing were a foil to this refashioned masculine appearance. Full skirts, small waists, soft colours, large bonnets, and ringlets created a dainty, childlike image. In contrast to the straight lines, practical materials and business-like image of men's clothes, women's fashion emphasized colour, detail, and flowing curved lines which both constricted the body and highlighted its shape. Clothes were a crucial part of gender segregation.

As a focus of gender, however, clothes could also be used to challenge this new emphasis on gender difference and fixed gender characteristics. In early French socialist communities, for example, unisex clothing was worn to affirm gender equality and express the ideal of the androgynous personality.[5] Forms of cross-dressing were closely allied to ideas of gender reversal and androgyny. In Britain, the Communist Church founded in the 1840s by Goodwyn and Catherine Barmby developed a similar critique of the idea of an essential masculinity and femininity which found expression in dress. Goodwyn wore his blond hair down over his shoulders, and Catherine advocated, and possibly emulated, the masculinizing bloomers of the Saint-Simonian women.[6]

The relation between clothes, fashion, and gender roles was complex. For example, David Kunzle's study of the Victorian controversy over tight-lacing shows that although this fashion was designed to emphasize femininity, it came to be attacked by conservative, anti-feminist men. These attacks were gynaecologically directed. Tight-lacing was said to damage the reproductive organs and cause sterility, to be an abortion device, and to be the

Victorian equivalent of the vibrator. It was seen as a denial of maternity and was lumped together with other feminist aspirations such as education, freedom from domestic drudgery, sport, and sexual self-expression. Kunzle concludes that by the late-nineteenth century young women were tight-lacing in protest against the stereotyped social role awaiting them.[7] He is too sanguine about the radical potential of tight-lacing but his account does show how gender typing could produce its own contradictions. Challenges were possible from within even the most constricted situations.

There seem to be fewer examples of male than female transvestism in nineteenth-century writing. *The Princess* is the most fully developed example I know of men dressing as women. Mr Rochester's disguise as a gypsy fortune-teller in *Jane Eyre* is striking, but this seems a more traditional use of the transvestite motif for discovery and revelation. It does, however, also involve a form of role reversal. As Maurianne Adams has pointed out, the gypsy image applies to Jane as well as Rochester, dramatizing an affinity which marks them off from the world of the Ingrams and the Reeds.[8] Jane is excluded from this world, and Rochester is announcing his intention to leave it. For the male, cross-dressing can be educative, forcing him to feel what it is like to be treated as a woman. Rochester's disguise, which unlike that of the prince does not involve any loss of power, is not exactly of this kind, but it nevertheless anticipates his blinding and maiming which at the end of the novel leaves him in a position of 'feminine' dependency. I shall return to the blinding and maiming motif in the following chapter. A semi-comic example of male transvestism and role reversal occurs in *Mary Barton*, where two middle-aged men are forced to make a journey with their orphaned baby grandchild. The baby refuses to be fed by the men, although it happily takes food from various women they meet on the journey. Eventually, one of the men borrows a chambermaid's night-cap in a desperate attempt to get the baby to eat. This figure of the male mother was given serious and sustained treatment a few years later by George Eliot in *Silas Marner* (1861), where Silas finds a new identity by adopting the conventional female role of mothering.

Other examples of feminized men will occur in the course of my discussion of female transvestism. Given the relational nature of gender definition, it was difficult to express dissatisfaction with dominant ideas of womanhood without also examining masculinity. But interrogations of masculinity were more than just a by-product of a more deeply felt and widespread resistance to contemporary norms of femininity. There is a widely expressed sense in Victorian writing that contemporary gender definitions were limiting for men as well as for women. The decline of the hero in nineteenth-century fiction is hardly a fresh observation, but it is worth repeating in this context. In many nineteenth-century novels 'masculine' and 'heroic' qualities have become villainous, and the 'hero' is noticeably feminized. The eponymous hero of *David Copperfield* is nicknamed Daisy. The heroic qualities of his own boyhood idol, Steerforth, become predatory and destructive. In this respect David and Steerforth stand in similar relation to each other as the prince and his father.

Androgynous female characters – women dressed, looking, or living like men – are much more common. Charlotte Brontë's *Shirley* (1849) is a particularly rich text for women's issues, and Shirley herself is probably the most fully developed example of the androgynous heroine in Victorian writing. This is how she announces herself on her first appearance: 'Shirley Keeldar, Esquire, ought to be my style and title. They gave me a man's name; I hold a man's position'.[9] She owns a mill, constantly refers to herself as a man, and is referred to as a man by others, including the narrator. She even whistles. She attacks Milton's depiction of Eve – 'Milton tried to see the first woman; but . . . . It was his cook that he saw' (Ch. 18, p. 252) – and has an alternative vision of Eve as a 'woman-Titan' (p. 253), equal with Adam before God. She is physically attractive, but described as wearing 'armour under her silk dress' (Ch. 23, p. 321). This recalls Ida, as well as Joan of Arc, and so too does the taming of Shirley's feminism at the end of the novel. She tells her future husband, Louis Moore, 'I am glad I know my keeper, and am used to him. Only his voice will I follow; only his hand shall manage me; only at his feet will I repose' (Ch. 36, p. 492). However, Louis is a far more shadowy character than the prince (he doesn't even appear until late in the novel), and it is the image of Shirley as the 'young squire of Briarfield' (Ch. 11, p. 161), which dominates the novel. It is also significant that despite her 'masculine' role, habits, and manner she remains beautiful and 'feminine'. This comes out particularly in the descriptions of her friendship with Caroline. The novel insists that for a woman to live in the world is not to be unwomanly or desexed. In passing, it is worth noting that Charlotte Brontë's heroines are resistant to being dressed *by* men. We have already seen this in the case of Jane Eyre, but it is even more striking in *Villette*. Lucy Snowe is the antithesis of the beautiful, androgynous Shirley. Physically plain, financially dependent and introspective, she is bullied into taking a male role in M. Paul's play but stubbornly refuses to dress for the part, insisting on wearing her usual clothes.[10] This assertion of her independence is also a refusal to be desexed or regendered by M. Paul, whom she is coming to love.

Dickens's novels are full of role confusion. The parent–child reversal is the most common one, but there are interesting examples of androgynous women as well. Here is David Copperfield's description of Betsey Trotwood's clothes:

> Her dress was of a lavender colour, and perfectly neat; but scantily made, as if she desired to be as little encumbered as possible. I remember that I thought it, in form, more like a riding-habit with the superfluous skirt cut off, than anything else. She wore at her side a gentleman's gold watch ... with an appropriate chain and seals; she had some linen at her throat not unlike a shirt-collar, and things at her wrists like little shirt-wristbands.
>
> (*David Copperfield*, Ch. 13, p. 249)

Betsey Trotwood has suffered from her husband and has partly redefined herself as a man. As David's mother dimly perceives, she is publicly masculine but privately feminine:

> In a short pause which ensued, she had a fancy that she felt Miss Betsey touch her hair, and that with no ungentle hand; but, looking at her, in her timid hope, she found that lady sitting with the skirt of her dress tucked up, her hands folded on one knee, and her feet upon the fender, frowning at the fire.
>
> (*David Copperfield*, Ch. 1, p. 53)

As Clara's eyes turn to her, Betsey's gentleness dissolves to be replaced by masculine attitudes. Betsey has tried to exclude men from her life, insisting before David's birth he will be a girl, and years later greeting her weary, unknown relative with the emphatic dismissal ' "Go along! No boys here" '. As the description of her clothes suggests, she has tried to free herself of a woman's usual encumbrances.

The use of women's clothing as an image of their encumbrances and restrictions is widespread. I have touched on this already, and it will appear again in Chapter 4 below on *Aurora Leigh*, where it is a recurring image for the cramped, confining social role of middle-class women. We see it at work in the description of Shirley and Caroline racing across fields and through hedges to warn the men at the mill that an attack is imminent; they are hindered by their long hair, tender skin, silks and muslins (*Shirley*, Ch. 19, pp. 268–9). The encumbrous nature of women's clothing is dramatized by male writers as well. In *The Woman in White* Wilkie Collins' resourceful heroine Marian Halcombe climbs out of an upstairs window and along a roof to overhear the plotting of Fosco and Glyde. She explains in her diary that to do so she must first remove all the layers of her underclothing: 'In my ordinary evening costume I took up the room of three men at least. In my present dress, when it was held close about me, no man could have passed through the narrowest spaces more easily than I'.[11] Undergarments, however, were not without their uses, as Henry Knight discovers in Hardy's *A Pair of Blue Eyes* (1873) when he is rescued from a cliff-face by an improvised rope knotted together from the yards of white linen which made up Elfride's undergarments. This, as Penny Boumelha has pointed out, involves an interesting example of role reversal. Elfride, the author of a pseudo-medieval romance, rescues her virgin knight in distress, inverting the roles proper to both romance convention and nineteenth-century bourgeois ideals.[12]

The Woman in White also has one of the classic images of androgyny in Victorian writing. Walter Hartright's first view of Marian Halcombe is from behind. He is struck by 'the rare beauty of her form . . . her waist, perfection in the eyes of a man, for it occupied its natural place, it filled out its natural circle, it was visibly and delightfully undeformed by stays' (*The Woman in White*, p. 25). (Tight-lacing was deplored by other novelists as well. Mrs Snagsby in *Bleak House* is described as 'something too violently compressed about the waist', the consequence, it is said, of her mother having laced her up every morning 'with her maternal foot against the bed-post for a stronger hold and purchase'. Body sculpture is also attacked in Trollope's *The Way We Live Now*.) But as Marian turns towards Hartright she is revealed as dark and ugly:

> never was the fair promise of a lovely figure more strangely and startlingly belied by the face and head that crowned it. The lady's complexion was almost swarthy, and the dark down on her upper lip was almost a moustache. She had a large, firm, masculine mouth and jaw; prominent, piercing, resolute brown eyes; and thick, coal-black hair, growing unusually low down on her forehead. Her expression ... appeared ... to be altogether wanting in those feminine attractions of gentleness and pliability without which the beauty of the handsomest woman alive is beauty incomplete. To see such a face as this set on shoulders that a sculptor would have longed to model – to be charmed by the modest graces of action ... and then to be almost repelled by the masculine form and masculine look of the features in which the perfectly shaped figure ended – was to feel a sensation oddly akin to the helpless discomfort familiar to us all in sleep, when we recognize yet cannot reconcile the anomalies and contradictions of a dream.
>
> (*The Woman in White*, p. 26)

Not until the appearance of the Countess in *What Maisie Knew* does a whiskered lady make such an impact in a Victorian novel.[13] However, in James's novel the joke is on the Countess. Maisie recovers quickly enough from the shattering of her Arabian Nights fantasy which the Countess's lavish and exotic house had conjured up. In *The Woman in White* it is the utterly conventional, stereotyped attitudes of Hartright which are exposed. Marian Halcombe is one of the most independent and attractive heroines in Victorian writing, and this initial perception of her as somehow Janus-faced is revised by the narrative which follows. Her grace and her strength are not, as first perceived by Hartright, antithetic qualities, but blended and harmonized, central to her strongly defined character. It is Fosco's admiration, indeed love, for Marian which exposes Hartright's Anglo-Saxon attitudes. Marian's darkness causes no problem for the Italian, who finds her magnificent. As Nina Auerbach has shrewdly remarked, 'Her very moustache may be the real object of Count Fosco's love'.[14] Fosco and Marian are doubles in wit, intelligence, and perception, and her 'masculinity' is echoed by his 'femininity'. Fosco's habits and style would be commonly regarded as effeminate, and so too is his dress. Here is Fosco on the lawn at Blackwater Park:

> He had a broad straw hat on, with a violet-coloured ribbon round it. A blue blouse, with profuse white fancy-work over the bosom, covered his prodigious body, and was girt about the place where his waist might once have been with a broad scarlet leather belt. Nankeen trousers, displaying more white fancy-work over the ankles, and purple morocco slippers adorned his lower extremities.
>
> (*The Woman in White*, p. 205)

Marian and Fosco are, of course, antipathetic as well as paired. Her goodness is pitted against his evil, but their energy and resourcefulness push the moral contest to one side, and each is drawn to what they are fighting. The interest and power of these two cross-gendered characters lies in their androgyny, their liberation, whether for good or evil, from the social categories of masculine and feminine.

Munby's fascination with masculinized women extended to actual cases of female transvestism, and he recorded many examples in his diary.[15] Gender reversal attracted him as much as class reversal. Typically, these entries stress the physical characteristics which produce gender uncertainty, as, for example, in the case of Thomas Walker, whose trial he attended:

> to the outward eye she looked a bluff and brawny young man ... A broad, bronzed face, fullcheeked and highboned; well cut straight nose, sharp eyes, determined mouth: rough dark hair, short as a man's ... Her head was bare, and so was her strong bull neck: about the waist, she wore nothing but a blue sailor's shirt, with the sleeves partly rolled up. Standing there, with broad shoulders squared and stout arms folded on the dock rail ... it was almost impossible to believe that she was not a man. No one suspected her, indeed; she confessed her sex to avoid the prison bath.[16]

This kind of detailed physical description could come from any mid-century novel, but the sympathy of the presentation is distinctive. The other spectators at the trial are 'roughs'; the Peeler who removes her from court is 'ruthless'; the magistrate is 'pompous and petulant and grandiose'. Thomas Walker stands alone in a hostile court, with only Munby to understand her. This fascination with female transvestism was not limited to working-class women. The only occasion Munby went to see his friend Mrs Martin (the actress Helen Faucit) on the stage was when she played Rosalind in *As You Like It*:

> I expected that it would be a shock, and a strange thing, to see one whom you know as a highbred accomplished lady, moving in good society & mistress of a fine house, to see her appear in public as an actress, and in men's clothing.[17]

Needless to say, Munby was not shocked but found the performance 'a delightful compound result'. He frequently had Hannah transformed into a man. She was photographed in male dress, and Munby cut her hair short like a man's.[18] They both considered Hannah acccompanying Munby on holiday disguised as a male companion. Although this obviously accorded with the cross-gendered nature of their relationship it was also prompted by the difficulties inherent in their different class positions. Gender and class wove a complex pattern.

Munby's sympathies and predilections were limited to female transvestism. When visiting a masked ball at some pleasure gardens in Camberwell he was disconcerted to discover examples of male transvestism:

> not a few of the youths were elaborately disguised *as women* of various kinds; and some so well, that only their voices showed they were not girls – and pretty girls. This is a new thing to me, and is simply disgusting.[19]

Munby's disgust must have been at what he would have understood as the implied homosexuality of male transvestism. Jeffrey Weeks has argued that transvestism was automatically regarded as an indication of homosexuality in the nineteenth century, and his fascinating account of the Boulton and Park trial of 1871 bears this out.[20] Munby recorded his uneasiness whenever homosexuality was discussed. Swinburne frequently upset him in this respect, praising Whitman, upholding 'that hateful theory' of Shakespeare's sonnets, and creating a scene with a male friend at the Arts Club where, 'incredibile dictu – they embraced one another in some indecent fashion'.[21] In these reactions Munby

Plate 6 Ernest Boulton (left) and Frederick Park parodying pictures of sisterly sentiment. Female impersonation was a widespread and acceptable form of entertainment but Boulton and Park carried their performances on to the streets of London and were arrested in 1870. They were were charged with conspiring and inciting persons to commit an unnatural offence. Others arrested with them included Lord Arthur Clinton, MP for Newark and son of the Duke of Newcastle, with whom Boulton had been living, masquerading as his wife. Clinton committed suicide while awaiting trial. Boulton and Park were acquitted after a long and much publicized trial, at which Park's father, a Master of the Court of Common Pleas, appeared as a defence witness.

would seem to be repressing a fear of his own possible homosexuality. In a similar way, the public knowledge of Ruskin's impotence seemed to provoke fears of his own incapacity. After an evening with Ruskin at the Working Men's College, he wrote:

> Those who only know Ruskin in the beauty & worth of his books, had better look no further: the doubts of his virility, and his appearance which confirms them, are alone sufficient to make one feel strangely in his presence.[22]

Munby's anxieties and uncertainty about his own sexual identity clearly fed his interest in female transvestism. As gender boundaries became sharper, transgression of those boundaries in the form of cross-gender behaviour acquired new importance and prominence. Munby fitted neither his gender nor his class, and his fascination with female transvestism and boundary transgression was an expression of suppressed discontent with dominant Victorian definitions of gender role and sexual identity.

A further dimension of the androgyny motif in female characters, one which I can only mention in passing, is the recurring pattern of paired female characters, one active and 'masculine', the other passive and 'feminine'. Almost invariably the active woman is dark and the passive one fair. Marian Halcombe's half-sister Laura is blond, pliant and conventionally feminine. Predictably, Walter Hartright marries her. Shirley Keeldar and Caroline Helstone are similarly paired. So too are Maggie Tulliver and her cousin Lucy Deane in *The Mill on the Floss*. Dorothea and Rosamund in *Middlemarch* can also be seen in this way, although Rosamund's passivity is unusually strong and Dorothea's activity easily diverted. Another suggestive pairing of this kind is that of Rosa Bud and Helena Landless in *Edwin Drood*. Helena is herself a twin, and much braver than her brother who recalls that when they ran away from their stepfather, 'she dressed as a boy, and showed the daring of a man'.[23] Rosa Bud's nature is sufficiently indicated by her name.

This splitting of female characters into opposed types, like the related androgyny motif, suggests the conflict between self and role which seems to have become stronger as the social definition of gender difference hardened. In each of the cases cited above, the conventional middle-class young lady has her anti-type whose dominant characteristics are those which the nineteenth century regarded as masculine. These anti-types challenge and resist contemporary gender polarization, blurring and confusing the distinctions which became essential to the middle-class family as it developed during the Victorian period. They meet a variety of fates. Marian remains single, a maiden aunt to Laura's children. Maggie is drowned. Dorothea escapes from Middlemarch to London. The most uncompromising – Ida and Shirley – are the most fully incorporated into orthodox family roles. It is only the older woman, Betsey Trotwood, a version of the old maid, who becomes a 'mother' while retaining her independence and remaining free of nuclear ties.

The use of androgyny to express dissatisfaction with gender stereotypes becomes very pointed in late-nineteenth-century writing. Angel Clare's name underlines the contrast with the emphatically masculine Alec Stoke-d'Urberville. Although angels were traditionally masculine, they always had bisexual potential, and in the Victorian period they became irrefutably female.[24] Angel Clare's rejection of Tess is a reversion to masculine values of a kind he has earlier resisted. There is a notable scene in *Jude the Obscure* where Sue Bridehead sits in front of Jude's fire wearing his best dark suit while her own clothes dry. As she sits and talks of her past, Jude is struck by her 'curious unconsciousness of gender'. However, clothes raise the question of gender even as Sue denies their significance: ' "I suppose, Jude, it is odd that you should see me like this and all my things hanging there? Yet what nonsense! They are only a woman's clothes – sexless cloth and linen..."'.[25] As Virginia Woolf wrote in *Orlando*, 'it is clothes that wear us and not we them'. The heroine of Lady Florence Dixie's transvestite feminist Utopia *Gloriana; or the Revolution of 1900* (1890) has no doubts about the significance of clothes. She disguises herself as a man, becomes an MP, successfully sponsors a Woman Suffrage Bill and finally becomes prime minister. The revelation of her true gender sparks off a feminist revolution.[26] It is an interesting sidelight on this fantasy that earlier in the century Margaretta Grey, cousin of the Whig prime minister Earl Grey and aunt of Josephine Butler, used to dress as a boy to gain admittance to Parliament to observe her cousin.[27] Clothes were also part of the defence system of the institutions of male power.

This more overt and polemical use of transvestism in later nineteenth-century writing was also reflected in controversy over dress fashion. Kunzle shows that late in the century a number of items of men's clothing shifted across to women's dress. One example of this was the masher collar, but even more conservative male fashion became radicalized when worn by women. These overt transvestite tendencies in late-nineteenth-century fashion were nicely captured by a Du Maurier cartoon in *Punch* in 1891, in which a young woman wearing her brother's shirt, tie, coat, and hat is taxed by her girlfriend with making herself 'look like a young man, you know, and that's so effeminate'.[28]

What conclusions can we draw from this preoccupation with transvestism? In any culture clothes operate as a signifying system. They are invested with social meanings and form part of a larger symbolic order. Although the use of clothes for disguise and role reversal has a long literary history, the examples I have been discussing indicate a changing use of this tradition in nineteenth-century writing. The frequent recurrence of the androgyny theme, its realization in terms of transvestism, and the blurring of gender lines it expresses, suggest a deep anxiety about gender in nineteenth-century Britain. This can be seen as a reaction to the increasing emphasis on gender difference. As masculinity and femininity were reconstructed in sharp binary opposition, discontent with the limiting nature of these stricter definitions of gender began to be expressed. This was most obviously the case with women who resisted the passive, home- and child-orientated stereotype, but it extended to dissatisfaction with male stereotypes as well. In fact, it was difficult to examine femininity without also taking account of its opposite and defining term. There was also a clear homosexual dimension to the transvestite motif. As sexual behaviour was increasingly categorized and regulated, and 'perverse' sexualities given stricter medical and legal descriptions, the resulting emphasis on heterosexual conjugality proved limiting and oppressive for those who did not wish to meet its requirements. Transvestism was also an expression of resistance to these normative pressures.

In general terms, then, transvestism questioned existing sex roles, argued for their redefinition and was used to explore new possibilities. This search for new definitions was at least as significant as the manner in which these texts tended eventually to fall back into an acceptance of more conventional ones. Toril Moi has made a useful distinction between alternative concepts of androgyny as either the *union* of masculinity and femininity, or the *deconstruction* of that duality and rejection of the social constructs of masculinity and femininity. Only the latter, she argues, can be regarded as authentically feminist.[29] Most Victorian texts which question gender definition are of the former kind, and none more so than *The Princess*. Yet to argue for the redefinition of gender roles is to expose existing norms as socially constructed rather than biologically inevitable. Although none of my major texts is authentically feminist in Moi's terms, each questions the binary opposition of masculine and feminine and in doing so opens up the possibility of a more radical deconstruction of sexual identity.

IV

Tennyson had the idea for *The Princess* at least as early as 1839, and John Killham has suggested a connection between the origin of the poem and the debate surrounding the Custody of Infants Bill.[30] In particular, he draws attention to Tennyson's friend J.M. Kemble, editor of the *British and Foreign Review*, a virulent opponent of the bill and of rights for women. Killham provides generous samples of Kemble's style, but he doesn't really pursue the connections between Kemble's writing and *The Princess*. In fact, Kemble sounds very like the northern king, although I hesitate to suggest him as a model; clearly there was no shortage of possible originals. Another connection which Killham ignores is that the issue of child custody and the rights of mothers figures prominently in Tennyson's poem, a point I shall return to later. But the feature which binds Kemble and *The Princess* most closely is a shared concern with the implications of feminism for the family. Kemble saw the Custody of Infants Bill as an attack on patriarchal power: 'remember that God himself has placed his greatest glory in being GOD THE FATHER', he wrote in a letter defending his hostility to the bill.[31] Sexual equality would lead to domestic anarchy:

> The *family*, the foundation of all society, would be at once, and completely destroyed; and this indeed is the avowed object . . . of many of those who, in France and elsewhere have advocated the doctrine of female emancipation.[32]

The Princess

The Princess is written within the same nexus of concern, although its ideological resolution is less reactionary. It is another family narrative, a poem about the disturbance of family, the severing of family ties in the name of alternative values, and their eventual reconstruction on what purports to be a reformed basis.

Section 1 of *The Princess* establishes a network of family relationships, actual, and prospective, within the two kingdoms and stretching between them. Thus Psyche and Florian, who are sister and brother, live in different courts as 'sister' and 'brother' to Ida and the prince, whose marriage has been contracted since childhood. This opening section also shows the rejection of family ties. Ida has withdrawn to her college, repudiating her father and brothers, thereby disturbing the relationships I have just outlined.

Throughout the poem feminism is presented as anathema to family. This antagonism is dramatized in the recognition scene between Psyche and Florian in Section 2. Psyche recognizes her brother and feels bound by her vow to the college to denounce him. Florian's response establishes the opposition between feminism and family.

> 'Well then, Psyche, take my life,
> And nail me like a weasel on a grange
> For warning: bury me beside the gate,
> And cut this epitaph above my bones;
> *Here lies a brother by a sister slain,*
> *All for the common good of womankind.*'
> (Sect. 2, ll. 187–92)

At first Psyche is adamant. Then she is appealed to in terms of her family and her past which confront her present self and rejection of family. Florian reminds her of their childhood together: ' "are you/That brother-sister Psyche, both in one?/You were that Psyche, but what are you now?" ' (Sect. 2, ll. 235–7). The repeated question, "Are you that Psyche?", is used to recall scenes from her 'gentler days' and increases the pressure on her to temper 'dogmatism' with love. This is forced home by a direct appeal to Psyche as "mother of the sweetest little maid,/That ever crowed for kisses" (Sect. 2, ll. 260–1), Florian's ' "little niece" '. Psyche's response ' "and why should I not play/The Spartan Mother" ' (Sect. 2, ll. 262–3), is by now largely rhetorical. Recollected family feeling proves too strong for recently acquired convictions, and she relents:

> '... I give thee to death
> My brother! it was duty spoke, not I.
> My needful seeming harshness, pardon it.
> Our mother, is she well?'
>
> (Sect. 2, ll. 287-90)

I shall return to this opposition of duty and love later. Here, with duty pushed aside, Psyche is able to ask about her mother and recapture her former 'self':

> and betwixt them blossomed up
> From out a common vein of memory
> Sweet household talk, and phrases of the hearth,
> And far allusion, till the gracious dews
> Began to glisten and to fall
>
> (Sect. 2, ll. 292-6)

These peaceful, soothing images of domesticity and family life, ratified by the tranquil evening scene, release an alternative set of values to those of the college into the poem, the antidote to Ida's feminism.

The scene ends in a tableau. Cyril holds Psyche's child, blowing out his cheeks to amuse it, while Psyche watches, smiling, and the child responds by pushing her hand against Cyril's face. It is one of those moments when Tennyson organizes his scene in what John Dixon Hunt has termed 'the picturesque mode of visual focus', using a painterly structure which suggests the genre picture.[33] It is a family tableau with clear parallels in mid-century genre and narrative painting. Later in the poem it is seen to be the first part of a triptych. In Section 6, after the tournament, this happy scene has been shattered. Psyche – 'Red grief and mother's hunger in her eye/ ... and half/The sacred mother's bosom, panting, burst/The laces toward her babe' (ll. 130-3) – pleads with Ida for the return of her baby. The child, lying 'like a new-fallen meteor on the grass' (l. 119), recognizes its mother and clamours to be returned. Ida towers above the scene:

> Erect and silent, striking with her glance
> The mother, me, the child; but he that lay

> Beside us, Cyril, battered as he was,
> Trailed himself up on one knee: then he drew
> Her robe to meet his lips, and down she looked
> At the armed man sideways
> (Sect. 6, ll. 136–41)

This second tableau is followed by a third, with the return of the baby, via Cyril, to Psyche. Ida:

> Laid the soft babe in his hard-mailed hands,
> Who turned half-round to Psyche as she sprang
> To meet it, with an eye that swum in thanks;
> Then felt it sound and whole from head to foot,
> And hugged and never hugged it close enough,
> And in her hunger mouthed and mumbled it,
> And hid her bosom with it
> (Sect. 6, ll. 191–7)[34]

The 'triptych' is completed.

One of the central features of the dialogue of literary, pictorial and dramatic forms in nineteenth-century writing and painting is the use of the tableau to provide what Meisel has termed 'vivid epitomes'. This extends beyond the obvious examples of the illustrations to novels and the use of pictorial dramaturgy in the theatre whereby 'the actors strike an expressive stance in a legible symbolic configuration that crystallizes a stage of the narrative'.[34] It is used extensively in the written texts of Victorian novels, and these scenes from *The Princess* show it at work in poetry as well, forming part of that collaborative narrative pictorial style which Meisel has analysed.

Most early-nineteenth-century genre painting has an implicit narrative interest. Wilkie's paintings *The Rent Day* and *Distraining for Rent* were the inspiration for Douglas Jerrold's domestic melodrama *The Rent Day*, and there are many other examples of dramatists developing the narrative hints of contemporary genre paintings into plays, and also using the pictorial original as tableaux within these plays. Painting itself grew away from the more static genre scene, drawing out the narrative interest of its subject and developing into the mid-century narrative picture. This prompted a renewed interest in the pictorial narrative series, which drew on Hogarth and other eighteenth-century precedents, but also had its own distinctive character. Pre-Raphaelite influence, for example, contributed to the renewed interest in the triptych, and mid-century painting saw other experiments in multiple framing.[35]

Probably the best known, certainly the most interesting, example of a mid-century multiple framed painting is Augustus Egg's three-part domestic drama *Past and Present* (1858). This is not really a serial picture but a triptych consisting of a centre-piece and two subordinate lateral paintings. The intricate cross-referencing of expressive detail within the triptych gives this painting what Meisel has called an 'echo structure',[36] a term which can usefully be applied to Tennyson's 'triptych' as well. Tennyson's sequence of three tableaux is a literary example of the use of multiple framing and echo structure. The first tableau shows a family in the process of being formed and anticipates the reformation of families at the end of the poem. The second depicts this embryonic family as threatened, with Ida's feminism momentarily triumphant but about to yield. The third dramatizes the restoration of family. Mother and child are reunited, and in returning the baby to its rightful mother Cyril also woos and wins Psyche as his wife. Ida's alternative concept of feminist motherhood disintegrates, and this clears the way for her marriage to the prince and her acceptance of a conventional idea of motherhood. This 'triptych' dramatizes a custody battle of sorts, not between a husband and wife but between a loving mother and an ideologically motivated usurper. In so far as it sympathetically presents the case for the mother, it can be seen as a liberal intervention in the question of infant custody. On the other hand, this mother is not in conflict with a husband insisting on his 'natural' rights but with another woman whose aim is to challenge that very idea of innate male superiority. In a way which is characteristic of the poem as a whole, and recognizable as a familiar kind of liberal argument, all 'extreme' positions, no matter what their ideological content, are held to be fundamentally similar. From this point of view, Ida and the northern king, feminism and male chauvinism, are identical in lacking the liberal virtues of tolerance and compromise which the poem pre-empts.

Egg's triptych works rather differently. *Past and Present* is a painting of the irretrievable breakdown of marriage, the collapse, not the consolidation, of family. There is no explicit questioning of the stern morality which is shown operating within the painting. The wife's infidelity leads to her expulsion from the home, her husband's death, and leaves her two legitimate children 'orphaned'. But the painting has a subtext, established through the more delicate aspects of its echo structure. Meisel points out correspondences between the suppliant figure of the mother in the centre-piece and that of her younger daughter in one of the pendants, and also between the attitude and profile of mother and elder daughter, both staring at the moon, in the paired lateral pictures. This compositional parallelism suggests connections which have survived the dissolution of this now fatherless family. Implicitly, it seems to ask whether such tragic consequences are not disproportionate to their cause. Although the centre-piece of Tennyson's 'triptych' is a scene of the severance of family ties, it is framed by scenes of promise and renewal. The child is the real focus of each tableau and the series is resolved with the return of the baby to its mother.[37] In Egg's triptych on the other hand, the illegitimate baby shelters with its mother on the side of the Thames. The narrative implication is that both will soon be dead.

Tennyson's pictorial mode of dramatization in these tableaux is an important part of the way in which the poem establishes its central values. These 'legible symbolic configurations' are indeed 'vivid epitomes', crucial stages in the process whereby the narrative breaches the defences of Ida's feminism. Like a Victorian problem picture they can really only be read in one way. Egg's painting is less plain-speaking, his tableaux dilations rather than epitomes.

The recognition scene in Section 2, with its summarizing tableau, therefore marks the beginning of the victory of family over feminism. Family ties have begun to subvert the college from within, a process which quickens in the following sections as embryonic 'orthodox' relations are seen forming – Florian and Melissa as well as Psyche and Cyril. In the case of Ida and the prince the debate between these two opposed models of personal and social relationships continues. The prince's challenge that Ida is denying herself 'what every woman counts her due,/Love, children, happiness' (Sect. 3, ll. 228–9), is angrily rejected, but the child theme surfaces again in Section 4 when after Psyche's disgrace and disappearance Ida decides to keep her child for herself. This apparent severing of yet another family relationship,

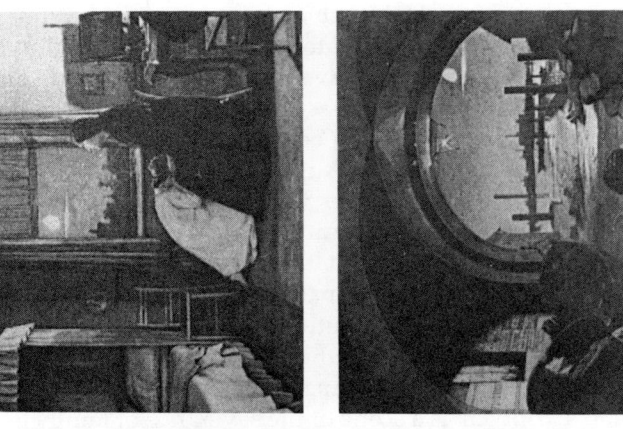

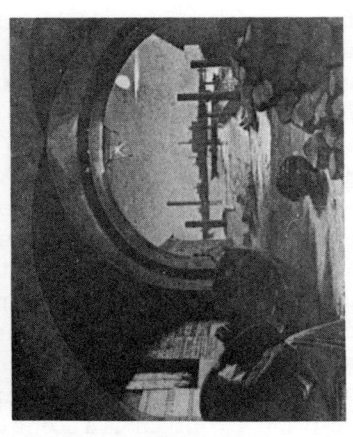

Plate 7   Augustus Leopold Egg, 'Past and Present', 1858

this time in the name of feminist motherhood, in fact signals the first stirrings of the return of family feeling in Ida. In the postscript to a letter to her brother she reports the comfort she gets from Psyche's baby:

> I took it for an hour in mine own bed
> This morning: there the tender orphan hands
> Felt at my heart, and seemed to charm from thence
> The wrath I nursed against the world
> (Sect. 5, ll. 424–7)

As Ida's heart is touched she begins the move back to more conventional motherhood.

This movement is underlined in the aftermath of the battle in Section 6, which is the forcing ground for the return of family feeling. The sight of the wounded prince and his grieving father helps prompt in Ida the memory of her own mother. When she lays down Psyche's child, places her hand on the wounded prince, and tells the king his son still lives, she clears the way for the restoration of broken family relationships. Psyche moves in to reclaim her child. The king is 're-fathered' (Sect. 6, l. 113). Ida takes on the nursing role, which is the prelude to her marriage to the prince. The return of feeling in Ida, begun by the child and sealed by her nursing the prince back to life, brings with it a return of the 'natural' order of family. The college becomes a hospital, men walk in and out 'at their will' (Sect. 6, l. 363), and the marriages, creating new families, complete the narrative of the prince. The real victor of the tournament is family; feminism is routed. Blanche, its sole remaining voice, is too corrupt to be assimilated, but her daughter Melissa remains behind (left by her mother in a final denial of family) and becomes one with the others through her marriage to Florian.

The frame-story does not have a marriage, but its conclusion is concerned with the family in a more broadly political sense as a paradigm of the 'natural' social order. This recalls Kemble's insistence that the family was the foundation of all society, and his warning of the dire consequences for the whole social system that would result from its destruction. Nothing could seem more permanent and reassuring than the peaceful rural scene viewed from Vivian-place at the end of the poem; 'a land of peace' (Conclusion, l. 42). Across the channel lies France, Britain's anti-type, a victim of anarchy as one of the students, a Tory member's son, sees it. But France is no more threatening to this naturalized vision of peace and order than Blanche is to the marriage of Ida and the prince. The narrator demurs from his companion's crude chauvinistic contrast of British calm and French chaos (rather as the prince does from his father's brutal male chauvinism), but he nevertheless derives political comfort from the same scene and 'happy crowd' (Conclusion, l. 75) which has provoked this contrast. He sees that 'This fine old world of ours is but a child' (Conclusion, l. 77), an affirmation which draws strength from the recurring imagery of the child earlier in the poem.

Underwriting this optimism is Sir Walter Vivian, with his family around him:

> Among six boys, head under head, and looked
> No little lily-handed Baronet he,
> A great broad-shouldered genial Englishman,
> A lord of fat prize-oxen and of sheep,
> A raiser of huge melons and of pine,
> A patron of some thirty charities,
> A pamphleteer on guano and on grain,
> A quarter-sessions chairman, abler none;
>
> (Conclusion, ll. 83–90)

Sir Walter is the ideal father which the inner narrative has lacked. This is no 'spindling king . . . swamped in lazy tolerance' (Sect. 5, ll. 432–3) like Ida's father, and nor is he like the prince's father:

> He cared not for the affection of the house;
> He held his sceptre like a pedant's wand
> To lash offence, and with long arms and hands
> Reached out, and picked offenders from the mass
> For judgement.
>
> (Sect. 1, ll. 26–30)

Sir Walter is seen among his family and his people as a true father. The swelling catalogue of his virtues in the lines quoted above, which stress the bounty of his nature, are rewarded by the shouts of affection and respect, 'More joyful than the city-roar that hails/Premier or king!' (Conclusion, ll. 101–2), which echo round his estate at the end of the day.

Of course, this is pastoral, in tune with the Prologue and

justified perhaps by the poem's disarming subtitle, 'A Medley'. But the mood of the poem has become more sombre in its concluding sections and this disturbs the continuity of Prologue and Conclusion. When the narrator reminds the Tory member's son that Britain too is 'full/Of social wrong' (Conclusion, ll. 72–3) the poem is momentarily wrenched back into the context of the 1840s and what had come to be called the 'Condition of England' question. The poem's concluding use of pastoral is therefore distinctly ideological, ushering in the feudal social vision of a benevolently hierarchical society whose leaders recognize their duties while their happy liege men and women toil in comfort for the mutual good of themselves and their masters. It is in this way that the frame-story draws out the contemporary political implications of its inner medieval narrative, with family as the common term of each.

V

The poem's concluding use of pastoral raises the whole question of its different modes; the principle of 'medley' common to the frame-story and the inner narrative. This 'strange diagonal' – the tension between its manner and its matter, its clash of genres and voices, the narrative indirection produced by these mixed modes – has interested most recent criticism of the poem. Christopher Ricks is refreshingly direct on the evasions of Tennyson's medley form: '*The Princess* comes armoured in those good-humoured self-incriminations which act as self-exculpations'. For Ricks, the artistic problem of the long poem, the moral issues of women's education, and the political concerns raised by the poem, are all evaded by a tone and a story which is both earnest and flippant: 'the poem is in its way a triumph of bringing the fearful within its purlieus and then tranquillizing everything'.[38] To this I would only want to add further and different instances of evasion. There is, for example, a strange displacement effected by the double narrative structure, which sets the contemporary issue of feminism in the remote past while surrounding the present with older chivalrous and feudal forms. If the principle of medley was used to examine the complexity of the issues the poem raises then it could be justified, along with the narrative indirection, as an exploratory form, necessarily open and multi-vocal. But it is only intermittently used in this way. More often, the questioning, challenging aspects of the poem are neutralized by the medley form which concedes a limited degree of seriousness without relinquishing its satirically reductive hold.

This general point has been made often enough before. There is, however, another level at which the poem is antagonistic to the subject it purports to be exploring. This is the level of language. Critics have often noted the distinctive language of *The Princess*. David Shaw has contrasted the 'laconic compressions' of 'Ulysses' with the 'florid expansions' of *The Princess*.[39] Ricks notes the 'liberated, almost sportive quality in the style of *The Princess*', seeing this as an experiment in 'linguistic propriety'.[40] Laurence Lerner draws attention to the poem's 'skin', pointing to its wonderful surface texture'.[41] However, there is a tendency among these critics to see this as a value in itself, somehow distinct from the more unsatisfactory aspects of the poem's form and treatment of its subject. After his strictures on the poem's evasions, Ricks turns with relief to the integral lyrics. His fine discussion of 'Tears, idle tears', 'Now sleeps the crimson petal', and 'Come down, O maid, from yonder mountain height' which follows, isolates these lyrics from their context and takes no account of the function of this kind of poetry in a poem like *The Princess*.

The opposition within the poem between the family and feminism, and between love and what is variously called law, system, or duty, is registered in a clash of languages. The sensuous descriptive language of the poem contrasts with Ida's precise, chiselled language, surrounding it and arguing with it. An obvious example of this is the movement from the intercalated song between Sections 3 and 4, an elegiac song of dusk, to the opening lines of Section 4:

> 'There sinks the nebulous star we call the Sun,
> If that hypothesis of theirs be sound'
> Said Ida;
>
> (Sect. 4, ll. 1–3)

This contrast between Ida's scientific, 'masculine' language and the nostalgia of the preceding song is almost immediately repeated; one of the party sings 'Tears, idle tears, I know not what they mean', which Ida scorns as 'fancies hatched/In silken-folded idleness' (Sect. 4, ll. 48–9).

The purpose for which Ida has established the college is consistently undermined by the language used to describe it. The women at study are described as being 'like morning doves/That sun their milky bosoms on the thatch' (Sect. 2, ll. 87–8). At dinner they are seen

> With beauties every shade of brown and fair
> In colours gayer than the morning mist,
> The long hall glittered like a bed of flowers.
> (Sect. 2, ll. 414–6)

This kind of language, which Ida dismisses as 'barren verbiage, current among men' (Sect. 2, l. 40), is consistently turned against the college. It is a language of feeling which is denied the women as long as they remain the prisoners of 'ideology', and it becomes more dominant, more insistent as the college breaks up. Having offered to open up the college and nurse the wounded, Ida is shown leading her 'maids' across the park to where the soldiers lie:

> A hundred maids in train across the Park.
> Some cowled, and some bare-headed, on they came,
> Their feet in flowers, her loveliest: by them went
> The enamoured air sighing, and on their curls
> From the high tree the blossom wavering fell,
> And over them the tremulous isles of light
> Slided, they moving under shade: but Blanche
> At distance followed:
> (Sect. 6, ll. 60–7)

As this delicate, scented language of idealization envelops the women, shutting out Blanche, the spokeswoman of ideology, the way is prepared for Ida's descent from the cold language of the mountain height to the warm and mellow sounds of the valley, where

> the children call, and I
> Thy shepherd pipe, and sweet is every sound,
> Sweeter thy voice, but every sound is sweet;
> Myriads of rivulets hurrying through the lawn,

> The moan of doves in immemorial elms,
> And murmuring of innumerable bees.
>
> (Sect. 7, ll. 202-7)

In this way the language of feeling ('poetry') conquers the language of ideals ('law' or 'system'), a victory which has been rehearsed throughout the poem. Ida's return of feeling allows the return of poetry of a kind she has earlier rejected but which the text itself has been practising throughout its length. The intercalated songs and the integral lyrics are essential to this process. They create what Humbert Wolfe called a 'cadence of expectation'[42] which makes the eventual restoration of family simultaneously a victory for poetry. Superb lyrics in their own right, in any discussion of *The Princess* they must be considered in the context of the whole poem which celebrates the language of feeling through its own rich, sensuous diction, asserting this against the cold, abstract language of ideals.

It is necessary to insist on the ideological nature of the resolution of this clash of languages. Lerner asks fatalistically, what else could Tennyson have done? Tennyson simply wrote rich, 'feminine' poetry, and if Ida was right to reject this, 'what could he do in return except betray her?'[43] This seems to imply that Ida somehow wrote her own lines, and sees Tennyson's language as constant, distinct from the subject it treats. Tennyson's poetry has many registers, and the dominant language of *The Princess* is distinctive; it isn't something Tennyson was stuck with. Indeed, 'Edwin Morris' voices suspicion of this particular register, and plays off a more colloquial, uncertain voice against what it terms the 'full-celled honeycomb of eloquence'. Nor, as Ricks implies, are the embellishments of language and the nostalgia and melancholy of the lyrics simply a warming up for the great poetry which was to follow. The language of the poem is its meaning; in *The Princess* it establishes the case against its subject.

Yet this dominant language cannot entirely silence the echo of Ida's earlier voice. As the narrative of the princess concludes, Walter Vivian's remark, 'I wish she had not yielded!' (Conclusion, l. 5), underscores something in the poem which resists the neatness and conservatism of its resolution. This is more than just a further example of the poem trying to have things all ways. In

Ida and the other feminist voices energies have been released which the poem cannot entirely contain.

VI

Tennyson wrote many other narrative poems of marriage and family. In most of these, families obstruct love marriages, insisting instead on marriages arranged on the basis of property, wealth or the payment of debt. This causes unhappiness, sometimes tragedy, and provokes denunciation of the social practices which keep love separate from marriage:

> Cursed be the social wants that sin against the
> strength of youth!
> Cursed be the social lies that warp us from the living
> truth!
> Cursed be the sickly forms that err from honest
> Nature's rule!
> Cursed be the gold that gilds the straitened
> forehead of the fool!
>
> ('Locksley Hall', ll. 59–62)

This stock situation has other recurring features. Historic conflict between the families of the lovers often complicates existing differences of class and wealth. The female lover usually has a tyrannical father or guardian, and a weak or dead mother. The male lover is often orphaned. Women, both mothers and daughters, are often weak, sometimes blamed for this weakness, but never evil. Fathers and male guardians are cruel and oppressive, slaves to 'filthy marriage-hindering Mammon' ('Aylmer's Field') and 'the rentroll Cupid of our rainy isles' ('Edwin Morris'). Family is almost always too powerful for love, although occasionally, as in 'Aylmer's Field', the victory is pyrrhic. These traditional situations are presented in contemporary, often Carlylean terms. This is 'the golden age' *(Maud)* in which 'Every door is barred with gold, and opens but to golden keys' ('Locksley Hall'). The family is exposed as an institution for preserving, increasing, and transmitting property and wealth, and marriage is the mechanism of this process. Love confronts family, but its challenge is pitifully weak; the individual is cruelly sacrificed to family and society.

These narrative poems of love and family, of class, 'mammonism', and the arranged marriage, are often grouped together and explained in terms of Tennyson's own frustrated love for Rosa Baring, and other similar experiences within his family. In his notes to a late poem, 'The Wreck' (1883–4) Christopher Ricks comments, 'It is another of T.'s poems on the wickedness of the arranged marriage; cp., among others, "Aylmer's Field" and "The Flight". T. never forgot Rosa Baring'.[44] However, arranged marriages in Tennyson's poems are not always incompatible with love. In *Maud* it is the breaking of a marriage arrangement because of antagonism between the families which leads to the tragedy of the lovers. Far from being inimical to love, the arranged marriage creates a felt obligation in Maud from which love grows. And in *The Princess* love and the arranged marriage eventually harmonize. Although this poem is not usually included in the group of so-called marriage poems, I see no reason why it shouldn't be. It treats the same subject, but does so differently. The differences are interesting.

In *The Princess* Tennyson is defending contemporary society rather than criticizing it. The poem expresses a more conservative vision than the anti-'mammonism' of 'The Flight', 'Locksley Hall', 'Edwin Morris', *Maud*, and 'Aylmer's Field'. In these poems the issues are predominantly personal. Individuals, primarily men, are pitted against social arrangements which frustrate their desire to translate love into marriage, and they fall victim to families whose acquisitiveness and materialism allow no place for love. Although this implies a criticism of society, which sometimes becomes explicit, the focus is on the lovers, and usually on the man. In *The Princess*, however, the issues are reversed. Family is obstructed and challenged by feminism, and in this changed context of radical social theories family no longer frustrates love but becomes its defender and guarantor; 'marriage-hindering Mammon' becomes 'marriage-hindering feminism'. In 'Locksley Hall' Amy is criticized for her lack of courage and independence in the face of family pressure, but when Ida's courage and independence take the form of feminism it must be tamed by those family structures it seems to threaten. It is difficult to avoid the conclusion that while social forms frustrate men's aspirations, they are endangered by women's.

This different treatment of family in *The Princess* is illustrated by comparing Sir Walter Vivian with his fellow baronet Sir Aylmer Aylmer, the mammonite father of 'Aylmer's Field'. Whereas Sir Walter offers reassurance as a bulwark against French ideas and social upheaval, and as a fatherly overlord of family, tenants, and county, Sir Aylmer, of similarly ancient family and extensive estates, is described as one of 'These old pheasant-lords, /These partridge-breeders of a thousand years,/Who had mildewed in their thousands, doing nothing/Since Egbert' ('Alymer's Field', ll. 381–4). The country gentry are not the cement of the social order in this poem. The greed and pride of Sir Alymer, this 'county God', leads to the death of his daughter, the suicide of her lover, and is associated with post-revolutionary France:

> ever-murdered France,
> By shores that darken with the gathering wolf,
> Runs in a river of blood to the sick sea.
> Is this a time to madden madness then?
> Was this a time for these to flaunt their pride?
> ('Aylmer's Field', ll. 766–70)

The poem is set in 1793, and these questions are addressed to Sir Aylmer and his wife, who in contrast to Sir Walter, are seen as encouraging, by their pride and neglect, the onset of revolution in Britain. Their treatment of their daughter implies a larger social irresponsibility. There is muttering on the estate as the tenants grieve for the young victims. Family, as so often in Tennyson's work, has abrogated its moral and social duties, becoming an enemy of love and a cause of personal tragedy. In *The Princess*, however, in the context of feminism, family becomes the repository of order and love, and the example of France is invoked as its anti-type.

The poem most closely related to *The Princess* in its treatment of family is 'Enoch Arden'. Enoch, as we have seen, although one of the very few good fathers in Tennyson's narrative poems, must keep his survival a secret. If he revealed himself, the reconstituted family which is innocent of the knowledge that he lives, would be destroyed and his wife exposed as guilty of bigamy. The new family must be preserved, and Enoch's suffering cannot justify its disruption. Like *The Princess*, therefore, this poem reverses the priorities of Tennyson's other family narrative ones. In both these poems the family is of overriding importance, too valuable to be sacrificed to individual desire. The stakes are too high.

VII

Reading the learned journals in the course of preparing this chapter, I have been struck by how congenial Tennyson's *via media* between feminism and male chauvinism has proved for most liberal criticism. Such criticism moves in effortlessly to occupy the middle ground established by the poem's resolution of opposites. This complicity with the poem's repudiation of 'extremes' leaves criticism with little to do apart from making clearer what the poem is saying and admiring the way it says it. While it is interesting that Tennyson should resolve the polarities of his poem in the way that he does, it is curious that late-twentieth-century criticism should be left repeating the same 'wisdom'.

This ideological complicity between *The Princess* and its liberal critics helps explain the rough handling the poem has had from radical ones. Terry Eagleton's *jeu d'esprit*, 'Tennyson: Politics and Sexuality in "The Princess" and "In Memoriam"'[45] is a mirror image of the liberal criticism described above. Eagleton attacks Tennyson's endorsement of the dominant values of his age, seeing his mild reformism as a subtle but necessary strategy for consolidating and extending the ideological hegemony of the Victorian ruling classes. His facetious but strenuous Lacanian reading has a 'strange diagonal' of its own between the mock and the serious, another instance of criticism complicit with the text it is discussing.

Of these approaches to the poem, one assumes that moderate reformism is always and inevitably the correct stance; the other assumes it is always, and merely, a cover for something more sinister. One implicitly reads *The Princess* as a prophetic anticipation of our own enlightened practices; the other regards it is a functionary of the ideological state apparatus. Neither reads the poem as part of a larger, conflictive discourse on the family, gender, and marriage. *The Princess* is concerned with deeply significant issues, but structures its treatment of these in such a way that an ideology of 'helpmeets', a picture of changing bourgeois marriage practices within the regulating context of the family, emerges as inevitable and inviolable. To say this, however, should neither be to sneer at a fascinating poem riven with tensions and contradictions, nor to endorse it as an apologia for our own family and marriage practices.

NOTES

1. A note on the text: *The Princess* was more extensively revised than Tennyson's other long poems. It was first published at the end of 1847. The intercalcated songs were added in the third edition (1850), the Prince's 'weird seizures' in the fourth edition (1851), and the Prologue was enlarged in the fifth edition (1853). For a fuller discussion of these revisions, see Christopher Ricks (ed.), *The Poems of Tennyson* (London and Harlow: Longmans, 1969), pp. 741–3.
2. 'Whether the marriage-relationship could survive the fulfilment of women's aspirations is the real point at issue.' John Killham, *Tennyson and The Princess: Reflections of an Age* (London: Athlone Press, 1958), p. 65.
3. Sandra M. Gilbert, 'Costumes of the mind: transvestism as metaphor in modern literature', in Elizabeth Abel (ed.) *Writing and Sexual Difference* (Brighton: Harvester Press, 1982), p. 199. Gilbert is drawing on the work of Natalie Davis.
4. The next two paragraphs come mainly from Leonore Davidoff and Catherine Hall, *Family Fortunes: Men and Women of the English Middle Class 1780–1850*, (London: Hutchinson, 1987), pp. 410–15.
5. Barbara Taylor, *Eve and the New Jerusalem* (London: Virago, 1983), p. 171.
6. ibid., p. 180.
7. David Kunzle, *Fashion and Fetishism; A Social History of the Corset, Tight-lacing and Other Forms of Body-Sculpture in the West* (New Jersey: Rowman & Littlefield, 1982), pp. 21, 42–5, 122ff.
8. Maurianne Adams, 'Family disintegration and creative reintegration: the case of Charlotte Bronte and *Jane Eyre*', in Anthony S. Wohl (ed.) *The Victorian Family: Structure and Stresses* (London: Croom Helm, 1978), p. 166.
9. *Shirley* (London: Dent, 1970), Ch. 11, p. 160.
10. *Villette* (London: Dent, 1974), Ch. 14, pp. 123–4.
11. *The Woman in White* (London: Nelson, n.d.), p. 289.
12. Penny Boumelha, *Thomas Hardy and Women: Sexual Ideology and Narrative Form* (Brighton: Harvester Press, 1982), p. 45.
13. 'She had a nose that was far too big and eyes that were far too small and a moustache that was well, not so happy a feature as Sir

Claude's', *What Maisie Knew* (Harmondsworth: Penguin, 1979), Ch. 19, p. 138.
14. Nina Auerbach, *Woman and the Demon: The Life of a Victorian Myth* (Cambridge and London: Harvard University Press, 1982), p. 137.
15. Derek Hudson (ed.) *Munby; Man of Two Worlds: The Life and Diaries of Arthur J. Munby 1828-1910* (London: John Murray, 1972), e.g. pp. 42–3, 110, 131, 255.
16. ibid., pp. 237–8.
17. ibid., p. 232.
18. ibid., photo facing p. 86.
19. ibid., p. 188.
20. Jeffrey Weeks, *Sex, Politics and Society* (London and New York: Longman, 1981), pp. 101, 111.
21. Hudson, pp. 223, 246, 270, 283.
22. ibid., p. 82.
23. *The Mystery of Edwin Drood* (Harmondsworth: Penguin, 1978), Ch. 7, p. 90.
24. Auerbach, p. 64.
25. *Jude the Obscure* (London: Macmillan, 1973), Part 3, Ch. 3, p. 152. Hardy's story 'The Distracted Preacher' is rich in examples of transvestism. Lizzy Newberry dresses in the clothes of her dead husband to help with the smuggling, and the smugglers themselves dress as women to ambush the excisemen.
26. Boumelha, pp. 65–6.
27. Janet Horowitz Murray, *Strong-Minded Women* (Harmondsworth: Penguin, 1984), p. 266.
28. Kunzle, pp. 25, 148.
29. Toril Moi, *Sexual/Textual Politics* (London: Methuen, 1985), p. 14.
30. This bill was introduced to Parliament in 1837 and was passed in 1839. It granted women the right to have their case for custody of their infant children considered. Prior to this act the father's right to custody was unchallengeable. Killham, pp. 154–5.
31. ibid., p. 166.
32. ibid., p. 155. This extract is from an article in the *British and Foreign Review* which Kemble had a hand in writing although the full extent of his contribution is uncertain.
33. John Dixon Hunt, ' "Story Painters and Picture Writers": Tennyson's *Idylls* and Victorian painting', in D.J. Palmer (ed.) *Tennyson* (London: G. Bell & Sons, 1973).
34. Martin Meisel, *Realizations: Narrative, Pictorial and Theatrical Arts in Nineteeth-Century England* (Princeton, NJ: Princeton University Press), p. 50.
35. ibid., pp. 24, 59, 142.

The Princess

36. ibid., p. 26.
37. Tennyson remarked of the poem as a whole that 'The child is the link through the parts'; Ricks's edn, p. 741.
38. Christopher Ricks, *Tennyson* (London: Macmillan, 1972), pp. 188, 190–1.
39. David Shaw, *Tennyson's Style* (Ithaca & London; Cornell University Press, 1976), p. 130.
40. Ricks, *Tennyson*, pp. 197–8.
41. Laurence Lerner, 'An essay on *The Princess*', in Lerner (ed.) *The Victorians* (London: Methuen, 1978), pp. 1, 209–10.
42. Humbert Wolfe, *Tennyson* (London: Faber & Faber, 1930), p. 28.
43. Lerner, p. 221.
44. *The Poems Of Tennyson*, p. 1335. 'The Wreck' is also a poem of retribution for neglecting the duties of motherhood and for breaking family relations. It is a cry to the Holy Mother, from a young mother, herself motherless and victim of an arranged marriage, who runs away with another man and deserts her own baby. The baby dies. Like most of the 'marriage poems' it is also about parenthood, unusual only in that it dwells on the mother rather than the father.
45. In F. Barker, J.Coombes, P. Hulme, C. Mercer and D. Musselwhite (eds) *1848: The Sociology of Literature* (University of Essex, 1978).

4
'A printing woman who has lost her place': Elizabeth Barrett Browning's *Aurora Leigh*

I

In England no one lives by verse that lives
(*Aurora Leigh*, Bk 3, l. 307)

The calculated ambiguity of this line expressed Barrett Browning's sense that English poetry was in decline, threatened by the ability of the novel to mediate more smoothly between art and life, and by the greater earning power of the prose writer. She had expressed these fears as early as 1842 in an article on Wordsworth for the *Athenaeum*,[1] but it was the popularity of 'Lady Geraldine's Courtship', the narrative poem she dashed off as a space-filler for her *Poems of 1844*, which suggested ways in which poetry could reclaim its lost ground. Subtitled 'A Romance of the Age', the fevered tone, contemporaneity, and smattering of Carlylean radicalism of 'Lady Geraldine's Courtship' proved a winning combination. It also prompted Robert Browning to seek out Elizabeth Barrett.

Her letters of late 1844 and early 1845 are full of her idea to write 'a poem comprehending the aspect and manners of modern life'.[2] The most detailed account of this idea is in a letter to Mary Russell Mitford:

And now tell me, – where is the obstacle to making as

interesting a story of a poem as of a prose work – echo answers *where*. Conversations and events, why may they not be given as rapidly and passionately and lucidly in verse as in prose – echo answers *why*. You see nobody is offended by my approach to the conventions of vulgar life in 'Lady Geraldine' – and it gives me courage to go on, and touch this real everyday life of our age, and hold it with two hands'.[3]

Crabbe was the poet she felt had most successfully anticipated her idea. 'Locksley Hall' she considered too general in its treatment of the age. In another letter she described Bulwer's *Eva, or the Unhappy Marriage* – 'a sort of poetical novel with modern manners inclusive' – as an example of the kind of thing she had in mind.[4]

In these letters Barrett Browning is struggling with the problem of form – how to give poetic shape and expression to matter both prosaic and contemporary. She had written to Mary Russell Mitford:

> I want to write a poem of a new class, in a measure – a Don Juan, without the mockery and impurity . . . under one aspect, – and having unity, as a work of art, – and admitting of as much philosophical dreaming and digression (which is in fact a characteristic of the age) as I like to use.[5]

The aim is to give that attention to everyday life which the novel manages so easily, without relinquishing the manner, power, and concentration of poetry. Several months later she used a modified term, 'novel-poem', to describe the new class of writing she sought. This occurred in a letter to Robert Browning in which she also expressed her determination to make her own story: 'I am waiting for a story, and I won't take one, because I want to make one, & I like to make my own stories, because then I can take liberties with them in the treatment'.[6] Here Barrett Browning is thinking like a novelist, impatient with the usual poetic practice of reworking earlier narratives. When Browning suggested her novel-poem should be based on the Prometheus myth, she replied heatedly:

> We want new *forms*, as well as thoughts. The old gods are dethroned. Why should we go back to the antique moulds? – Let us all aspire rather to *Life*, and let the dead bury their dead. If we have but courage to face these conventions, to touch this low

ground, we shall take strength from it instead of losing it; and of that I am intimately persuaded. For there is poetry *everywhere*.[7]

In similar vein Aurora Leigh attacks 'the poet who discerns/No character or glory in his times,/And trundles back his soul five hundred years,/Past moat and drawbridge, into a castle court' (Bk 5, ll. 189–92), which I take to be directed at the medievalism and obscured contemporaneity of *The Princess*.

In *Aurora Leigh*, published in 1857 many years after those early letters to Mary Russell Mitford, Barrett Browning did indeed make her own story out of the materials of her age. The work is a first-person narrative, told by Aurora, of her childhood, adolescence, struggle to become a writer, and eventual marriage. Her Italian mother dies when she is 4, and she is raised in Italy by her English father until his death when she is 13. Aurora is then sent to England and brought up by an aunt who does all she can to turn her niece into a perfect lady. Aurora inwardly resists this conditioning, reads avidly and plans to become a writer. At 20 she has an offer of marriage from Romney, her cousin and heir to the family estate, Leigh Hall. He is a social reformer and wants Aurora to abandon her writing and assist him with his work. Aurora angrily rejects the terms of Romney's proposal. The aunt dies and Aurora inherits a small amount of money, moves to London, and tries to establish herself as a writer.

Romney pursues his reforming and philanthropic schemes, in the course of which he rescues Marian Erle, the outcast daughter of brutal, degraded parents. As a gesture towards ending class divisions he decides to marry her. Aurora learns of this projected marriage from Lady Waldemar, who wants Romney herself, and asks Aurora to try and prevent it. However, when Aurora meets Marian she sanctions the marriage. Marian fails to turn up for the wedding. Romney, humiliated, returns to his work. Aurora finishes a new book of poems and decides to return to Italy. In Paris she accidentally meets Marian, who has had a baby. Aurora learns that Marian has been persuaded to abandon Romney by Lady Waldemar, and then abducted, raped, and abandoned. Aurora, Marian, and the little boy set up home together in Florence.

Lady Waldemar has been helping Romney establish a socialist community on his estate, and Aurora believes they are married.

However, Romney arrives in Florence unwed and blinded after a riot at Leigh Hall which has destroyed his social experiment. He renews his offer of marriage to Marian but is rejected. Persuaded by the power of Aurora's recent book and the failure of his own schemes, Romney recants his dismissal of Aurora's work. They confess their love for each other and marry.

II

There was, however, more at issue in the gestation of *Aurora Leigh* than the claims of the present over the past. Barrett Browning was intensely conscious of herself as a woman writer, and this, too, impelled the search for new forms. In *Aurora Leigh* she tried to resuscitate the almost lost form of epic:

> Never flinch,
> But still, unscrupulously epic, catch
> Upon the burning lava of a song
> The full-veined, heaving, double-breasted Age
> (Bk 5, ll. 214–17)

The striking female image of the Victorian age all but obscures that word 'unscrupulously'. A little earlier in Book 5 Aurora has asked whether it is possible to write an epic in this 'pewter age' which seems so unheroic. Milton had asked a similar question in writing his epic – whether 'an age too late .../... damp my intended wing' (*Paradise Lost*, Bk 9, ll. 44–5). But although *Paradise Lost* challenges and rejects many epic conventions, Milton could never be described as 'unscrupulous', and his Christian epic rests upon the sacred source of biblical narrative which ensures its superiority to classical epic. Barrett Browning's epic, on the other hand, really is unscrupulous. It is contemporary and its sources are profane and female. These sources have been well documented, and comprehensive accounts have been given of the influence of Madame de Stael's *Corinne*, George Sand's *Consuelo*, Elizabeth Gaskell's *Ruth*, and *Jane Eyre*, to name but a few.[8] But these writers were novelists. Barrett Browning extended their work into territory long occupied by male writers. Cora Kaplan has described this venture into epic and dramatic verse as an 'unmannerly intervention in the "high" patriarchal discourse of bourgeois culture'.[9] 'Unmannerly' teams well with 'unscrupulous'. *Aurora Leigh* isn't an epic in any conventionally recognizable sense of the term, and the preoccupation of contemporary reviewers with the poem's form – what was it? what gave it unity? was it unified? – was understandable, even if their discussion of these questions was laboured and sometimes obtuse. Barrett Browning appropriated the term 'epic' and redefined it, using it polemically to emphasize the significance of contemporary life and the centrality of women and women's writing. It was less a venture into a male stronghold than the construction of her own out of new materials, with the ancient name of epic then placed defiantly over the entrance.

Aurora Leigh also, however, questioned and reworked Tennyson and Clough's treatment of the woman question. Barrett Browning wrote bitingly of *The Princess*:

> What woman will tell the great poet that Mary Wolstonecraft [sic] herself never dreamt of setting up collegiate states, proctordom & the rest ... which is a worn-out plaything in the hands of one sex already, & need not be *transferred* in order to be proved ridiculous?[10]

Aurora Leigh's refusal to abandon her vocation implicitly criticized the terms of Ida's marriage in *The Princess*, and Clough's treatment of the cross-class marriage theme in *The Bothie* is interrogated. I shall return to these points later in the chapter. But *Aurora Leigh's* mainspring was the work of contemporary and near-contemporary women writers. By the middle of the nineteenth century this constituted a visible tradition which *Aurora Leigh* drew on and contributed to. G.H. Lewes acknowledged this tradition when in 1852 he surveyed many of those texts which were to be sources for *Aurora Leigh* and recognized both their literary and broader significance: 'The appearance of Woman in the field of literature is a significant fact. It is the correlate of her position in society'.[11] Most reviewers also placed *Aurora Leigh* in this broad context, although Coventry Patmore in the *North British Review* seemed unaware of it and complained that as Barrett Browning was almost the only modern example of a woman poet, the story of *Aurora Leigh* was uninteresting from its very singularity.[12] Other reviewers, however, granted the work a certain representative character without necessarily welcoming it:

'The extreme independence of Aurora detracts from the feminine charm . . . she is made to resemble too closely some of the female portraits of George Sand, which were never to our liking'.[13]

The more interesting criticisms of *Aurora Leigh* concentrated on the problem of its form – was it a poem? – and the associated question of its engagement with contemporary issues. The *Blackwoods* reviewer was categorical:

> It is not the province of the poet to depict things as they are, but so to refine and purify as to purge out the grosser matter; and this he cannot do if he attempts to give a faithful picture of his own times. . . . All poetical characters, all poetical situations, must be idealized. The language is not that of common life, which belongs essentially to the domain of prose. Therein lies the distinction between a novel and a poem.[14]

This reviewer then quoted lines from the poem which he had laid out as prose, and asked, rhetorically, whether this was poetry? The *Westminster Review* did precisely the same thing and criticized the poem for lapsing into coarseness, attributing this to an attempt by Barrett Browning 'to prove her manhood'.[15] The poet and painter William Bell Scott also noted Barrett Browning's 'manly manner'.[16] Barrett Browning herself hated the concept of 'manly': 'I am not very fond of praising men by calling them *manly*. I hate and detest a masculine man'.[17] What is most striking about these reviews is the way in which the question of language and form repeatedly raised that of gender, and then extended further to the position of women and other extra-literary areas of ideological and social practice. To understand more fully why this should have been, it is necessary to have some sense of the social and political context in which *Aurora Leigh* was produced and read.

The work was written and read against the background of widespread public debate over the related questions of married women's property rights, divorce, custody, and women and work. In the public mind these issues were also linked with prostitution, another burning issue of the 1850s. The Marriage and Divorce Bill was submitted to Parliament in 1854 as a measure narrowly concerned with the jurisdiction of the ecclesiastical courts and Parliament over divorce, but over the next three years it broadened into a debate about the legal status of married women and about the marital relationship itself. This began when Caroline

Norton, whose fight for the custody of her children had prompted the 1839 Infants' Custody Act, took up the case for the protection of the property of divorced, separated or deserted wives. Far more radical, however, was Barbara Leigh Smith's demand for the right of all married women to own property and have an independent legal existence. This was a direct attack on the common-law doctrine of spousal unity, or coverture, whereby a married woman had no legal identity apart from her husband. A petitioning campaign for a married woman's property law followed, and Parliament was forced to consider this question and the related issue of equalization of the grounds for divorce. The 1857 Divorce Act, however, confirmed the sexual double-standard whereby a woman could be divorced for adultery but could divorce her husband only if his adultery was aggravated by incest, bigamy, or extreme cruelty. It also forestalled a Married Woman's Property Bill which would have abolished the doctrine of spousal unity with respect to married women's property. The 1857 Act dealt only with the property rights of separated and deserted wives, where the marriage was for all practical purposes at an end. Marriage itself remained intact, and the Divorce Act simply gave legal recognition to *de facto* marital breakdown. It was the demand for married women's property rights which had been the really significant issue. This was based on the assumption that marriage involved two separate individuals, and was perceived by most members of both Houses as posing a fundamental threat to the unity of the family.[18]

This fear for the family also surfaced in parliamentary debates on the frequent attempts to remove the ban on marriage with deceased wife's sister. One such bill was debated and defeated in 1856 while Parliament was also considering divorce and married women's property, and the issues became intertwined. The main argument for reform was the need for widowers to find mothers for their children, and the bill did not attract feminist support. Opponents of reform, however, expressed fears about sullying the purity of the English home, thereby tangling the issue with that of divorce and married women's property rights. Both measures were felt to threaten the family.[19] At least one novel was written on this subject, Mrs Frewin's *The Inheritance of Evil, or The Consequences of Marrying a Deceased Wife's Sister* (1849).[20]

It was also during the 1850s that the question of women and

work became the subject of widespread public debate. Educational and professional opportunities for women were slowly and unevenly beginning to open up. There was also growing middle-class concern about the fate of its single women, whose numbers were felt to be increasing as male emigration stepped up, and the rising material expectations and cost of middle-class marriage meant that men were marrying later than previously.[21] Barbara Leigh Smith's pamphlet 'Women and Work' (1856) discussed employment for middle-class women and was widely debated and criticized. The organizers of the married women's property petitioning campaign established the *Englishwoman's Journal* in 1857, and this became the centre for organizations such as the Association for the Promotion of the Employment of Women founded in the late 1850s.[22]

The reviewer of a number of books on the woman question in the *North British Review* in 1857 announced that the employment of women was one of the great matters of the age. Young women, the reviewer argued, were raised only to become dependants: 'We bring them up with the assumption that they may marry; and that then there will be an end of them. They will be absorbed into the man, and become "non-existent"'. The use of 'non-existent' refers to an earlier *North British Review* article on the Marriage and Divorce Bill and is aimed at the doctrine of spousal unity. The reviewer then went on to argue that the lack of jobs for poorer women was a major cause of the rapid growth of prostitution.[23] It was in 1857 that William Acton's classic account of prostitution in London and other large cities appeared, and there had been a spate of writing and painting on the subject since the 1840s. Thomas Hood's poem 'The Bridge of Sighs' (1844), on the recovery of the body of a prostitute from the Thames, was enormously influential. D.G. Rossetti's 'Jenny', begun in 1847, and Meredith's 'London by Lamplight' in *Poems 1851*, were other notable poetic treatments of this subject, and we have already seen it touched on in *The Bothie*. Gaskell had tracked and developed the twin themes of the fallen woman and prostitution in the figure of Aunt Esther in *Mary Barton* (1848), her story 'Lizzie Leigh', which appeared in *Household Words* in 1850, and at full novel length in *Ruth* (1853). The figure of Martha in *David Copperfield* (1849–50) is narrowly rescued from the same fate as the subject of Hood's poem. Leading mid-century painters picked up the theme: G.F. Watts in *Found Drowned* (1850), Spenser Stanhope in *Thoughts of the Past* (1852), Millais in *Virtue and Vice* (1853), and Rossetti in his unfinished *Found,* begun in 1853. Other well-known paintings – Ford Madox Brown's *Take Your Son, Sir* (1851) and Holman Hunt's *The Awakened Conscience* (1853), for example – have an obvious bearing on this subject as well. Another important source and symptom of this interest was Mayhew's writing on prostitution, particularly in his work for the *Morning Chronicle.* His revelations about prostitution among needlewomen which appeared in 1849 had caused a sensation.[24]

These sketchy outlines are an attempt to give some sense of the context within which *Aurora Leigh* was produced and read. They should not, however, be seen as mere 'background', any more than *Aurora Leigh* should be regarded as some merely superstructural efflorescence. Published in 1856, it inevitably became part of wider political and social debate about the status of women, their position in mid-nineteenth-century society, and the implications of re-emergent feminism for the family and the social structure in general. Certainly, it was perceived in this way by the periodical press. The review of *Aurora Leigh* in *The National Magazine* was sandwiched between a hostile rejoinder to Caroline Norton's claim for mothers to have custody rights, and a piece entitled 'London Children', which contrasted the paradise of the countryside with the purgatory of the city, and was heavy with the fear of prostitution, although the subject itself was never made explicit. This was followed by the magazine's regular feature 'The Home', a lengthy column of advice on domestic economy.[25] The layout of the magazine connected the literary text *Aurora Leigh* with adjacent and connected areas of social and political practice. *The North British Review* article on the employment of women, referred to above, appeared in the same issue as Patmore's review of *Aurora Leigh,* and the author cited the poem in the discussion of prostitution, adding that more use would have been made of the work if there had not been a separate article devoted to it. And as *Aurora Leigh* was being reviewed by most of the leading periodicals, the Divorce and Married Women's Property Bills were being hotly debated in their pages.[26] In this way we can begin to see how the literary text *Aurora Leigh* was part of a broader ideological clash. It was not simply that *Aurora Leigh* mirrored many of these conflicts but that, as Terry Eagleton has argued in relation to

Clarissa, it was a material part of these struggles, an agent rather than an account.²⁷ The work *Aurora Leigh* was not just a literary text, nor was Aurora herself merely a fictional character.

The work itself was immensely popular. It had gone through twenty editions by 1887 and was reprinted regularly until the end of the century. The letters of leading writers of the period give a sharp impression of the interest and controversy it provoked. Its most ardent admirer was Ruskin who gave the work his imprimatur in *The Elements of Drawing* which appeared just after *Aurora Leigh* had been published: 'Mrs. Browning's *Aurora Leigh* is, as far as I know, the greatest poem which the century has produced in any language'.²⁸ The poem spoke to and out of the heart of mid-century British culture, provoking a wide range of response and generating an unusually large body of written comment which took it well beyond the confines of literary circles and out into the public world. This process was assisted by the translation of *Aurora Leigh* into other cultural forms. 'She' appeared at the Royal Academy exhibition in 1860 in a painting by William Maw Egley, best known for his scenes of contemporary life such as *Omnibus Life in London*.²⁹ In the same year the Pre-Raphaelite painter Arthur Hughes completed his oil *Aurora Leigh's Dismissal of Romney (The Tryst)* now owned by the Tate Gallery. Nina Auerbach has commented on the way in which Victorian characters, especially female ones, escaped their originating condition – the text – and stepped out into new and transforming contexts. Dickens's characters are an obvious example of this process. Auerbach includes among her examples Mary Cowden Clarke's *The Girlhood of Shakespeare's Heroines* (1850), which invented childhood histories for Shakespeare's women characters, and she also discusses the Victorian practice of making paintings of literary characters.³⁰ *Aurora Leigh* is a good example of this process whereby the individual literary text was transformed into a cultural event.

The complexity of this process of reception and translation needs to be emphasized, however. Ruskin's admiration was not necessarily more benign than the hostility of the *Blackwoods* reviewer. Reading *Aurora Leigh* made no difference to his views on the position of women in Victorian society, and within a few lines of celebrating the work he was able to describe Patmore's *The Angel in the House* as 'the sweetest analysis we possess of quiet modern domestic feeling'.[31] Many of the apparently generous responses to *Aurora Leigh* involved a neutralizing of its more radical elements by a process of assimilation and incorporation. Eagleton has described Richardson's novels as organizing forces of the bourgeois public sphere, assisting in the process of carving out a space for the eighteenth-century middle class in the domain of public discourse.[32] If, following Eagleton, *Aurora Leigh* is understood as carving out a space in public discourse for mid-nineteenth-century women and as one of many organizing forces of an emergent female public sphere, it must be added that no sooner was this space won than it was invaded.

The obvious but crucial difference between Richardson and Barrett Browning is that of gender. By comparison with the eighteenth-century middle class, women in mid-nineteenth-century England had hardly begun to construct a public discourse of their own. This meant that *Aurora Leigh* was more exposed and vulnerable to assimilation than *Clarissa*. Eagleton shows how Richardson as a master printer was at the centre of an ideological network – 'the nub of a whole discursive formation'.[33] Barrett Browning, by contrast, spent years reading and writing in a darkened room, sending messages (poems, letters, reviews) out into a world from which she was cut off. The collective, open-ended, revisionary mode of production which Eagleton emphasizes in Richardson[34] had its Victorian equivalents, Dickens for example, but was not available to women writers forced to operate within a more private sphere.

With the advantage of hindsight it is probably true that in the nineteenth century writing was the form of public discourse most open to women. It cannot always have seemed so to women writers at the time, even when reassured to the contrary. The author of the *North British Review* essay on women and work could write, 'There is no injustice done to women here. The road is open. The race is fair. If woman be the fleeter, she wins. . . . Women who can write, do write'.[35] But as Barrett Browning had made clear in her criticism of *The Princess*, serious women writers did not see themselves as running the same race as men. They were seeking their own track, their own pace, their own language, and it was precisely here that their difficulties were greatest. Barrett Browning wrote of this to her friend and fellow writer Mary Russell Mitford:

you, who are a woman and a man in one, will judge if it isn't a
hard and difficult process for a woman to get forgiven for her
strength by her grace. You who have accomplished this, know it
is hard – and every woman of letters knows it is hard'.[36]

It is a bitter phrase, 'to get forgiven for her strength by her grace',
and still a relevant one. The Greenham Common women who
have cast off conventional notions of 'grace' have been all the
more virulently attacked for their strength. The requirement that
female grace compensate for '(wo)manly' strength was a powerful
strategy for resisting the emergence of a female public sphere with
its own forms, ideologies, and language. Every contemporary
review of *Aurora Leigh* I have read criticized it for lapses of taste,
by which, it is clear, was meant a fall from 'feminine grace' –
strength exposed rather than veiled.

There is nevertheless considerable relevance to Barrett Browning and *Aurora Leigh* in Eagleton's description of Richardson's
method of production as sustaining a constant circulation of
discourse, generating further texts and converting the process of
his art into an act of ideological solidarity.[37] There were special
difficulties for the woman writer of this period in transforming
literary production into effective social practice. However, the
ways in which Barrett Browning drew on women's texts, argued
with male texts, won a hearing for a woman's voice on the woman
question, and prompted further writing by women was an act of
ideological solidarity whereby seemingly private literary production became social practice.

III

The central dilemma of *Aurora Leigh* – how to live as a woman
rather than a pattern lady – is posed through the question of
Aurora's writing, and it is around this issue that gender definitions
are reworked. In the treatment of these issues the unorthodoxy of
Aurora's parenting and upbringing is presented as crucial, and it is
here that I shall begin. Consideration of the distinctive handling of
the writing and gender themes will grow out of this discussion
later in the section.

Aurora's unusual childhood immunizes her against the values
of the world she is suddenly removed to after her father's death. It

enables her to reject Romney's initial proposal and to pursue the vocation of writing undeterred by the expectations of the kind of life a young woman such as Aurora should lead. Egley's painting from *Aurora Leigh* took a significant childhood scene, its title quoting lines from Book 1: 'Father, then, and child we lived among the mountains many years . . . and old Assunta, to make up the fire, crossing herself, whene'er a sudden flame, . . . made alive that picture of my mother on the wall'.[38] Scenes of childhood in Victorian paintings often show an implicit concern with the adult life to come. Another Egley painting, *Military Aspirations* (1861), in which a boy is shown tormenting his sisters in the nursery, projects forward in this way and was intended as part of a triptych showing the life of a boy who wanted to join the army. This preoccupation with the child as father to the man is also present, though less insistently, in the paintings of children by Thomas Webster and the Cranbrook group.[39] In Egley's painting from *Aurora Leigh* the child is mother to the woman. The memory of her mother, intensified by the picture on the wall, and the daily influence of her father ensure her later independence. Viewed in this light, Arthur Hughes's painting *Aurora Leigh's Dismissal of Romney* becomes a sequel and companion-piece to Egley's.

From the age of 4, when her Italian mother dies, Aurora is raised by her father and her nurse in mountain isolation above Pelago, outside Florence. It is a childhood significantly free from the usual social conditioning of the bourgeois family. Her father, formerly 'an austere Englishman' (Bk 1, l. 65), had been 'flooded with a passion' by Aurora's mother and the influence of the Italian sun and landscape, and transformed into an apostle of love. His dying injunction to his daughter, 'Love, my child, love, love' (Bk 1, l. 212), rings as an imperative through the poem and helps protect her from the full weight of social conditioning which falls on her at the age of 13, when her father dies and she is sent to live with her aunt in England. Under the stern regimen of her aunt, Aurora's femininity is carefully constructed:

> She liked a woman to be womanly,
> And English women, she thanked God and sighed
> (Some people always sigh in thanking God)
> Were models to the universe.
> (Bk 1, ll. 443–6)

Aurora's life is now filled with modelling flowers in wax and reading books on womanhood, but the upbringing she received from her father enables her inwardly to resist this conditioning:

> The trick of Greek
> And Latin he had taught me, as he would
> Have taught me wrestling or the game of fives
> If such he had known

Mrs Sara Ellis and her kind are no match for such a father:

> Thus, my father gave;
> And thus, as did the women formerly
> By young Achilles, when they pinned a veil
> Across the boy's audacious front, and swept
> With tuneful laughs the silver-fretted rocks,
> He wrapt his little daughter in his large
> Man's doublet, careless did it fit or no.
>   (Bk 1, ll. 722–8)

There is a neat reversal involved in this comparison of Aurora and her father with Achilles and his mother, Thetis, and the association of clothing and gender is one of several such instances in the poem. The clothing figure, in particular, becomes significant and will be explored later. The important point here is that her father's disregard of gender roles assists Aurora in resisting the shaping pressures of contemporary definitions of womanhood.

The culmination of these pressures is Romney's proposal, which has the full weight of family and property behind it. Romney is Aurora's cousin, and on the death of their aunt will inherit all the Leigh estates, a clause in the entail excluding offspring by a foreign wife having left Aurora disinherited. Romney's father had long ago suggested to Aurora's that their children should marry. Personal factors complicate these lineage pressures. Several commentators on the poem seem to enjoy pointing out that Aurora has loved Romney from the beginning, although only admitting this to herself in the final book. In this they echo the aunt's accusation (Bk 2, ll. 688–91), which should make them hesitate. Aurora's denial is not simply disingenuous, nor is her blush a brand of guilt. Love between Aurora and Romney remains potential until they come to share a common definition of that term. The proposal scene in the garden that June morning, which is also the morning of Aurora's twentieth birthday, shows that their definitions of love are antagonistic. Love is the poem's imperative, but not regardless of the terms. Until new terms are discovered, independence is paramount, although recognized as incomplete in itself. Romney, in fact, must travel the same journey as that taken, rather more economically, by Aurora's father, whose conversion from good works and social questions – he had come to Florence to 'note the secret of Da Vinci's drains' (Bk 1, l. 72) – to passion prefigures Romney's history. When Romney first visits Aurora he comes with a gift of hothouse grapes in one hand but a book of 'mere statistics' (Bk 1, 1. 525) in the other. Set against Romney's blue-book is Aurora's book of poems which they argue about during the proposal scene, and which figures so prominently in Arthur Hughes's painting. As an improbably boyish Romney looks sorrowfully at Aurora, she clutches her book (its marker visible) and stares resolutely ahead, the other arm free to point his dismissal.

Specific details link and counterpoint Aurora's father with Romney in the early books of the poem. There is, for example, Romney's first sign of tenderness to Aurora;

> Once, he stood so near,
> He dropped a sudden hand upon my head
> Bent down on woman's work, as soft as rain –
> But then I rose and shook it off as fire,
> The stranger's touch that took my father's place
> Yet dared seem soft.
>
> (Bk 1, ll. 543–8)

Romney's action recalls one of Aurora's earliest memories – 'My father's slow hand . . . /Stroke out my childish curls across his knee' (Bk 1, ll. 20–1) – and is experienced as a usurpation. Her father's action was unselfishly caring. Romney's is an act of false homage inspired by the sight of Aurora engaged in 'woman's work' and implying proprietorial rights. The symbolism of hands, head, and hair is important. It expresses Aurora's father's respect for his daughter's otherness, as when nursing her – 'His large man's hands afraid to touch my curls,/As if the gold would tarnish' (Bk 1, ll. 96–7) – and the aunt's determination to refashion her niece – 'I broke the copious curls upon my head/In braids, because she liked smooth-ordered hair' (Bk 1, ll. 385–6). It

Plate 8 Arthur Hughes, 'Aurora Leigh's Dismissal of Romney' ('The Tryst'), 1860

is also associated with the ivy crown-wreath with which Aurora adorns herself on the morning of the proposal and which Romney catches abruptly, halting Aurora before making his offer. Romney is left in no doubt that Aurora's head is not for his hands, and when he approaches her again after their aunt's funeral and begins the tediously protracted offer of part of his wealth, he is considerably more cautious: 'he touched, just touched/My hat-strings, tied for going' (Bk 2, ll. 970–1). Only when Romney is able to accept Aurora's life as having independent value, and her writing as more than mere 'women's work', can their love be actualized.

But this is to anticipate. Aurora's earliest memory is of her mother at the nursery door, divided between quelling infant riot and participating in it. It is a gentle picture, but the note of division it quietly sounds becomes stronger in the passages concerning Aurora's mother which follow. Aurora feels her life to have been gained at the cost of her mother's: 'my life/A poor spark snatched up from a failing lamp/Which went out therefore' (Bk 1, ll. 31–3) – the poem's first example of a pattern of light/dark imagery which is to run throughout its length. This sense of guilt intensifies in the immediately following violent image of life and death – 'She could not bear the joy of giving life,/The mother's rapture slew her' (Bk 1, ll. 34–5) – and spreads to her father as well, with his grief at her mother's death: 'I, Aurora Leigh, was born/To make my father sadder' (Bk 1, ll. 45–6). This sense of original sin mixes with the child's strong sense of 'mother-want' to produce the startlingly contradictory images of her mother concentrated in the picture on the wall which Assunta's fire lit up. This picture, painted after death but with Aurora's mother dressed not in a shroud but 'the last brocade/She dressed in at the Pitti' (Bk 1, ll. 131–2) holds the life–death opposition within its frame. It fascinates the young Aurora:

> I, a little child, would crouch
> For hours upon the floor with knees drawn up,
> And gaze across them, half in terror, half
> In adoration, at the picture there –
>
> (Bk 1, ll. 135–38)

The ambivalence of Aurora's response, emphasized here by the enjambment, continues throughout her childhood. The picture becomes the point of reference to which all childhood experience is assimilated. It is, by turns:

> Ghost, fiend, and angel, fairy, witch, and sprite,
> A dauntless Muse who eyes a dreadful Fate,
> A loving Psyche who loses sight of Love,
> A still Medusa with mild milky brows
> All curdled and all clothed upon with snakes
> Whose slime falls fast as sweat will; or anon
> Our Lady of the Passion, stabbed with swords
> Where the Babe sucked; or Lamia in her first
> Moonlighted pallor, ere she shrunk and blinked
> And shuddering wriggled down to the unclean;
> Or my own mother, leaving her last smile
> In her last kiss upon the baby-mouth
> My father pushed down on the bed for that, –
> Or my dead mother, without smile or kiss,
> Buried at Florence.
> (Bk 1, ll. 155–68)

This is an extraordinary passage of densely packed and violently contradictory images. Conventionally gentle imagery of motherhood – 'mild, milky brows' – is weirdly attached to Medusa and then hideously distorted in the grisly image of snakes, slime, and sweat. Sucking (a recurring image in the poem) is followed by stabbing in the sado-masochistic picture of Our Lady of the Passion. The mother is both comforting and menacing, alive and dead, a dualism expressed in the Lamia image which is to recur later.

Most recent writing on *Aurora Leigh* sees this passage as a symptom of Aurora's 'mother-want' and an expression of her consequent difficulty in understanding and accepting her psychosexual identity. In the absence of a living mother she projects on to the portrait the range of contradictory images and myths of women she has learnt. Internalizing this essentially male tradition of ways of seeing women, she develops contradictory, often hostile attitudes to her own femininity, including a male view of women's inferiority. In particular, this finds expression in the conflict between the woman as artist and mother.[40] Much of this is helpful. 'Mother-want' and its resolution is a dominant theme in the poem, and in the passage immediately above, the Muse eyeing its Fate and Psyche losing sight of love both seem to be anticipations of Aurora's adult life. Some of these emphases are, however, distorting. For one thing, the role played by Aurora's father is ignored. Fathering in Aurora's history is not synonomous with patriarchy, and the 'single parenting' she receives leaves her unusually immune from conventional gendering and socialization. Aurora's responses to the portrait are primarily to do with guilt about her mother's death and resentment at her disappearance. The conflicts in her position as a woman are not really perceived and experienced until after she is sent to England and exposed to conventional social pressures. In this, *Aurora Leigh* echoes and reworks Madame de Stael's *Corinne*, in which the central opposition between, on the one hand, art and love, and on the other, domesticity, is expressed in the contrasting half-sisters Corinne and Lucy. They represent antithetical conceptions of womanhood. Corinne is part-Italian, dark, passionate, and gifted; Lucy is wholly English, fair, modest, and conventional. England is presented as the domestic country par excellence, and Corinne, try as she does to suppress her genius and conform to the ideals of timid, subdued womanhood, is unassimilable. Aurora makes no concessions and will eventually bridge the divide between Italy and England, art and domesticity.

Once Aurora is sent to England the image of her mother ceases to be Janus-faced, and memories of her become associated wholly with loss. There is a strong identification between her mother and Italy – culminating in Book 5 when Aurora's intended return to that country and its hills is imaged as a return to the breast (ll. 1267–71) – and both are now lost. Within the confines of English domestic life her mother's image is thrown into harsh relief by the aunt's hatred of this Italian woman she never met: 'And thus my father's sister was to me/My mother's hater' (Bk 1, ll. 359-60).

As unfamiliar social pressures are experienced, Aurora's parents become the standard for all she knows and understands of love. In a speech during the proposal scene in which Romney invites Aurora to enter his world, 'Ah, my sweet, come down' (Bk 2, l. 385), echoing those lines which softened Ida in *The Princess*, 'Come down, O maid, from yonder mountain height', but here without success, he invokes the image of her mother's face. She throws it back at Romney:

> I answered slowly; 'you do well to name
> My mother's face. Though far too early, alas,
> God's hand did interpose 'twixt it and me,
> I know so much of love as used to shine
> In that face and another. Just so much;
> No more indeed at all. I have not seen
> So much love since, I pray you pardon me,
> As answers even to make a marriage with
> In this cold land of England.'
>
> (Bk 2, ll. 392–400)

The memory of her mother and father has now become a protection against social and family pressures and central to her bid for independence. This she wins through the death of the aunt, which is for Aurora pure gain: 'Henceforth none/Could disapprove me, vex me, hamper me' (Bk 2, ll. 958–9). And the unexpected bonus of a small legacy completes the package: 'With three hundred pounds/We buy, in England even, clear standing-room/To stand and work in' (Bk 2, ll. 983–5). By the end of the second book Aurora has indeed won 'clear standing-room'. She has £300, a room of her own, and is fully orphaned. Free of that tangle of family relationships the opening books explore, she has reached the condition enjoyed by Charlotte Brontë's heroines – a condition of freedom and of difficulty.

Aurora Leigh, like many Victorian novels and poems, uses the metaphor of life as a journey beset with difficulties, applying this particularly to the passage from childhood to maturity:

> When any young wayfaring soul goes forth
> Alone, unconscious of the perilous road,
> The day-sun dazzling in his limpid eyes,
> To thrust his own way, he an alien, through
> The world of books!
>
> (Bk 1, ll. 740–4)

Most Victorian texts, however, would stop short of the last two words. *Aurora Leigh* is insistently and distinctively a poem about books – about reading and writing. The words 'write', 'writing', and 'written' occur in each of the poem's opening four lines, striking its keynote. Almost one-third of the opening book is concerned with Aurora's reading and early development as a poet.

'Books, books, books!' she apostrophizes in introducing the passage which tells excitedly of the discovery of her father's books piled high in a garret in her aunt's house. It is this 'quickening inner life' fed by her reading and writing which helps Aurora keep her aunt's world at arm's length. But this is not a simple opposition between art and life, the personal and the social. 'The world of books is still the world', the poem repeats insistently as it makes its frequent identifications between world and book, and develops its metaphors of books, writing, language, and grammar. Aurora's early poetry is 'Like those hot fire-seeds of creation held/In Jove's clenched palm before the worlds were sown' (Bk 3, ll. 252–3). Stars shine out like 'secret writing from a sombre page' (Bk 8, l. 91). Aurora repeatedly sees herself and her life as a book (e.g. Bk 4, l. 41; Bk 7, ll. 1042–52). Our incomplete understanding of the world is imaged as an incomplete sentence, the verb and pronoun missing (Bk 8, ll. 667–73). Aurora's mistaken belief that Romney has married Lady Waldemar is described by Romney as 'monstrous forgeries/For the legible life signature of such/As I, with all my blots' (Bk 8, ll. 1233–5). This is a small sample from the poem's constant use of the writing figure.

When Romney recants in Book 8 it is appropriate he should accuse himself of semi-illiteracy, having 'obliterate [d] good words with fractious thumbs/And cheat[ed] myself of the context' (Bk 8, ll. 326–7) in his earlier denigration of Aurora's writing. For Aurora, to write is to live. Her existence is grounded in writing, and Romney must accept Aurora's writing/herself before she can ever accept him. Another important example of the writing figure is the book/body metaphor. Here is Aurora announcing the completion of her book:

> Behold, at last, a book.
> If life-blood's necessary, which it is, –
> (By that blue vein athrob on Mahomet's brow,
> Each prophet-poet's book must show man's blood!)
> If life-blood's fertilising, I wrung mine
> On every leaf of this, – unless the drops
> Slid heavily on one side and left it dry.
>
> (Bk 5, ll. 353–8)

This is the book which brings Romney sight in blindness and provokes his recantation. It is through her art that Aurora finally wins love. To have sacrificed art to love would have been to lose both. Aurora's book becomes assimilated to Romney's body:

> 'for the book is in my heart,
> Lives in me, wakes in me, and dreams in me:
> My daily bread tastes of it, – and my wine
> Which has no smack of it, I pour out,
> It seems unnatural drinking.'
> (Bk 8, ll. 265–9)

Prophet-poets administer the eucharist while their readers experience the miracle of transubstantiation. And with Romney's heart full of Aurora's book it is entirely appropriate that Lady Waldemar's love for him should be 'wiped wholly out/Like some ill scholar's scrawl from heart and slate' (Bk 9, ll. 122–3). Only when Romney comes to accept Aurora on her own terms can she admit her father's imperative and concede that 'Art is much, but Love is more' (Bk 9, l. 956). Romney comes to Italy, which since Aurora's return to the settings of her childhood, has stubbornly refused to 'mix its tenses' (Bk 7, l. 1158), keeping past and present apart, and the language of that childhood is , at last, recovered. In form and theme the poem has celebrated the triumph of writing, and through it, love: 'the world of books is still the world'.

I can think of no other early- or mid-Victorian text in which the writing theme is as central and insistent. *Aurora Leigh* is *the* Victorian *kunstlerroman*. *David Copperfield*, by comparison, is a *bildungsroman*, its writing theme murky and undeveloped. *Pendennis* (1849–50) gives a vivid picture of London literary and journalistic life and its central character writes a successful novel, but of the silver-fork kind. The writing theme gets lost in Thackeray's more general interest in the hazardous, often comic journey from adolescence to maturity of Arthur Pendennis. Lady Carbury in Trollope's *The Way We Live Now* (1875) writes in order to supplement her small income, but only turns to novels because a publisher tells her they do better than anything else – 'She would have written a volume of sermons on the same encouragement'.[41] This emphasis on writing as a means of earning a living, often to maintain social position in reduced circumstances, is the most common later in the century. Diana Merion in Meredith's *Diana of the Crossways* (1885), a character based on Caroline Norton, is a more liberated version of the Lady Carbury figure struggling to earn a living by writing novels. Gissing takes this furthest, in *New Grub Street* basing a whole novel on such a figure. Hardy's *The Hand of Ethelberta* (1876) is unusual in showing more interest in writing as a vocation based on a strong personal urge, and in the special problems of being a serious woman writer. Hardy had already touched on the question of the woman writer in *A Pair of Blue Eyes* (1873), but it is more central in the later novel. Ethelberta Chickerel is a poet, not a writer of society novels. Her first volume, *Metres by E*, earns her notoriety rather than fame. These poems, described as 'not quite virginibus puerisque', are reproved in terms which recall Barrett Browning and *Aurora Leigh*. One character remarks of them: 'Really, one would imagine that women wrote their books during those dreams in which people have no moral sense, to see how improper some, even virtuous, ladies become when they get into print'.[42] Following this, Ethelberta tries to make her way as a public story-teller. The writing theme is again connected with the need to earn a living and support others – unlike Aurora, Ethelberta is part of a large family – but this is less overriding than in the other novels I have mentioned.

These novels however, are all by men. It is strange that writing as a vocation does not figure at all prominently in women's texts. For all its difficulties, writing was one of the few openings into the public sphere available to women. The writing theme is strikingly absent in George Eliot's work, for example. Mary Garth does, it is true, produce a book – *Stories of Great Men, taken from Plutarch*– but it is 'a little book for her boys', and her writing is simply an aspect of her mothering. Ellen Moers was no doubt right to emphasize *performance*, the dramatic presentation of self through singing or acting as paralleling the writing theme.[43] Preaching seems as central to Dinah Morris's life as writing is to Aurora's. Again, however, this helps establish the distinctiveness of *Aurora Leigh*. Dinah Morris gives up her preaching career with what Ellen Moers describes as 'a flutter of glad submission'.[44] Christina Rossetti's Maude, a young writer, turns away from marriage but also renounces life. Aurora Leigh writes, and therefore lives, and eventually loves. In the end nothing is lost.

Nor, however, is it easily won, and *Aurora Leigh* explores the special problems which confront the woman as writer. At a party in Book 5 Aurora rebukes her friend and host, Lord Howe, for tossing her some conventional sounding compliments:

> 'my dear Lord Howe, you shall not speak
> To a printing woman who has lost her place
> (The sweet safe corner of the household fire
> Behind the heads of children), compliments,
> As if she were a woman. We who have clipt
> The curls before our eyes may see at least
> As plain as men do.'
>
> (Bk 5, ll. 805–11)

This proud assertion of the independence of the woman writer and her emancipation from gender stereotypes has undergone painful self-examination earlier in Book 5. The image of clipped hair is in any case an ambiguous one in this poem, and the almost contemptuously cosy picture of domestic contentment has been treated very differently several hundred lines earlier. Writing, Aurora has felt, means a loss of place, of home and family.

The first 500 or so lines of Book 5 are an extended soliloquy in which Aurora contemplates the failure of her art to move humankind (and Romney in particular), and keeps returning to her own loneliness. Slowly this concentrates into a series of pictures of domestic happiness, each of which Aurora is excluded from, and yet, ironically and bitterly, her writing feeds. While Aurora sits 'On winter nights by solitary fires' (Bk 5, l. 440), engaged lovers read to each other from one of her books. A father returning home to the 'luminous round of lamp and hearth' (Bk 5, l. 458) greets his delighted children and gives to the eldest a present of Aurora's latest book. This then develops into a further run of such pictures which unite the domestic and the literary. Aurora describes several leading writers of the day, envying neither their abilities nor their success, but rather their domestic circumstances. One has a loving mother to whom he can show glowing reviews of his work. Another has a loving wife and son. 'Who loves me?' she asks (Bk 5, l. 540), and returns to the memory of her parents – 'Dearest father, – mother sweet' – whose deaths first estranged her from home and family, a condition exacerbated by her life as a writer. Aurora's defiant reply to Lord Howe is therefore decidedly edgy, and it is followed, ironically and aggravatingly, by an offer of marriage which Howe bears from one John Eglinton, a sizeable landowner and patron of the arts.

Eglinton wants, as Aurora says, not a wife but 'A star upon his stage' (Bk 5, l. 915). This offer by proxy, devoid of love, is it seems the only kind to which Aurora's celebrity entitles her. It is after this party that Aurora, convinced Romney is about to marry Lady Waldemar, decides to leave 'unfostering England' (Bk 5, l. 936) and return to the land of her birth:

> my Italy,
> My own hills! Are you 'ware of me, my hills,
> How I burn toward you? do you feel to-night
> The urgency and yearning of my soul,
> As sleeping mothers feel the sucking babe
> And smile?
> (Bk 5, ll. 1266–71)

This tension between the pen and the hearth, between vocation and family, is of course peculiar to women writers, as Book 7 underlines when Aurora's artist friend Carrington writes and tells her of his marriage. Love and marriage merely effect a change in Carrington's style (Bk 7, l. 592); he will continue to work at his vocation. The warm response to Aurora's latest book which Carrington's letter also relates highlights the human cost of such success. Believing Romney to be already married, and learning of Carrington's happiness, Aurora lives unhappily in the land of her dead parents with the 'orphaned' Marian and her fatherless child.

Aurora's reproof to Lord Howe suggests that writing has somehow ungendered her. As I mentioned earlier, clothing imagery is important in the poem's examination of gender roles, women's clothing often being imaged as an impediment to her activity and development. During the proposal scene Aurora tells Romney:

> A woman's always younger than a man
> At equal years, because she is disallowed
> Maturing by the outdoor sun and air,
> And kept in long-clothes past the age to walk.
> (Bk 2, ll. 329–32)

Women are sheltered like plants in a greenhouse, and their garments cramp their movement. Aurora's effort to become more than a 'mere' woman writer involves the metaphoric discarding of conventional female dress: 'This vile woman's way/Of trailing garments shall not trip me up' (Bk 5, ll. 59–60). And several books later the same figure is applied more generally to the difficulties Aurora faces:

> I cannot see by road along this dark;
> Nor can I creep and grope, as fits the dark,
> For these foot-catching robes of womanhood:
> A man might walk a little ... but I!
> (Bk 7, ll. 148–51)

The nightmare quality of this picture is gender-specific. Women cannot keep pace with men, and their clothing serves as a precise image of society's constricting definition of womanhood. Acceptance of conventional dress implies acceptance of a conventional role, as we see when Lady Waldemar, finally abandoning her scheme to net Romney, remarks tartly that in future she will admit 'No socialist within three crinolines' (Bk 9, l. 136).

But in all this Aurora Leigh stops well short of George Sand, whom Barrett Browning admired so much and so uneasily. George Sand's notoriety in early Victorian England was, as Patricia Thomson has shown, based as much on her divorce, her adoption of a male name, and her liking for wearing men's clothing, as on her writing.[45] Barrett Browning wrote two sonnets to George Sand which first appeared in her 1844 collection and which were both preoccupied with George Sand's androgyny. The first of these, 'To George Sand – A Desire' begins, 'Thou large-brained woman and large-hearted man,/Self-called George Sand!', calling attention to this gender confusion. The second, 'To George Sand – A Recognition', partly dispels this image, rehabilitating Sand as a woman in terms which recall *Aurora Leigh*:

> True genius, but true woman! dost deny
> The woman's nature with a manly scorn,
> And break away the gauds and armlets worn
> By weaker women in captivity?
> Ah, vain denial!

George Sand has thrown off the trappings of women's subjection yet remains a woman:

> Thy woman's hair, my sister, all unshorn
> Floats back dishevelled strength in agony,
> Disproving thy man's name:

Aurora Leigh, as I said, stops short of actually putting her metaphors into practice. But the piece of her clothing most frequently referred to has Sandish associations. This is her cloak. In Book 3 Kate Ward has asked her for its pattern, and later, in Book 7, when Carrington writes and tells Aurora of his marriage to Kate, we learn that she has insisted on wearing this cloak for her portrait. She has also insisted on holding Aurora's recent book, an interesting anticipation of Hughes's painting. Aurora's cloak is, of course, the traditional mantle of the prophet-poet, but it is also contemporary and gender-specific. Aurora's life and achievements are an example to other women. Carrington writes how Kate 'has your books by heart more than my words,/And quotes you up against me' (Bk 7, ll. 603–4); how women 'Grow insolent about you against men' (Bk 7, l. 615); and how there are women who believe 'that if you walked on sand/You would not leave a footprint' (Bk 7, ll. 621–2). This must surely be one of the most developed examples of what Ellen Moers has termed performing heroinism. And it is clear, too, that Aurora's cloak goes naturally with that 'large Man's doublet' her father had wrapped her in as a child.

In passing, it is interesting to note how Barrett Browning insisted on dressing her own son. When Pen was only 2 his parents were already at odds over how he should be dressed, as Elizabeth described in a letter to her sister Arabel:

> Robert wants to make the child like *a boy*, he says – (because he is a man) – and I because I am a woman perhaps, like him to be a baby as long as possible . . . it vexes Robert when people ask if he is a boy or a girl – (oh, man's pride!) and he will have it, that the lace cap and ribbons help to throw the point into doubt.[46]

If Robert's objection to his 2-year-old son wearing a lace cap under his hat seems fastidious, by the time he was 10 Pen himself was in conflict with his mother over his clothes. He was still wearing a velvet blouse with his long curls hanging down over it, and in a letter to another sister, Henrietta, Elizabeth described their differences: 'Pen tugs at me in vain for very thick shoes – which he thinks manly – because he has seen great boys wear them. I won't let him wear a shoe except of the soft polished leather'.[47] When Elizabeth died in 1861 it was not only his mother that Pen lost. Four days after Elizabeth's funeral Robert wrote to his sister, 'Pen, the golden curls and fantastic dress, is gone just as Ba is gone: he has short hair, worn boy-wise, long trousers, is a common boy all at once'.[48] It must have been a traumatic few days for the twelve year old Pen, and the central part played by clothes in this little conflict over gender is particularly interesting.

Aurora Leigh frequently uses other metaphors which confuse the masculine and the feminine. In its recurring use of animal imagery, for example, the poem seems oblivious of gender difference; Aurora is indiscriminantly lion and lioness, doe and stag. Barbara Charlesworth Gelpi reads this gender blurring as a symptom of the anti-feminine biases Aurora has internalized. Her identification with learning and poetry, seen as male prerogatives, becomes a derogation of the feminine and a denial of her own womanhood. Only when she overcomes this ambivalence towards femininity can she recognize her love for Romney and give undivided voice to her own poetic powers.[49] This kind of reading uncritically accepts 'masculine' and 'feminine' as fixed categories, whereas this is precisely what the poem is questioning. Gelpi's assumptions are shared by Steinmetz and Rosenblum. These critics all see the poem as Aurora's inner quest for the recovery of her parents, and hence herself, rather than as an exploration of the problem of how to live authentically outside family structures and in pursuit of her vocation. For Gelpi, Romney's scepticism about Aurora's powers is '*only* an expression, a projection of her own divided feelings about herself' (my emphasis).[50] The 'psychologism' of this approach excludes the social construction of masculinity and femininity with which the poem is centrally concerned. The poem's metaphorical language has a social as well as psychological reference, and plays with the categories of 'masculine' and 'feminine'. Late in the poem Aurora tells Romney:

> 'I'm plain at speech, direct in purpose: when
> I speak, you'll take the meaning as it is,
> And not allow for puckerings in the silk
> By clever stitches. I'm a woman, sir –
> I use the woman's figures naturally,
> As you the male license.'
> (Bk 8, ll. 1127–32)

There is something more complicated than an acceptance of her womanhood going on in these lines. The metaphor is derived from 'woman's work' and recalls the scene referred to above in which Romney first showed tenderness to Aurora (Bk 1, ll. 543–8). Aurora uses it as a means of asserting *her* femininity while denying Romney's understanding of this term. She is 'plain at speech, direct in purpose', which for Romney are masculine qualities. Her 'natural' use of the 'woman's figure' is challenging – women do have a language of their own – and ironic. She distances herself from the kind of femininity suggested by silk and clever stitches (the reference here is to Lady Waldemar, who Aurora still thinks is Romney's wife) without denying her sex. Gelpi is right in showing how so much of the metaphorical language of the poem blends and blurs masculinity and femininity, but the use to which this androgynous language is put is altogether more subtle and radical than she allows. It is not so much that Aurora must become reconciled to her own womanhood, but that the world, and Romney in particular, must revise its definition of femininity and learn to accept the kind of woman she is. Unlike George Eliot's fictional world, not all the adjustments have to be made by the heroine.

IV

George Eliot's novels are a useful starting point for moving out from the isolated text, *Aurora Leigh*, into its surrounding literary context. Ellen Moers's judgement on Eliot could, it might seem, also be applied to Barrett Browning:

> Eliot, as her readers have always been surprised to discover, was not feminist. That is, her aim as a novelist was not to argue for a diminishing of the social inhibitions and a widening of the options that affect the lives of ordinary women; instead, like Mme. de Stael, George Eliot was always concerned with the superior, large-souled woman whose distinction resides not in her deeds but in her capacity to attract attention and arouse admiration.[51]

There is no doubt that Barrett Browning's primary concern and identification was with the woman as artist. But the significant difference between Aurora Leigh and, say, Dorothea Brooke, is that Aurora does something. Dorothea does nothing, while remaining superior to other women who cannot understand her, let alone emulate her. Women artists in Eliot's work are rare, and usually unhappy. Deronda's mother abandoned motherhood for a singing career and lives an empty, bitter life. In *Aurora Leigh*, on the other hand, the affirmative presentation of the figure of the woman artist makes her a paradigm for other possible activities and vocations for women.

Barrett Browning was a trenchant critic of the traditional roles open to women. Although honouring Florence Nightingale for her work in the Crimea, she had no illusions about its general implications for women:

> I confess myself to be at a loss to see any new position for the sex, or the most imperfect solution of the 'woman's question', in this step of hers. If a movement at all, it is retrograde, a revival of old virtues! Since the siege of Troy and earlier, we have had princesses binding wounds with their hands; it's strictly the woman's part, and men understand it so. – Every man is on his knees before ladies carrying lint, calling them 'angelic she's', whereas, if they stir an inch as thinkers or artists from the beaten line (involving more good to general humanity than is involved in lint), the very same men would curse the impudence of the very same woman. For my own part (and apart from the exceptional miseries of the war), I acknowledge to you that I do not consider the best use to which we can put a gifted and accomplished woman is to *make her a hospital nurse*.[52]

This point was made in the course of a comparison between Nightingale and Harriet Beecher Stowe. Barrett Browning thought more highly of Stowe's achievements. It was also a riposte to Tennyson. Although the emphasis is clearly on the 'gifted and accomplished woman', this figure is enlisted to challenge the strict limits within which all women's activity was confined. This emphasis on an active role for women prevents the self-abnegation within marriage which happens to several of George Eliot's heroines. Just as Aurora Leigh rejected the terms of Romney's first proposal, so too Elizabeth Barrett loathed the idea of woman's secondary, supporting role in marriage:

> A German professor selects a wife who can merely stew prunes – not because stewing prunes and reading Proclus make

a delightful harmony, but because he wants his prunes stewed for him and chooses to read Proclus by himself. A fullness of sympathy, a sharing of life, one with another, is scarcely ever looked for except in a narrow conventional sense. Men like to come home and find a blazing fire and a smiling face and an hour of relaxation. Their serious thoughts, and earnest aims in life, they like to keep on one side. And this is the carrying out of love and marriage almost everywhere in the world – and this, the degrading of women by both.[53]

If this could be a light sketch of Dorothea's chilling marriage to Casaubon, it could also be a picture of her later marriage to Ladislaw. Although Dorothea's 'wifely help' to her MP husband is regretted by 'many who knew her', this is because of their dislike of Ladislaw, and Dorothea's taste for self-sacrifice is unquestioned. In 'Finale', Eliot writes of Dorothea and Ladislaw: 'They were bound to each other by a love stronger than any impulses which could have marred it' (*Middlemarch*, p. 576). In *Aurora Leigh*, love is similarly important but rather less immune from other impulses.

A further interesting point of comparison with Eliot is the treatment of the fallen woman figure. There doesn't seem much to be said for Barrett Browning's depiction of Marian Erle until one reads other contemporary versions of this figure in the novels of Dickens, Gaskell, and Eliot. Although Barrett Browning's treatment of working-class life is weaker than these novelists, her handling of the fallen woman theme is more sympathetically and consistently engaged. Marian's child isn't her badge of shame; he becomes the central concern of her life. Mother and child both live, whereas in *Adam Bede* the child is killed by its mother, and in Gaskell's *Ruth* the mother dies. Marian's 'fall' is blameless and is treated as such, unlike those other fictional women who suffer blameless falls and are then forced to atone for their 'sin'. There is no unnecessary penitence, and it is Aurora, not Marian, who is forced to adjust her attitudes. Marian is actually glad when she discovers she is pregnant (Bk 7, ll. 56–63). The counterpointing of Marian and Aurora is far more subtle than that of Hetty and Dinah in *Adam Bede*, being based on affinity as much as on difference. An interesting shadow relationship develops between the two involving a series of correspondences between their respective histories.

Both are outsiders lacking a place in the world, although Marian's situation is more extreme and is class- as well as gender-based. Both are orphaned, Marian more horribly so – her mother having tried to sell her. Marian, against all the odds, has acquired a love of literature, which has to an extent insulated her from the terrors of her childhood. A similar imagery of flowers, birds, animals, and hunting is attached to them both. They are, of course, linked through Romney, and after Aurora's rediscovery of Marian in Book 6 they repeatedly refer to each other as 'sister'. Marian in her turn is shadowed by the figure of Rose Bell, a childhood friend and another orphan, who has become a 'ruined creature' (Bk 4, l. 1049) frequenting Oxford Street by night (Bk 3, ll. 927–8).

The physical descriptions of Marian are interesting. Her most distinctive feature is her hair with its 'opulence of curls' (Bk 3, l. 813), and this provides another linking detail with Aurora. Her mother's violent treatment of her hair as she offers her daughter for sale recalls the aunt's insistence that Aurora have her curls cut off. Long wild hair as an image of passionate womanhood occurs in the second George Sand sonnet (see above p. 155), and again in *Aurora Leigh* at the end of Book 5, when Aurora returns home from Lord Howe's party:

> My loose long hair began to burn and creep,
> Alive to the very ends, about my knees:
> I swept it backward as the wind sweeps flame,
> With the passion of my hands.
>
> (Bk 5, ll. 1126–9)

Marian is a victim rather than a pioneer, and given neither the voice nor the dramatic strength of Aurora, but her otherwise rather thin characterization is tempered by these associations.

There is a further association. The description of Marian's 'opulence of curls' is followed by these lines:

> Too much hair perhaps
> (I'll name a fault here) for so small a head,
> Which seemed to droop on that side and on this,
> As a full-blown rose uneasy with its weight
>
> (Bk 3, ll. 815–18)

Looking at the well-known portrait of Barrett Browning on the cover of my edition of *Aurora Leigh*, these lines seem to be a self-portrait. This extends still further the connections and correspondences which make her fallen woman figure more central and complex than those of the novelists I've referred to.

Aurora Leigh uses many other conventions found in mid-century narratives. It examines both the cross-class and arranged marriage, and, like most Victorian narratives, ends in a love marriage. Again, however, the treatment of these conventions is markedly different. Cross-class marriages are usually an act of closure, and function as an image of class reconciliation or the supersession of politics by love. They are also usually hedged with qualifications. In *Jane Eyre*, for example, there is a striking discrepancy between Jane's actual class position and her rightful status. Her marriage to Rochester sets this right, helped by the legacy she inherits. In Clough's *Bothie*, as we saw, the cross-class marriage was followed by emigration, so that the difficulties raised by such a marriage were never confronted. In *Aurora Leigh*, on the other hand, the cross-class marriage is attempted in mid-narrative (Bk 4), and its difficulties and self-deceptions are explored. The arranged marriage is another echo of the Victorian novel, but its treatment in *Aurora Leigh* most obviously recalls *The Princess*. In both poems the arranged marriage does finally take place, but only after it has been rearranged by love. The arrangement itself is an obstacle rather than an aid to marriage – an idea which Dickens takes much further in *Edwin Drood* – and it is only when a different basis for marriage has been discovered that the arrangement can be ratified.

It is hardly necessary, however, to spell out the different basis for marriage in these two poems. Ida renounces her feminism; Aurora remains a writer. Ida nurses the wounded Prince back to health as a prelude to their marriage, but in *Aurora Leigh* the nursing theme is treated ironically. Lady Waldemar nurses the injured Romney, who then returns to Aurora. Ida's college becomes a hospital, but Aurora escapes being Florence Nightingale. The resolution of *The Princess* and *The Bothie* rests on the idea of marriage as a relation of 'helpmeets'. This is also the basis of Romney's proposal in Book 2, where it is examined, found wanting, and rejected. It is exposed as meaning, in effect, that the woman helps the man. As with cross-class marriage, we find a contemporary narrative convention scrutinized and subverted. A comfortable resolution is discomfitingly searched by being introduced into the body of the narrative. It is many years before Romney's offer is taken up, by which time its terms are very different.

The resolution of *Aurora Leigh*, however, makes more predictable and less interesting use of mid-nineteenth-century narrative convention. Romney has come to see Aurora and her art very differently, acknowledging both her gift and its utility (Bk 9, ll. 915–24), but only at the cost of his blindness which leaves him dependent and the relationship unequal:

> Shine out for two, Aurora, and fulfil
> My falling-short that must be! work for two
> (Bk 9, ll. 910–11)

And Aurora's admission that 'Art is much, but Love is more' (Bk 9, l. 956), involves the further concession that her refusal to be 'a woman like the rest' (Bk 9, l. 960) and her insistence on analysing, confronting, and questioning have been mistaken (Bk 9, ll. 660–73). This gives away far more than Romney now wants, and amounts to a repudiation of her life up to this point. It reverses the positions of the first proposal scene. It is also, given Romney's reduced state, a little hollow. The dominant impression left by *Aurora Leigh* is of its hero's blindness and not, as in *The Princess*, the heroine's recantation.

The blinding and maiming motif in the treatment of male heroes by Victorian women writers has been noted by several commentators. Elaine Showalter explains it as a symbolic immersion of the hero in feminine experience so that he too can feel and understand its dependency, frustration, and powerlessness. The mid-century texts she refers to are *Jane Eyre*, *Shirley*, *Aurora Leigh*, and *The Mill on the Floss*.[54] *Jane Eyre* is the obvious point of reference for *Aurora Leigh*, but if maiming and blinding are not taken literally, then Gaskell's *North and South* offers another. At the end of *North and South* Thornton returns to Margaret Hale (in *Jane Eyre* the women returns to the man) and renews an offer of marriage made much earlier in the novel. Since this first proposal, Thornton has suffered financial ruin and lost control of his mill, which has been inherited by Margaret. He has now modified many of his mill-owner's values which Margaret had challenged, and his second proposal is made in very different terms. Thornton, powerless and propertyless, is now accepted by Margaret and gets his mill back, the gift confirming her power.[55]

The blinding of Romney can certainly be explained. It exploits the paradox of sight in blindness, with Romney as a Gloucester figure. Showalter's suggestion of emotional education through symbolic role reversal is apposite. Romney's blinding is the equivalent of the feminization of Aurora's father discussed earlier. He was transformed by the melting influences of Italy and love alone. Romney has been a more resistant subject and in his case feminization must precede the fulfilment of love. Nevertheless, his blinding is difficult to justify. A recent reworking of *Aurora Leigh* for stage and radio by Michelene Wandor left Romney with his sight, a decision explained by the author in these terms: 'If Aurora and Romney's reconciliation were to have real potential for equality in the future, I could not see how it could be credible if male domination was simply replaced with female domination'.[56] Also, in Michelene Wandor's re-reading/writing Aurora no longer repudiates her need to analyse, confront, and question. These changes seem right, not just for a late-twentieth-century reading but also in bringing the conclusion into a more consistent relationship with the rest of Barrett Browning's poem.

Despite the overkill of the last book, however, Aurora's marriage to Romney and her re-entry into family seems less compromised than most other contemporary versions of this myth. *Aurora Leigh* does, in the main, carry through its resistance to conventional gender roles, contemporary definitions of womanhood, and orthodoxies about love, marriage and family. In doing so it contemplates alternative family arrangements such as Aurora, Marian, and her baby with its 'two mothers' (Bk 7, l. 124), and although this *ménage* does not survive Romney's return, the poem challenges any automatic assumption that women and children need men. Marian's rejection of Romney certainly clears the way for his marriage to Aurora, but Cora Kaplan's suggestion that Marian's 'fall' has made her 'unmarriageable' is misleading.[57] Romney's offer is sincere if unenthusiastic, and Marian's refusal speech emphasizes that she no longer feels unworthy of Romney (Bk 9, ll. 326–33) and that her earlier attachment to him was based not on love but on worship (Bk 9, ll. 378–9). She doesn't want him any more. Marriage for the fallen woman does not necessarily mean re-entry into society anyway, as Martha in *David Copperfield* discovers. Mr Peggotty describes her gone to Australia and living with her husband 'fower hundred mile away from any voices but their own and the singing birds'. Aurora's admission that 'Art is much, but Love is more' only becomes possible when Romney no longer sees art and love as alternatives. It also incorporates the recognition that love itself is not enough, and that love defined in terms of subordination is no love. Only when Aurora and Romney share a similar understanding of love, and its relation to work and marriage, can their relationship be sealed.

V

In the introduction to a new edition of *Aurora Leigh* in 1898, Swinburne wrote 'there is not a dead line in it', but few, it seems, still agreed. Soon after the turn of the century the stream of editions dried up. There were no new editions between 1905 and 1978. By 1932, when Virginia Woolf wrote of Elizabeth Barrett Browning, 'Nobody reads her, nobody discusses her, nobody troubles to put her in her place', the work seems almost to have slipped out of sight. As Woolf continued, one takes *Aurora Leigh* from the shelf 'not so much in order to read it as to muse with kindly condescension over this token of bygone fiction, as we toy with the fringes of our grandmothers' mantles and muse over the alabaster models of the Taj Mahal which once adorned their drawing-room tables'.[58]

There is something curious about this disappearance of *Aurora Leigh* just as the next major wave of feminism was breaking. It was not, apparently, a text that spoke to the era of the Women's Social and Political Union. One obvious reason for this is that *Aurora Leigh*'s politics are consistently hostile to socialism. By the mid-nineteenth century the earlier, mainly Owenite, alignment of feminism and working-class radicalism had disappeared. Sex oppression and class exploitation had become separate objects of separate struggles, and the new feminism of the 1850s was middle class and free of any taint of socialism or atheism.[59] Romney's phalanstery – his socialist experiment with an extended communal family of the kind found in Owenite communities – is rejected much more sharply than the bourgeois family, notwithstanding the poem's sustained critique of patriarchal power. *Aurora Leigh*'s main ideological affinity is with the more pragmatic middle-class feminism of the 1850s and 1860s, and the poem is not at all concerned with women gaining political power through the ballot box.

Yet the sexual politics of *Aurora Leigh* has remained of central importance to feminism, and there must be a further reason for its disappearance in the early years of this century. This, I think, lies in its status as a Victorian classic. The reception and reputation of a work inevitably affects the ways in which it is read and understood, becoming an important determinant of its meanings. The reviewers, the Royal Academicians, the moderate reformism of the High Victorian period, and all those other determinants of how *Aurora Leigh* was received and understood, were largely successful in neutralizing its more radical feminist elements. Barrett Browning's relatively early death and her canonization as England's female laureate assisted in this. *Aurora Leigh* was not available to early-twentieth-century feminists as a feminist text; effectively, it had been rewritten.

However, neither the originating moment of a text nor the immediate determinants of its meanings can limit its later identities. Raymond Williams, in arguing that literary studies should be concerned with exploring the social conditions of production of literary texts, has emphasized that these conditions of production include the conditions of making a text contemporary: 'All the forces which keep the text current are among its conditions of production'.[60] Subsequent determinations 'remake' the text, which is itself no passive spectator of its own fate. Virginia Woolf saw *Aurora Leigh* as a Victorian curio, but acknowledged that it remained, 'with all its imperfections, a book that still lives and breathes and has its being'.[61] These traces of life discerned in the Victorian corpse of *Aurora Leigh* by the leading woman writer of her age helped its resuscitation in our own time. The new feminist presses have given the kiss of life to many apparently dead texts, and the successful republication of *Aurora Leigh* by the Women's Press is a leading example of this. It has been made available to us in a new way, and is therefore a different text from the one which was left to hibernate earlier in this century.

As *Aurora Leigh* has been brought into a freshly relevant relationship to our time, it has once again shown that potential for translation which marked its early history. It has been dramatized by Michelene Wandor and performed by feminist theatre groups. Michelene Wandor also adapted it for radio.[62] In 1979 an article in *Time Out* described *Aurora Leigh* as 'a Victorian female voice speaking acutely of the relationships between gender, art and politics'.[63] Barrett Browning would have recognized this description. Lost meanings have been rediscovered in the text as well as new meanings created.

NOTES

1. Gardner B. Taplin, *The Life of Elizabeth Barrett Browning* (New Haven: Yale University Press, 1957), p. 104.
2. Frederic G. Kenyon (ed.) *The Letters of Elizabeth Barrett Browning* (London: Smith, Elder, 1898), Vol. 1, p. 204.
3. Betty Miller (ed.) *Elizabeth Barrett to Miss Mitford* (London: John Murray, 1954), p. 321.
4. Kenyon, Vol. 1, p. 212.
5. Miller, p. 231.
6. Elvan Kintner (ed.) *The Letters of Robert Browning and Elizabeth Barrett Browning 1845-1846* (Cambridge, Mass.: Harvard University Press, 1969), Vol. 1, p. 31.
7. Alethea Hayter, *Mrs Browning: A Poet's Work and Its Setting* (London: Faber & Faber, 1962), p. 151.
8. See Hayter; Cora Kaplan, Introduction to *Aurora Leigh and Other Poems* (London: The Women's Press, 1978), – all references to the text are to this edition; Ellen Moers, *Literary Women* (London: The Women's Press, 1978); Patricia Thomson, *George Sand and the Victorians* (New York: Columbia University Press, 1977).
9. Kaplan, p. 8.
10. Barbara Hardy, 'Gossip made permanent', *Times Literary Supplement*, 1 July 1983.
11. 'The Lady Novelists', *Westminster Review*, July 1852, p. 129.
12. *North British Review*, February 1857, p. 454.
13. *Blackwoods Edinburgh Magazine*, January–June 1857, p. 33.
14. ibid., p. 34.
15. *Westminster Review*, October 1857, p. 401.
16. W.M. Rossetti (ed.) *Ruskin: Rossetti: Pre-Raphaelitism* (London: G. Allen, 1890), p. 147.
17. Kaplan, p. 30.
18. This summary has come mainly from Mary Lyndon Shanley, ' "One Must Ride Behind": married women's rights and the Divorce Act of 1857', *Victorian Studies* 25 (3).
19. This summary has come from Cynthia Fansler Behrman, 'The

Annual Blister: A sidelight on Victorian social and parliamentary history', *Victorian Studies* 11 (4).
20. Kathleen Tillotson, *Novels of the Eighteen-Forties* (Oxford: Oxford University Press, 1962), p. 15.
21. J.A Banks and Olive Banks, *Feminism and Family Planning in Victorian England* (Liverpool: Liverpool University Press, 1965), pp. 27–9.
22. Ray Strachey, *The Cause: A Short History of the Women's Movement in Great Britain* (London: G. Bell & Sons, 1928), pp. 91–4.
23. *North British Review*, February 1857.
24. E.P. Thompson and Eileen Yeo (eds) *The Unknown Mayhew* (Harmondsworth: Penguin, 1973) pp. 25–34.
25. *The National Magazine*, Vol. 1, 1857. The subject of this particular column was the Condensed Air-Bath.
26. E.g. *Edinburgh Review*, January 1857; *Quarterly Review*, July 1857; *North British Review*, August 1857.
27. Terry Eagleton, *The Rape of Clarissa* (Oxford: Basil Blackwell, 1982), pp. 4ff.
28. E.T. Cook and Alexander Wedderburn (eds) *The Works of John Ruskin* (London: George Allen, 1904), Vol. 15, pp. 227.
29. Algernon Graves, *The Royal Academy of Arts: A Complete Dictionary of Contributors and Their Work From Its Foundation in 1769 to 1904* (Wakefield: S.R. Publications, 1970), Vol. 2, p. 34.
30. Nina Auerbach, *Woman and the Demon: The Life of a Victorian Myth* (Cambridge and London: Harvard University Press, 1982), pp. 191–219.
31. Cook and Wedderburn, p. 227.
32. Eagleton, p. 6.
33. ibid., p. 7.
34. ibid., pp. 10–13.
35. *North British Review*, February 1857, pp. 328–9.
36. Barbara Hardy.
37. Eagleton, p. 12.
38. Graves, p. 34.
39. See Raymond Lister, *Victorian Narrative Paintings* (London: Museum Press, 1966), p. 96; Christopher Wood, *Victorian Panorama: Paintings of Victorian Life* (London: Faber & Faber, 1976), pp. 65–8.
40. See Barbara Charlesworth Gelpi, 'Aurora Leigh: the vocation of the woman poet', *Victorian Poetry* 19 (1); Virginia V. Steinmetz, 'Images of "Mother-Want" in Elizabeth Barrett Browning's *Aurora Leigh*', *Victorian Poetry* 21 (4); Dolores Rosenblum, 'Face to face: Elizabeth Barrett Browning's *Aurora Leigh* and nineteenth-century poetry', *Victorian Studies* 26 (3). Although each of these essays has its own approach, they are broadly in agreement about the significance of the portrait of Aurora's mother.

Aurora Leigh

41. Anthony Trollope, *The Way We Live Now* (Oxford: Oxford University Press, 1982), Vol. 2, p. 364.
42. Thomas Hardy, *The Hand of Ethelberta* (London: Macmillan, 1975), Ch. 10, p. 99.
43. Moers, Ch. 9.
44. ibid., p. 194.
45. Patricia Thomson, *George Sand and the Victorians* (New York: Columbia University Press, 1977), pp. 11–20.
46. Taplin, pp. 244–5.
47. ibid., p. 388.
48. ibid., p. 404.
49. Gelpi, passim.
50. ibid., p.42.
51. Moers, p. 194.
52. Hayter, p. 184.
53. ibid., p. 188.
54. Elaine Showalter, *A Literature of Their Own* (London: Virago, 1977), pp. 150–2.
55. Another similarity between these texts is in the scene where Margaret throws herself in front of Thorntorn to protect him from an angry demonstration by his workers, and the parallel one in *Aurora Leigh* where Romney is threatened by the disappointed working-class crowd at the wedding and Aurora tries to protect him.
56. Michelene Wandor (ed.) *Plays by Women* (London: Methuen, 1982), Vol. 1, p. 134.
57. Kaplan, p. 25.
58. Virginia Woolf, *'Aurora Leigh', Collected Essays* (London: Hogarth Press, 1971), Vol. 1, pp. 209–10.
59. Barbara Taylor, *Eve and the New Jerusalem* (London: Virago, 1983), pp. 263–4, 276ff.
60. Raymond Williams, *Politics and Letters* (London: New Left Books, 1979), Ch. 5, esp. pp. 328–9, 344–5. See also Tony Bennett, 'Text and history', in P. Widdowson (ed.), *Re-Reading English* (London: Methuen, 1982).
61. Woolf, p. 218.
62. This was broadcast on BBC Radio 3 in 1981 and rebroadcast the following year.
63. *Time Out*, August–September 1979.

5
Who needs men? Christina Rossetti's *Goblin Market*

I

Goblin Market was written in 1859, published in 1862, and in manuscript was dedicated to Christina Rossetti's sister Maria.[1] It has the appearance of a children's fairy story and was a nursery favourite in the Victorian period. It will still engage a young listener when read aloud. But rather like 'The Ancient Mariner' or *Alice in Wonderland,* it is a text for both adults and children which can be read in a disconcerting number of ways. In recent years it has been read as a Christian allegory; a feminist Christian allegory with a female Christ figure; an allegory of sexual desire; a female rites of passage poem; a lesbian manifesto; a poem about the erotic life of children; a metaphoric statement about patterns of social destructiveness in Victorian England; and in psychoanalytic terms as a power struggle between mothers and children. Only the last of these seems to me self-evidently silly. Its 'underground reputation as a forgotten feminist classic'[2] was blown by the appearance of an abbreviated version of the poem with pornographic illustrations in *Playboy* in 1973, where it was described as 'the all-time hard-core pornographic classic for tiny tots'.[3] As this should make clear, there has been a marked revival of interest in *Goblin Market* in the last fifteen years during which time it has perhaps been reread more extensively than any other Victorian poem.[4] And the appearance of the first volume of Crump's long-needed edition of Rossetti's poetry has now made it much easier to read

Goblin Market in relation to her other poetry of the 1850s and 1860s.

The poem tells the story of two sisters, Laura and Lizzie, living together without family, who are tempted at evening by goblin men selling fruit. Goblins and fruit are clearly associated with illicit pleasures. The sisters know they must not look at goblin men, heed their song, or buy their fruit. Laura, however, succumbs, paying for the fruit with a lock of her hair and then satiating herself. She takes a kernel-stone home where her sister reminds her of the story of Jeanie, who yielded to the goblin men, was never able to find them again, pined, and died; no grass grows on her grave. Goblins sell only once to each buyer, and Laura will never again hear or see them. Next day Laura is sick and discontented. She longs for the night, but when evening comes and the sisters return to the brook and the glen where the goblin men appear, she can no longer hear their 'fruit-call'. This goes on night after night. She plants the kernel-stone but it fails to grow. Tormented by 'baulked desire' Laura goes into a decline. She can no longer work or eat. Lizzie longs to buy goblin fruit to comfort her but remembers Jeanie and fears the cost. However, when Laura seems close to death, Lizzie overcomes her hesitations and putting a silver penny in her purse goes out to meet the goblin men and buy their fruit. She gives them her penny but they insist she eats with them. They try to force her to do so, attacking her, and squeezing their fruit against her closed mouth. Lizzie remains firm and eventually they give up, fling back her penny and disappear with their fruit. She returns home dripping with juices from the fruit they have pressed on her. Laura kisses her with 'hungry mouth' and once more experiences the forbidden tastes. This time, however, the taste is repellent. Laura collapses and spends the night close to death tended by her sister, but next morning she is fully recovered and laughs 'in the innocent old way'. Her grey hair has returned to gold and the light has come back into her eyes. The poem finishes with a picture of the two sisters many years later, both now mothers with children of their own. Laura tells them her story, less as a cautionary tale than to highlight the example of a sister's love.

I want to start by looking at some of the recurring patterns in Rossetti's poetry before *Goblin Market*. Guilt, illness, and adolescent crisis; sisterhood and the two sisters configuration; the frustration and repression of desire; the problem of how a woman is to live in this world: these are recurring features of her poetry in the 1850s, and narrative is the most common form in which they occur. In the next two sections I shall examine Rossetti's treatment of these themes and her changing use of narrative form as a curtain-raiser to the discussion of how in *Goblin Market* they make their most individual, heterodox, and spectacular appearance. My approach is in broad agreement with McGann's suggestion that the recurring patterns in Rossetti's poetry need to be understood in terms of certain social and historical formations which they dramatize.[5] In order to uncover and elucidate some of these patterns, I shall begin with *Maude*, written in 1850 when Rossetti was only 19.

II

Maude is another of those mixed-genre works, blends of poetry and fiction, which appeared around mid-nineteenth century. It is a novella interspersed with poems whose narrative justification is that they are written by the central character, Maude Foster. *Maude* was not published until 1897, three years after Rossetti's death, and its first editor, her brother William, aptly described it as a 'Tale for Girls'.[6] The central characters are all adolescent females of similar age — between 15 and 16 when the story opens, and at least eighteen months older when it ends. Apart from Maude herself, there are her cousins Agnes and Mary, and Magdalen, a mutual friend. In different ways these three girls are all foils to Maude. Most obviously, Maude is placed between Mary and Magdalen. Mary is an amiable, conventional, and trivial young woman who gets married. Magdalen is her opposite, a serious and spiritual young woman who becomes a nun. Maude is a budding poet, proud of her talent but guilty about it. She rejects the conventional role Mary adopts but is unable to commit herself to the conventual alternative represented by Magdalen. The text explores different possible courses open to adolescent females as childhood is left behind and decisions about a future way of life have to be faced. It is very specifically about adolescent female crisis. Males are almost totally absent from the text. None of the girls seems to have a father. The family and social events around which the narrative is organised — a birthday party, a tea party, Christmas, and preparations for Mary's wedding — are attended entirely by women. (One family at the birthday party consists of six daughters.) The only male who speaks is a clergyman, something imposed on the text by the Church of England's refusal to ordain women.

Impatient of the social round which satisfies Mary, and unfitted for the renunciation and discipline of the sisterhood, Maude is full of guilt and a sense of her own unworthiness. This comes to a head in her refusal to take Christmas communion: 'No: at least I will not profane Holy Things; I will not add this to all the rest.' (*Maude*, p. 52). W. M. Rossetti found Maude's guilt inexplicable, excessive, and irritating.[7] Lona Mosk Packer echoes this but then, as always, goes on to explain it biographically in terms of Rossetti's putative love affair with William Bell Scott, whom she sees as the hidden god of Rossetti's life, immanent in all her writing.[8] However, the text makes clear the sources of Maude's guilt; they are her family and her writing.

The narrative opens with Maude's mother entering the sitting-room where her daughter, 'surrounded by a chaos of stationery, was slipping out of sight some scrawled paper'. (*Maude*, p. 29). Balancing this scene several pages later is one in which Mary's mother enters the sitting-room of their home and finds her daughter arranging flowers. A pointed contrast is made between the conventional, mother-pleasing activities of one, and the dubious, private acts of the other. A good deal of Maude's guilt derives from the tension between her mother's expectations and her own desires. When Maude asks if she would mind her becoming a nun, the reply is affectionately crushing and final: 'Yes my dear; it would make me miserable' (*Maude*, p. 59). On her death-bed at the end of the book Maude expresses her guilt about her mother: 'I have been her misery from my birth, till now there is no time to do better'. (*Maude*, p. 71).

This guilt, as we saw above, is closely connected with her writing. Although Maude is admired for her skill at writing, as, for example, when she improvises *bouts-rimés* sonnets at the birthday party, poetry is not presented as a possible vocation for a young woman. In this *Maude* contrasts sharply with *Aurora Leigh*. Serious writing is a dubious practice for a young woman, potentially a more active and challenging alternative to women's domestic role than conventual sisterhood. Guilt about it is clearly inscribed in the text. Much of Maude's writing is copied into a 'locking manuscript book' which is kept hidden and finally buried with her. (This is an uncanny anticipation of her brother Gabriel inhuming his poems with Elizabeth Siddall. It seems possible that *Maude* gave him the idea. The latter exhumation of his poems was, however, unprompted.)

Not only is writing a guilty act, but it is associated with illness. In the opening scenes, Maude's pallor contrasts with Mary's fresh complexion, just as her writing contrasts with Mary's 'natural' interest in flower arrangement and clothes. Maude's illness is, on the one hand, an emblem of her difference, her guilt, her inability to take up her allotted social role. On the other hand, however, it frees her to write. She withdraws from a Christmas Eve gathering with a headache and is then free to retire to her bedroom and copy her sonnets into the locking manuscript book. Florence Nightingale understood this when she wrote *Cassandra* two years later:

> Mrs A. has the imagination, the poetry of a Murillo, and has sufficient power of execution to show that she might have had a great deal more. Why is she not a Murillo? From a material difficulty, not a mental one. If she has a knife and fork in her hands for three hours of the day, she cannot have a pencil or brush. Dinner is the great sacred ceremony of this day, the great sacrament. To be absent from dinner is equivalent to being ill. Nothing else will excuse us from it. Bodily incapacity is the only apology valid. If she has a pen and ink in her hands during another three hours, writing answers for the penny post, again, she cannot have her pencil, and so *ad infinitum* through life.[9]

In Maude's case illness leads to early death. In fact she dies from injuries received in a cab accident on her way to Mary's wedding but this is merely convenient, a melodramatic conclusion to a decline which has been going on throughout the narrative. From the opening lines of the sonnet Maude is writing at the beginning of the book – 'Yes, I too could face death and never shrink:/But it is harder to bear hated life' – the intercalated poems express a turning away from life and a yearning for the peace and certainty of death. Maude's death fulfils these yearnings and seals the association of writing and illness.

Guilt, writing, and illness can all be seen as aspects of an adolescent crisis which Maude can find no way through. She has no wish to follow Mary into a conventional domestic role. She is unable to reject the world, as Magdalen does, but she is also unable to live in it with the calm objectivity of her other cousin and alter ego, Agnes. The religious dimension of this crisis is important. Maude's refusal to take Christmas communion confirms the impossibility, for her, of the convent option, but it is also a displaced expression of other, secular difficulties about negotiating pubescence and entering womanhood. In a general way it recalls Hewson's phrase from *The Bothie*, 'the growing distress, and celled-up dishonour of boyhood' – offering a specifically female account of a similar guilt about growing up. The accident which leads to Maude's death is another example of displacement. It has no dramatic status in the narrative. It happens off-stage. We are not told of any injuries Maude suffers. It is simply the occasion of her death, a means of actualizing the death yearnings of the intercalated poems, and has to be seen as a kind of final collapse precipitated by Mary's wedding and the news that Magdalen has completed her noviciate and entered the Sisterhood of Mercy. Maude is left the bride neither of God nor of man.

If Maude is not a bride, what can she be? The most common answer to this in Rossetti's poetry is that she can be a sister, although frequently this proves to be no answer at all. In *Maude*, the different kinds of alternative represented by the term 'sisterhood' are all blocked. The work has no developed idea of secular sisterhood such as we find in *Goblin Market*. Maude does not have a sister, although her cousin Agnes is a sister surrogate who has the important task of sorting Maude's papers and writing after her death. Unlike Lizzie, however, Agnes is a passive 'sister', able to sympathize but not to help. Maude's remains are put in order, but her life cannot be saved. The dominant idea of sisterhood in *Maude* is a religious one, and Magdalen is the text's true 'sister'. Conventual sisterhood has a powerful attraction within the poem and is consistently used to denigrate marriage. When Maude sits down to write an epithalamium for Mary, she actually produces a poem entitled 'Three Nuns'. Religious sisterhood is a possible course for Maude as Magdalen makes clear when she envisages her as 'pale Sister Maude' (*Maude*, p. 58).

Maude's question to her mother about becoming a nun was one that was being asked in the 1840s. During this decade the first

Anglican sisterhoods since the sixteenth century were established, and one, founded and directed by Pusey, was set up in the Rossettis' London parish. Packer records that a number of respectable young women left their family, friends, and suitors at this time to enter monastic life, and met with disapproval:

> The special vocation of a Sister, the character involved and the claims of such a character, were altogether unknown.... That young ladies (of good families) should shrink from society, and entertain thoughts of celibacy in the face of an eligible marriage was almost inconceivable.[10]

It seems that the refusal to marry could be almost as disturbing as promiscuity. Later in the century, when Mrs Oliphant attacked *Jude the Obscure*, she found Sue's sexual reserve even more disgusting than Arabella's concupiscence.[11] In certain social contexts chastity can be a radical act.

Religious sisterhood in *Maude* has these radical implications, and this compounds Maude's guilt and is a further reason why she cannot follow Magdalen's example. She feels that her motives for being drawn to the Sisterhood are suspect. It offers a serious purpose in life and a release from the social round of birthday and tea parties. It also offers an escape from normative definitions of female sexuality and the incorporation of this into marriage and family. Perhaps it even offers an escape from writing and its associated guilt.[12] Religious sisterhood in *Maude* seems to offer an alternative kind of family – women united in the service of God rather than divided in the secular families of Victorian England. Sisterhood therefore becomes a refuge from guilt but also a source of guilt. Maude is resolute in turning away from marriage (in its way the text is as cynical about bourgeois marriage as *Amours de Voyage*) but is unable to embrace religious sisterhood. Writing does not offer an alternative course. She cannot accept this impasse, and therefore her death becomes inevitable.

This inevitability highlights the problem inherent in *Maude's* mixed-genre form. In terms of the realist narrative conventions of most of the text, its conclusion is absurd and makes the ending of *The Mill on the Floss* seem like a master-stroke. The intercalated poems are far too intense for the novel of manners in which they are embedded. The death impulse expressed in these lyrics is most awkwardly translated into realist prose narrative as lyric intensity collapses the thin narrative surface. *Maude* was Rossetti's one attempt at mixing genre. She wrote many narrative poems and published two volumes of fiction in the 1870s, but never again attempted to combine poetry and prose. Like other related mixed-genre works of this period *Maude* can be seen as an experiment in form which enabled Rossetti to explore the possibilities of different genres. She discovered, for her, the limitations of realist narrative and the irreconcilability of overtly social narrative with her own lyric and narrative impulses. Her subsequent narrative poetry was to draw on the resources of dream and fairy tale.

III

Dream and fairy tale enabled Rossetti to dramatize matters which the form of *Maude* had not easily accommodated. They offered the latitude necessary for a poetry whose ingrained subject was the tension between the life of this world and that other world of the after-life, between flesh and spirit, eros and agape. They freed the poet from the kind of realism which had constrained *Maude*, while permitting the implied comparisons between dream worlds and real ones which is central to these poems. I want now to look briefly at several examples of the use of dream narrative in Rossetti's poetry of the 1850s, and then to pick up some other treatments of those recurring themes and patterns outlined at the end of Section 1, the point in both cases being to understand better the typicality and distinctiveness of *Goblin Market*.

'My Dream' (1855) tells of cannibalism among jewelled crocodiles in the Euphrates. One crocodile, larger and more richly bedecked, turns on the others with 'execrable appetite' and devours them:

> He battened on them, crunched, and sucked them in.
> He knew no law, he feared no binding law,
> But ground them with inexorable jaw:
> The luscious fat distilled upon his chin,
> Exuded from his nostrils and his eyes,
> While still like hungry death he fed his maw.

Gorged, satiated, and asleep, the crocodile shrinks back to normal size unaware of the approach of a white vessel which calms the swollen Euphrates and humbles the now 'prudent crocodile'. In the concluding lines the poem disclaims any knowlege of its own meaning, a teasing challenge to detailed interpretation which I shall resist. 'My Dream', however, does anticipate *Goblin Market* in several respects. Appetite in both poems is clearly sexual and treated with a similar blend of fascination and horror. Unlike 'My Dream', however, in *Goblin Market* there are forms of desire which are not simply reducible to appetite. Each poem has a redeemer figure – Lizzie is the white vessel in *Goblin Market* – which subdues the threateningly presented forces of desire. Also, the language of both poems has a strikingly limpid quality.

This same pellucidity recurs in other dream narratives in Rossetti's poetry of this period which explore the incompatibility of different kinds of love. 'The Convent Threshold' (1858), a longer poem, has two vivid dream sequences at its centre. The second of these is a chilling image of the death of human love as unrequited necrophilia:

> I tell you what I dreamed last night:
> It was not dark, it was not light,
> Cold dews had drenched my plenteous hair
> Thro' clay; you came to seek me there.
> And 'Do you dream of me?' you said.
> My heart was dust that used to leap
> To you; I answered half asleep:
> 'My pillow is damp, my sheets are red,
> There's a leaden tester to my bed:
> Find you a warmer playfellow,
> A warmer pillow for your head,
> A kinder love to love than mine.

'From House to Home' (1858) is a closely related poem which also uses dream and repeats the movement of 'The Convent Threshold' away from eros and towards agape, from the 'house' of life to the 'home' of Christ, from earthly family to the family of God.

Rossetti's use of dream narrative in these and other poems is related to her construction of fairy-tale worlds in *Goblin Market* and 'The Prince's Progress'. It is tempting but reductive to explain the use of these narrative forms as something imposed on her by 'the narrowness of the age'. Cora Kaplan makes too much of this in her interesting essay on Rossetti's poetry, arguing that dream form enabled her to express feelings and enact dramas which were taboo in genteel households, and to present distorted or unclear images with impunity.[13] Rossetti's imagery is complex, but as the extracts above show, it is hardly distorted or unclear, and I would want to explain her use of dream and fairy tale less in terms of the constraining influence of Victorian prudery than in the restrictions inherent in certain literary forms. *Maude* had exposed the limitations of overtly social narrative, and it is no cause for regret that Rossetti took up other forms. These were not expedients but experiments, and they enabled her to express feelings and enact dramas which other forms could not. Nor did the use of dream and fairy tale make her writing in any way less contemporary than *Maude*. The themes and patterns are similar and retain a cultural significance. The failures of modern love, for example, were all around her. McGann points to the well-known example of the writer Letitia Elizabeth Landon, whose suicide prompted Elizabeth Barrett Browning's poem 'L.E.L's Last Question' (1839) and a later poem by Rossetti, 'L.E.L' (1859), and reminds us of the example of her brother Dante Gabriel.[14]

The two sisters pattern is a significant recurring feature of Rossetti's poetry between *Maude* and *Goblin Market*. There is a literary tradition at least as old as the Bible that archetypal female pairs should be sisters or cousins. Rossetti is drawing on this, but there are also many analogues in contemporary writing. Some of these have been touched on in Chapter 3.[15] *Maude*, as we have seen, is a variant of this pattern. The two sisters poem which most obviously links *Maude* with *Goblin Market* is 'The Lowest Room' (1856). It picks up the connected themes of illness and vocation from *Maude* but treats them differently. The speaker of this poem, the elder sister, is pale and greying; the younger sister is golden-haired and radiant. The contrast of sickness and health recalls Maude and Mary, but in 'The Lowest Room' the Mary figure also has Magdalen's seriousness and purity. She has carried Magdalen's sense of vocation into her marriage, the roles of wife and mother are seen in semi-religious terms, and the home she establishes is like an ante-chamber of heaven, an anticipation of an after-life in the family of God. The poem has none of *Maude*'s scepticism about marriage and family. Like *Goblin Market* it concludes with a picture of both sisters many years later, but in this poem the elder has lived alone sustained only by her faith in the promise of an after-life. Unlike *Goblin Market* there is a tension in the sisters' relationship, a private guilty envy of the younger sister by the elder. This tension becomes open hostility and rivalry in several other poems of sisterhood, 'Noble Sisters' (1859–60) and 'Sister Maude' (date of composition unknown; first published in the 1862 collection *Goblin Market and Other Poems*). 'Cousin Kate' (1859) is another poem of this kind.

These two sister poems are all concerned with the repression or loss of strong feelings. In 'The Lowest Room' the elder sister learns to subdue her discontent with her dull, passionless existence and to immunize herself against 'Homer's sting'. Reading Homer provokes powerful feelings – 'He stirs my sluggish pulse like wine,/He melts me like the wind of spice' – which the poem eventually cancels. In 'Noble Sisters' and 'Sister Maude' envy, lies, and the disclosure of secrets result in one sister killing the other's love. The speaker in 'Cousin Kate' has been discarded and replaced by her cousin, and left with an illegitimate child – 'My fair-haired son, my shame, my pride' – with whom she taunts her cousin's childlessness. (Rossetti's use of the fallen woman figure is more radical and startling than in any Victorian writer before Hardy or George Moore.) In each of these poems the two sisters or cousins are pitted against each other, their rivalry either open or suppressed. In this they contrast with *Goblin Market* where Lizzie and Laura, though different in character, are true sisters.

All these poems centre round the problem that if, on the one hand, the frustration of desire brings pain and loss, its satisfaction seems necessarily to involve transgression. Hence the recurring question of Rossetti's poetry of this period: how to live in this world? This was a time-honoured question, but one of particular urgency for mid-nineteenth-century women. One extraordinary poem of protest against the frustration of desire is 'The Heart Knoweth Its Own Bitterness' (1857), a passionate cry against the world's inability to meet the poet's pitch of intensity:

> You scratch my surface with your pin,
> You stroke me smooth with hushing breath:-
> Nay pierce, nay probe, nay dig within,
> Probe my quick core and sound my depth.
> You call me with a puny call,

> You talk, you smile, you nothing do:
> How should I spend my heart on you,
> My heart that so outweighs you all?[16]

The fervid tone and visceral imagery of these lines is in startling contrast to the need expressed elsewhere to supress such feelings, and although the poem does conclude by moving its sexual imagery on to a religious level in the manner of Donne's religious sonnets, the object of reproach in these lines is manifestly of this world. More usually, however, it is the danger of desire and the need to resist it which is emphasized. This is usually associated with a turning away from the things of this world, the recurring *contemptus mundi* theme, as in 'The World' (1854). In this sonnet, fruit, flowers and the satisfaction of appetite are the world's snares, seductive by day but horrifying by night:

> By day she wooes me to the outer air,
> Ripe fruits, sweet flowers, and full satiety:
> But thro' the night, a beast she grins at me,
> A very monster void of love and prayer.
> By day she stands a lie: by night she stands
> In all the naked horror of the truth
> With pushing horns and clawed and clutching hands.

Fruit as an image of the temptations and delusions of sensual pleasure, and its association with repellent mongrel creatures connects this poem with *Goblin Market*. In 'The World', however, the clawed and horned beast is obviously the devil, whereas the goblin men are more ambiguous and seductive. And in *Goblin Market* there is no suppression of feeling or turning away from the world. Instead, desire is expressed and finds an object, and the opposition of flesh and spirit, sickness and health, sister and sister is resolved in a poem which uses the form of the fairy tale to dramatize matters which lay at the heart of Victorian culture.

IV

Kendrick Smithyman has described *Goblin Market* as an allegory of sexual desire.[17] Unlike 'The World', where to succumb to temptation is to 'take hold on hell', it dramatizes a secular version of the fortunate fall. By tasting the forbidden fruit Laura opens the way for her redemption and the poem's vision of sisterhood. Like the sisters in other Rossetti poems, Laura and Lizzie are paired opposites, but in *Goblin Market* their different personalities are not discordant but harmonious:

> Golden head by golden head,
> Like two pigeons in one nest
> Folded in each other's wings,
> They lay down in their curtained bed:
> Like two blossoms on one stem,
> Like two flakes of new-fall'n snow,
> Like two wands of ivory
> Tipped with gold for awful kings.
>
> (ll. 184–91)

This delicate and beautiful nightpiece is drawn immediately *after* Laura has eaten the fruit. It is not a tableau of innocence which the goblin men destroy but one which persists after they have done their worst. Here Lizzie lies down with Laura uncorrupted. And in comparison with *Maude*, possible retreat into religious sisterhood becomes in *Goblin Market* an active, engaged secular sisterhood.

I noted the absence of males in *Maude*. In *Goblin Market* they figure prominently but only as a corrupt and corrupting presence. The goblins' maleness is repeatedly emphasized; they are goblin men rather than just goblins. The poem dramatizes a totally uncompromising clash of gender. In *The Princess* and *Aurora Leigh* the seeds of reconciliation are there from the beginning, but in *Goblin Market* there is no hint of *détente*. The goblins are not only men but brothers, pitted against the two sisters whom they tempt and torture. This brotherhood of goblin men has attracted speculation. It has been suggested that the poem is actually about the demise of the Pre-Raphaelite Brotherhood.[18] Less strenuously, Smithyman notes that the animal resemblances in the goblin men are drawn from animals which attracted the Rossetti brothers. The 'one like a wombat', for example, seems decidedly Gabriel whose device and pet was a wombat.[19] Ellen Moers suggests that the depiction of the goblin brothers derives 'from the night side of the Victorian nursery – a world where childish cruelty and childish sexuality came to the fore'. She argues that the sister–brother relationship had a particular significance for many women in the

Victorian intellectual middle class:

> The rough-and-tumble sexuality of the nursery loomed large for sisters: it was the *only* heterosexual world that Victorian literary spinsters were ever freely and physically to explore. Thus the brothers of their childhood retained in their fantasy life a prominent place somewhat different in kind from that of the father figures who dominated them all.[20]

It seems clear that there is an element of personal reference in *Goblin Market*, but Smithyman is right to emphasize its teasing and whimsical nature. I take it that Gabriel saw at least part of the joke. Moers' approach is interesting and suggestive but her argument is left at the point where Lizzie is being mauled. Lizzie demonstrates not only the contrast between true sisters and false brothers but also that the goblin men are false in a sense other than that of duplicity. They are false also in being spurious or hardly real.

It is clear from the opening lines that the temptation the goblin men represent is experienced by all 'maids', and the cautionary element in the poem's conclusion warns the next generation of daughters of the need for vigilance. Lizzie's fear of the goblin men is as important as Laura's attraction to them. She dares not look at them nor listen to their song. As they tramp down the glen, she runs home. She is preoccupied with the story of Jeanie. She has an overwhelming sense of their irresistibility, but this is based on hearsay rather than experience. It is only when her sister is near death that Lizzie overcomes her fears, 'And for the first time in her life/Began to listen and look' (ll. 327-8). The timid, untested nature of her innocence is underlined by her primly polite approach to the goblins: '"Good folk", said Lizzie,/Mindful of Jeanie:/"Give me much and many"' (ll. 363-5). This reminds me of the way Alice addresses the troubling inhabitants of her dream world. The accents of the drawing-room confront the 'sugar-baited words' of the goblin men, which change to grunts and snarls as Lizzie stands her ground. As their attack intensifies, Lizzie discovers her own strength. The run of similes describing how 'White and golden Lizzie stood', from 'a lily in a flood' through 'a beacon. . . /In a hoary roaring sea' to 'a royal virgin town/Topped with gilded dome and spire' (ll. 409-21) is a carefully developed sequence which expresses Lizzie's triumphant discovery of her ability to withstand the goblin men. As they squeeze the fruit against her face, she 'laughed in heart'.

Steven Connor has argued that Lizzie's refusal to eat 'has a kind of prurience about it, so that abstinence becomes a kind of masochistic indulgence in erotic assault'.[21] There is something in this. In *Goblin Market* Laura's indulgence seems to be rewarded and Lizzie's abstinence enjoys some unusual satisfactions. The gratification of desire is a major element of the poem. Nevertheless, Lizzie's 'inward laughter' as she returns to Laura, her talismanic silver penny bouncing in her purse, is prompted by delight in the discovery of her own power rather than by complicity in the goblins' erotic assault. The similes underline this. The goblin men have been overcome and the story of Lizzie's victory can be added to that of Jeanie's defeat in the fables of maids.

The exemplary nature of Lizzie's courage goes beyond her confrontation with the goblin men. As Dorothy Mermin has put it, in returning to Laura she offers as an alternative a gift of love and an example of a better way of life.[22] The discovery of the poem is that sisters don't need brothers; alternative models of relationship are available. The terms of Lizzie's return to Laura are startling. She calls to her sister:

> 'Did you miss me?
> Come and kiss me.
> Never mind my bruises,
> Hug me, kiss me, suck my juices
> Squeezed from goblin fruits for you,
> Goblin pulp and goblin dew.
> Eat me, drink me, love me;
> Laura, make much of me:
> For your sake I have braved the glen
> And had to do with goblin merchant men.'
> (ll. 465–74)

Laura responds:

> She clung about her sister,
> Kissed and kissed and kissed her:
> Tears once again
> Refreshed her shrunken eyes,

> Dropping like rain
> After long sultry drouth;
> Shaking with aguish fear, and pain,
> She kissed and kissed her with a hungry mouth.
>
> (ll. 485–92)

The fusion of eucharistic and sexual language in this scene makes it one of the most powerful in the poem, and it dominates the final sections. It also confirms that Ellen Moers was wrong to describe the poem as being about the erotic life of children. Laura and Lizzie are not 'little girls'[23] but 'maids' – adolescent females of perhaps the same age as Maude. Jeanie's transgression was clearly sexual; she 'should have been a bride;/But who for joys brides hope to have/Fell sick and died/In her gay prime' (ll. 313–16). Laura's 'fall' is given similar metaphoric expression; she purchases the fruit with a lock from the maiden head.[24] These transactions – 'trade' was a term widely used in the mid-nineteenth century for any kind of sexual barter[25] – have killed Jeanie and left Laura 'Thirsty, cankered, goblin-ridden'. The passionate reunion of Laura and Lizzie, on the other hand, is restorative. Laura collapses and spends the night close to death tended by her sister, but wakes next morning restored to health and innocence. Heterosexuality, it seems, is redeemed by homosexuality.

There are problems about how we read this scene. Moers hastens to make clear she is not suggesting *Goblin Market* belongs to the history of pornography as a Victorian celebration of oral sex.[26] I understand her discomfort. Readings of the poem which make literal its metaphors seem inevitably reductive, and yet the suggestiveness of metaphor and its decoding is central to the reading of poetry. A common response to this kind of difficulty is to argue that contemporary readings see meanings which were not available to a Victorian reader. *Playboy*'s inverted Bowdlerization of the poem, with the clean bits left out, is an extreme example of this kind of response. In the case of *Goblin Market* I would reverse the terms and suggest that we fail to see meanings which a Victorian reader would have taken for granted.

Carroll Smith-Rosenberg has shown that in nineteenth-century American society there were no taboos on close female relationships.[27] There is no reason to believe that British society was any different. She argues that intense female love was socially acceptable and fully compatible with heterosexual marriage, and that it was one of the few emotional and behavioural options available to nineteenth-century women:

> society was characterized in large part by rigid gender-role differentiation... leading to the emotional segregation of women and men. The roles of daughter and mother shaded ... into each other, while ... frequent pregnancies, childbirth, nursing, and menopause bound women together in physical and emotional intimacy... within... such a social framework ... a specifically female world did indeed develop, a world built around a generic and unselfconscious pattern of single-sex or homosocial networks. These supportive networks were institutionalized in social conventions or rituals which accompanied virtually every important event in a woman's life, from birth to death. Such female relationships were frequently supported and paralleled by severe social restrictions on intimacy between young men and women. Within such a world of emotional richness and complexity devotion to and love of other women became a plausible and socially accepted form of human interaction.[28]

Women lived in a world inhabited by children and other women. It was a world of 'mutual valuation' in which sharing was paramount and hostility and criticism discouraged. In such a world relations between women were close, devoted, and long-lasting. Girls routinely slept together, kissed, and hugged. Sometimes, but certainly not always, this emotional closeness became intense and physical. Males were differently socialized, relatively segregated, and often remained distant even after marriage. The months immediately preceding marriage were spent almost exclusively with other women; sisters, cousins, or even friends frequently accompanied the newly married couple on their wedding trip; married life was structured about female rituals, with lengthy seclusions, supervised by other women, either side of childbirth. Smith-Rosenberg concludes that women's relations with each other in the nineteenth century were characterized by closeness, freedom of emotional expression, and uninhibited physical contact, and that the opposite was frequently true of male–female relations. As she observes, all this has more or less been reversed in our own century.

The Woman in White is an interesting example of the traumatic though temporary break-up of an intimate sibling relationship at marriage. Laura, most reluctantly, has to do without her half-sister's company on her European honeymoon. Nevertheless, her husband is perfectly happy to accept that Marian should live with them when they return to England. It is only this arrangement which saves Laura from the evil plans of her husband and Count Fosco. The intense relationship between the half-sisters goes relatively umarked in the context of the novel's mystery and suspense. Yet Marian's solicitude for Laura has both the care and the passion that we see in Lizzie's feelings for her Laura in *Goblin Market*. On the eve of Laura's wedding Marian creeps into her bedroom for a last 'stolen look at Laura in her pretty little white bed – the bed she has occupied since the days of her girlhood'. (This recalls that other, less benevolent but similarly marriage-deploring visit by another dark-haired woman on the eve of a marriage in *Jane Eyre*.) Marian records in her diary, 'I waited, looking at her, as I have seen thousands of times, as I shall never see her again . . . . My own love! with all your wealth, and all your beauty, how friendless you are!' (p. 175). And when Laura is about to return from her goblin honeymoon, Marian writes:

> Six months to look back on – six long, lonely months since Laura and I last saw each other!
> How many days have I still to wait? Only one!. . . . I can hardly realize my own happiness – I can hardly believe that the next four-and-twenty hours will complete the last day of separation between Laura and me. (p. 177)

Marian's language, unlike Lizzie's, is rhetorically hackneyed, but the kind and intensity of emotion expressed is that conventionally associated with male–female relationships. The diaries and letters upon which Smith-Rosenberg based her study were full of similarly intense passages, as in the following example of a woman describing her feelings for a friend: 'I love her as wives do love their husbands, as friends who have taken each other for life – and believe in her as I believe in my God.'[29] This extract even has the same mixing of the languages of secular and religious passion we find in *Goblin Market*.

The more-than-sexual emphasis of Smith-Rosenberg's essay is instructive and salutory. In relation to *Goblin Market* it illuminates the unselfconscious emotional and physical intimacy of the sisters, the absence of condemnation in Lizzie's fear of what Laura has done, and also, perhaps, the invisibility of the husbands at the end of the poem. An exclusively sexual reading of *Goblin Market* is reductive. Having said that, however, the sexuality of the passages quoted above is surely explicit and conscious. The common assumption that Rossetti could not really have intended to write what she seems to be saying reduces the poem to a kind of accident which its order and patterning belies. *Goblin Market* is not a Coleridgean fragment but a tightly controlled narrative. Smith-Rosenberg's essay, however, helps us to see that the poem is less aberrant or inexplicable than some critics have suggested. There is nothing unusual in the sisters' relationship, but it does undergo a physical intensification on the night Lizzie returns to Laura smeared with goblin juices. This is made clear by the lines describing Laura's awakening next morning:

> Laura awoke as from a dream,
> Laughed in the innocent old way,
> Hugged Lizzie but not twice or thrice;
>
> (ll. 537–9)

Restored to health and nature – birds chirp, buds open, reapers go out to harvest – Laura's physical needs have moderated; one hug will now do. The new morning brings restraint after the abandon of the previous evening and the restorative intensity of sisterhood can, even should, be relaxed.

Does this mean, therefore, that *Goblin Market* follows the trajectory of most Victorian family narratives and ends safely at home? At the beginning of the poem the sisters are maintaining a home based on self-sufficient productive labour and mutuality. This is contrasted with an outside world of exchange transactions dominated by the 'goblin merchant men'. The goblins are traders, and 'buy' is the central verb of this poem which constantly plays on 'buying' and 'paying'. Laura purchases the fruit with a piece of herself – 'a precious golden lock' – and even carries away a kernel stone for future investment. Of course, it fails to grow in home soil. Lizzie's purity is confirmed by the unspent silver penny whose jingle in her purse is 'music to her ear' as she runs home after her victorious confrontation with the goblin men. Trade and money are associated with sex, features of an outside world whose values threaten those of home. Home is the haven towards which Lizzie urges Laura. Once Laura has been corrupted by this outside world she is unable to help sustain the domestic economy on which the values of home are based. She neglects cooking, housekeeping and care of the animals. Lizzie's braving of the world outside to win redemption for her sister is an apparent victory for those values home embodies. Like a crucifix in a vampire film her incorruptibility annihilates the goblin men, who disappear. Laura recovers and home is restored, shown in full pastoral setting with a picture of reapers walking to the fields at harvest time. Natural fertility has replaced unnatural sexuality. The poem ends with a family tableau, a mother telling a cautionary tale to the children. Home and family have survived, been strengthened, and will persist as long as lessons are heeded.

Goblin Market, however, is not as placidly orthodox as this reading suggests. The husbands are kept out of the text, and merely implied by the description of Laura and Lizzie as 'wives'. In the concluding tableau Laura is not necessarily telling the story just to her own children:

> Laura would call the little ones
> And tell them of her early prime,
> Those pleasant days long gone
> Of not-returning time:
>
> (ll. 548–51)

These seem to be Lizzie's children as well, and the logic of the narrative suggests they are all girls. The apparent absence of conventional nuclear families opens up the possibility of alternative family arrangements. This is reinforced by the poem's concluding lines, which emphasize sisterly love rather than the need to resist temptation:

> Then joining hands to little hands
> Would bid them cling together,
> 'For there is no friend like a sister
> In calm or stormy weather;
> To cheer one on the tedious way,
> To fetch one if one goes astray,
> To lift one if one totters down,
> To strengthen whilst one stands.
>
> (ll. 560–7)

Even the poem's didactic tag is sisterly rather than cautionary. *Goblin Market* is not another Victorian text about the road to marriage and the creation or restoration of family. The marriages at the end of the poem are merely a gesture. The husbands have no more dramatic status than the totally absent parents. The dominant, indeed exclusive, relationship is that of the sisters. The poem offhandedly acknowledges the literary and social convention of marriage but refuses to use it. It offers instead a celebration of secular sisterhood.

This reading of the poem is governed by its language, which works directly on the senses and is full of appeals to sight, taste, and sound. Doubtless it is this sensuousness of language which has drawn so many illustrators to the poem, re-enacting Laura's enticement.[30] These appeals are far stronger than any moral duty to resist temptation which might seem to be the message of the poem. Lizzie closes her eyes, shuts her mouth, and blocks her ears, but the poem is one long temptation to peep, listen, and taste. Its language has pressures and energies which undermine the apparent resolution of the narrative and overwhelm the flat language of precept and example of its concluding lines. The drama of needs and desire which culminates in the passionate sexual and religious language of Lizzie's return to Laura, and provides the poem's most powerful effects, is not fully absorbed by the desexualised vision of sisterhood which Laura offers to the children.

This reading of the poem suggests a kind of triple-layered ending. Most obvious is the 'happy family' one. Lizzie and Laura become wives and mothers, and the temptation and threat represented by the goblin men is repudiated by the establishment of orthodox family structures. This, I have argued, is undermined, even contradicted, by the poem's vision of secular sisterhood. The ideal relationship is not with brothers or husbands but sisters (and daughters). This alternative model of personal and social relationship is the second, and dominant, ending. In the concluding lines of the poem it has been desexualized, but this platonic resolution cannot entirely contain, and indeed is covertly reinforced by, the poem's drama of satisfying sexual needs. The alternative model of sisterhood finds its most intense expression in the sexually charged imagery of Lizzie's return and Laura's recovery. For once in Rossetti's work desire finds its object and is gratified. The serene domesticity of the final tableau, orthodox as it seems, is in fact the result of this fulfilment of desire. Home, far from being emptied of sex, has actually been redeemed by it. Once Laura has been saved and satisfied, however, passion and erotics are replaced by feeling and sympathy, or at least given a relative rather than absolute significance. The goblins, like *Playboy*, are obsessional. Within new structures, sexuality can take its place alongside other aspects of life.

V

Wasting illnesses occur frequently in Rossetti's poetry. Maude's decline is hastened but not caused by her accident. Laura deteriorates from the moment she can no longer hear or see the goblin men. In 'The Prince's Progress' (1861/1865)[31] a princess lies wasting on her bed while her betrothed prince tarries on his journey to claim her. When he finally arrives she is dead. In manuscript the poem had been entitled 'The Prince Who Arrived too Late', and it recalls a contemporary painting by W. L. Windus, 'Too Late' (1858), in which a man returns to find the young woman he is to marry dying of consumption. The man hides his eyes from the wasting consumptive figure, but also from her glassy stare and the equally unrelenting gaze of the little girl at her side. The only comfort in the painting is being offered to the dying woman by a companion, and this heightens its accusatory nature. Its composition, in which the woman and her attendants confront the man, is similar to the arrival scene in 'The Prince's Progress' and the attendants' 'bride-song':

> Too late for love, too late for joy,
> You loitered on the road too long,
> You trifled at the gate:
> The enchanted dove upon her branch
> Died without a mate;
> The enchanted princess in her tower
> Slept, died, behind the grate;
> Her heart was starving all this while
> You made it wait.
> (ll. 481–90)

The heavily stressed last line convicts the prince, and the

Plate 9 William Lindsay Windus, 'Too Late', 1857–8

attendants' white poppies are preferred to his roses ('Your roses are too red') to adorn the head of the princess.

There are many examples of female decline in nineteenth-century writing, and these are commonly associated with unrequited or prohibited love, as in the examples immediately above.[32] In *Sense and Sensibility* Marianne Dashwood languishes after her rejection by Willoughby, and the resulting enfeebled condition and emotional distress leads directly to her catching a chill and almost dying. Anne Eliot, in *Persuasion*, suffers a much less intense but more protracted decline after her unwilling rejection of Wentworth. In both cases the fading beauty of these young women as decline sets in is emphasized. *Shirley* is probably the longest, most detailed study of wasting illness in nineteenth-century writing. Caroline's fading, again associated with unrequited love, begins early in the novel and develops into a serious decline which threatens death. This process stretches across much of the novel. In Caroline Helstone's case, however, the causes of her illness are deeper than unrequited love for Robert Moore. Moore becomes the *focus* of all she desires but is not, in himself, everything she desires. At the start of the novel Caroline is 18, in a borderland between adolescence and womanhood: 'at eighteen, drawing near the confines of illusive void dreams, Elf-land lies behind us, the shores of Reality rise in front'(Ch. 7, p. 75). Sitting alone in her room the shores of reality look inhospitable:

> she had the thin illusion of her own dim shadow on the wall. Turning from the pale phantom which reflected herself in its outline, and her reverie in the drooped attitude of its dim head and colourless tresses, she sat down – inaction would suit the frame of mind into which she was now declining – she said to herself – 'I have to live, perhaps, till seventy years. As far as I know, I have good health: half a century of existence may lie before me. How am I to occupy it? What am I to do to fill the interval of time which spreads between me and the grave?'
> (Ch. 10, p. 138)

What am I to become? is a frequently heard question in women's writing of this period. In this case the answer to Caroline's questions is there in the room with her, in the 'pale phantom', 'drooped attitude', and 'colourless tresses' dimly reflected on the wall and prefiguring her future self. This passage occurs in

Chapter 10, 'Old Maids', in which Caroline visits two elderly spinsters and again sees her own likely future. There is also a particular and ironic significance in Caroline's reference to her good health. It is at this point in the novel that her decline begins.

Caroline's illness is presented as a consequence of the restrictions of her life. Her secret love for Moore is one important factor, but so too is the unacceptability of her uncle's blunt summary of her position: 'stick to the needle – learn shirt-making and gown-making, and pie-crust making, and you 'll be a clever woman some day' (Ch. 7, p. 76). Significantly, Caroline is not cured by requited love but by the discovery of her mother. The onset of her illness is associated with her anxious need to discover and know her mother, and when her wasting turns to fever, and death threatens, Caroline's life is saved only by Mrs Pryor's revelation that she is Caroline's mother. And just as Caroline's illness is more than lovesickness, her case has representative as well as individual significance. Shortly before her illness reaches its crisis there is a long passage in which reflections on her own condition develop into a general, more authorial address to the men of England about the plight of their daughters:

> Can you give them a field in which their faculties may be exercised and grow? Men of England! Look at your poor girls, many of them fading round you, dropping off in consumption or decline; or, what is worse, degenerating to sour old maids, – envious, back-biting, wretched, because life is a desert to them: or, what is worst of all, reduced to strive, by scarce modest coquetry and debasing artifice, to gain that position and consideration by marriage which to celibacy is denied. Fathers! cannot you alter these things?
>
> (Ch. 22, p. 311)

Rossetti's bitter, brilliant sonnet 'A Triad' (1856) has three different female figures – the prostitute, the wife, and the spinster (or nun):

> One shamed herself in love; one temperately
> Grew gross in soulless love, a sluggish wife;
> One famished died for love. Thus two of three
> Took death for love and won him after strife;
> One droned in sweetness like a fattened bee:
> All on the threshold, yet all short of life.
>
> (ll. 9–14)

In the passage above Brontë presents three closely related or identical figures – the consumptive, the old maid, and the wife. The possibilities for women are illness or disease, loneliness or marriage, and for both writers the last of these seems the least desirable.

In *Shirley* it is clear that decline is not wholly caused by lovesickness and that it also functions as a displaced expression of more general dissatisfaction with life and its possibilities. There is an element of this, much less explicit, in my earlier examples from Austen. Marianne's disappointed love for Willoughby is the focus of more extensive pressures on her to control her sensibility, and her recovery from illness is not only an acceptance of the end of that love but of a whole range of past errors. Illness in *Sense and Sensibility* is a necessary part of Marianne's education. In *Shirley* it is pure waste. In neither case is it simply a matter of disappointed love. Anne Eliot's decline is much less dramatic, a slow fading which expresses her unrewarding existence but does not threaten her life. The emphasis has shifted from *Sense and Sensibility*. In *Persuasion* we see the cost of self-denial rather than its necessity. The fading of Anne's beauty and her low spirits are centred on the loss of Wentworth, but more generally connected to the bleakness of her future – her alienation from the world and values of her father and elder sister, her lack of enthusiasm for the drawing-room existence she is forced to lead, her likely future role as maiden aunt to her younger sister's children. Wentworth's return eventually changes all this, but it is the prospect of a different kind of future – with a world of her own and no longer a subordinate in that of others – as much as requited love which restores her beauty.

A conspicuous symptom of most wasting illnesses in nineteenth-century writing is a refusal or inability to eat. This is marked in *Shirley* where food is thrust on Caroline but is 'as ashes and sawdust to her'. In *Wuthering Heights,* after Heathcliff's return and the quarrel between Catherine and Edgar, Catherine fasts and begins the decline which leads to her death in childbirth. In both these examples the refusal or inability to eat is an extreme attempt to escape an intolerable situation. Jane Eyre, locked in the red room for her insubordination considers 'never eating or drinking more, and letting myself die' as a way of escaping the 'insupportable oppression' of her position (Ch. 2, p. 47). There is no romantic love involved for the child Jane, but her response is similar to those in which it is a factor. Jane's incarceration is followed by illness, an ambiguous submission to authority in which care of her person is handed over to others in exchange for a different kind of treatment.

This refusal to eat seems to be a form of anorexic suicide. Cora Kaplan has suggested that a medical analogy for Laura's decline might be anorexia, pointing out that anorexia is now thought to be associated with pubescent crisis at the onset of adult female sexuality. Such 'diagnosis', she insists, must be hypothetical, but it does coincide with those 'mysterious ailments' common in nineteenth-century writing.[33] Anorexia has been described as being about identity, autonomy, and the control of one's own life and body. It is a hunger strike against what seem the intolerable conditions of one's situation provoked by the question: how to live? It involves a refusal to grow up and take one's allotted social role.[34] Treated as case histories, Marianne, Caroline, Maude, and Laura have a good deal in common. Adolescents facing womanhood, with their future – how to live? – uncertain or only too certain, in any case likely to be unrewarding, each turns away from life, refusing to grow up and accept the social and sexual role allotted them.

Cora Kaplan is right to be wary of the medical diagnosis of fictive characters, but the preoccupation with adolescent female illness in nineteenth-century literary discourse is also found in medical, educational, and moral writing of the period. Medical knowledge played a crucial role in ideas about gender difference as they evolved during the nineteenth century. Most theories of women's social role were based on her biological function as the bearer of children.[35] Foucault identified two of the main elements of the deployment of sexuality as the medicalization of female sexuality (also described as the hysterization of women's bodies) and the problematization of adolescent sexuality. There is a significant conjunction of these two elements in this phenomenon of adolescent female illness. All specifically female biological functions – menstruation, pregnancy, menopause – came to be seen as pathological, and puberty was regarded as a period of particular stress and crisis during which girls needed protection and often invaliding. It was seen as a difficult transition period when the female role was ill-defined and the future role uncertain and causing tension.[36] A variety of illnesses were 'discovered' which were either peculiar to female adolescents or likely to commence at puberty. These were all ultimately derived from the reproductive system and thought to be sexual as well as female in character. Neurasthenia, chlorosis (green sickness), and amenorrhoea were illnesses of this kind commonly diagnosed in young women. Their symptoms were similar – lassitude, anaemia, nervous debility, pallor, menstrual irregularity – hardly distinctive, and by the early twentieth century it was widely accepted that they were unable to provide a coherent explanation of the symptoms they encompassed.[37]

Any of these symptoms could also have been seen as evidence of hysteria, which was widely diagnosed throughout the century. Nervousness, depression, and fatigue were common symptoms, but the most characteristic and dramatic was the hysterical fit which began with pain, usually in the uterine area, developed into something like an epileptic seizure, and could culminate in a death-like trance of varying duration. On the other hand, hysterical seizure could be so minor as to escape the notice even of the patient herself. As this suggests, symptoms were not solely physical and in nineteenth-century medical writing a hysterical female character emerged based on personality and mood as much as physical symptoms. The 'hysteric' was emotionally self-indulgent, egocentric, narcissistic, morally weak, and lacking in will power. Hysteria was heavily sexualized. It commenced with puberty, ended with menopause, and masturbation was thought to be a frequent cause.[38]

Hysteria and related conditions were not illnesses in the same sense as whooping cough or even schizophrenia. They were medical constructions placed on a widespread social phenomenon, the construction itself then reinforcing the illness. Smith-Rosenberg concludes that hysteria was a socially recognized behaviour pattern which was produced by, and functional within, a specific set of social circumstances.[39] Why did it occur? How was it functional? Duffin sees the illnesses she discusses as a means of escaping tedious social duties and points out that women often wrote in the time they stole. We have seen this happening in the case of Maude. She also argues that illness was a means whereby married women could avoid repeated pregnancy.[40] In other words, illness was a kind of survival technique. Smith-Rosenberg points to new stresses within the family, in particular the few domestic-role alternatives available to women and the rigid definition of those that were. Implicit in hysteria was a refusal to accept the role women were expected to play, forcing others to perform the caring expected of them. It expressed a dissatisfaction with their lives, using illness, which is unavoidable, to make the protest acceptable.[41] It was a form of passive protest, a way of being noticed and proclaiming their existence while remaining submissive and obedient. Smith-Rosenberg has neatly summarized the paradoxes and contradictions of this passive protest:

> Hysteria as a chronic, dramatic and socially accepted sick role could thus provide some alleviation of conflict and tension, but the hysteric purchased her escape from the emotional – and frequently – from the sexual demands of her life only at the cost of pain, disability, and an intensification of woman's traditional passivity and dependence . . . a complex interplay existed between the character traits assigned women in Victorian society and the characteristic symptoms of the nineteenth-century hysteric: dependency, fragility, emotionality, narcissism.[42]

These illnesses were perhaps the only acceptable way for young women to express their discontent, anger, and pain. Smith-Rosenberg concludes that certain symptoms were available and many women resorted to them.[43] These symptoms were not necessarily specific to adolescence but that was when they were first likely to commence and also, importantly, when they were first looked for. The problematization of adolescent female sexuality by parents, doctors, and educationalists helped create and intensify the stresses of this particular life stage, but it also provided an escape route for young women on the threshold of adult life. This route, however, as we saw above, was circular. The freedom gained was at the cost of further loss of independence.

The lives of Elizabeth Barrett Browning, Christina Rossetti, and Alice James illustrate this paradox. Elizabeth Barrett Browning became one of the most famous Victorian invalids, but it is her adolescent illness rather than the much later and well-known Wimpole Street period which interests me. This began in 1821, when she was 15, and lasted more than a year. Barrett Browning ascribed it to a spinal injury from a strain when saddling a pony, but biographers have attributed it to nervous hysteria. It seems to have been connected with the severing of her intense relationship with her brother Edward (Bro) when he was sent off to school.[44] In her early letters Barrett Browning frequently referred to her sealed-off existence, variously describing herself as a walled-up nun, a prisoner used to chains and dungeons, and as Marianna in the moated grange.[45] Her illness confirmed her prison but also permitted her voracious reading and extensive self-education. Her later illness, intensified but not caused by Bro's drowning in 1840, had different symptoms from the earlier one and is more properly considered an example of adult invalidism than 'hysterical illness'.

In 1845, at the age of 15, Christina Rossetti suffered an undiagnosed illness which transformed her from a healthy child into a sick, delicate adolescent. Her brother William drew a parallel between Maude's constantly weak health and Rossetti's,[46] and Packer has argued that by becoming an invalid Christina escaped her sister's fate of governessing and won the privileges and immunities necessary for writing.[47] Rossetti's ill health was acute between 1845 and 1850 but persisted beyond adolescence. In a letter to William in 1855, when she did have a temporary position as a governess, she wrote, 'I am rejoiced to feel that my health does really unfit me for miscellaneous governessing *en permanence*'.[48] Gwendolen Harleth, when faced with the same dismal prospect of governessing, wondered about the stage and then turned to marriage; illness would have been safer.

Alice James was the most precocious, spectacular, and persistent of these examples. She started to think about dying before she reached adolescence, and mysterious pains and prostrations soon followed. In her late teens she suffered what she described in her diary as 'violent turns of hysteria', and then her first breakdown. Her second, when she was 30, seems to have been precipitated by the marriage of her deeply loved brother William. Brothers are ubiquitous in these histories. She then became a full-time invalid and died in 1892 in her early forties.[49]

What interests me in these three case histories is the recurrence of nervous illness in adolescence as a response to deeply unsatisfactory life situations. Illness seems a destructively self-enclosing solution to the problem of how to live authentically, and yet for each of these women it won them space and often attention they would not otherwise have received. This was certainly true for Alice James, whose share of parental attention increased as her ill health became more constant. Her brother William became a philosopher, Henry became a writer, and Alice became an invalid. In a sense she never came through her adolescent crisis whereas Barrett Browning and Rossetti did, both saved by writing rather than love.

Goblin Market dramatizes one such adolescent crisis. In fact it is really two crises, because Laura's 'fall' forces Lizzie to confront the goblin world. However, it is Laura's experience which is central and decisive. Her drama is a highly unorthodox one in which illness is caused by requital rather than its lack. Laura falls ill after tasting 'joys brides hope to have'. Of course, her illness is intensified by 'baulked desire', and so frustrated desire plays a part as well, but the movement of the poem is towards her recognition that what she thinks she desires is really 'wormwood to her tongue'; it cannot satisfy.

Laura's symptoms suggest the kind of nineteenth-century female illnesses discussed above. She 'dwindles', her hair grows 'thin and gray', her eyes sink and her mouth fades. She withdraws from life, neither doing household work nor eating. The culmination of this steady decline is her seizure and collapse following Lizzie's return, which is strongly suggestive of an hysterical fit. Laura also has the kind of personality which was labelled hysterical. Compared with Lizzie she is self-indulgent, egocentric, and lacking in will power. The important difference between her presentation and discussions of the hysterical personality in medical writing, however, is that Laura is treated objectively. Her character is made clear, but there is nothing unsympathetic in its presentation. In a cautionary tale she would be 'foolish Laura'; in *Goblin Market* there is nothing more severe or less ambiguous than 'sweet-tooth Laura'. A further point of connection with hysteria is the way Laura's illness is heavily sexualised, in its cause, its character, and its cure.

Today Laura would probably be diagnosed as anorexic, and there is a particular appropriateness about such a diagnosis in a poem which is centrally about food, about tasting and eating, and being unable to taste or eat. Even goblin fruit itself 'feeds': 'Who knows upon what soil they fed/Their hungry thirsty roots?' (ll. 44–5). Denied a second taste of goblin fruit Laura is unable to eat at all. When, thanks to Lizzie's courage, she tastes the fruit again, it is inedible: 'She loathed the feast' (l. 495). Only now, unable to eat goblin fruit, can she again eat naturally grown and produced food. The reapers going out to harvest 'golden sheaves' signal the end of Laura's 'anorexia' and the victory of whole food over evil and artificial substitutes. The 'anorexic' yearning for the deadly goblin fruit has been replaced by the return of appetite for healthy and life-sustaining food.

The allegory is clear but heterodox. It involves the rejection of brothers (men), purveyors of satanic food and illness, for the palatable, health- and life-giving alternative of the love of sisters. Unlike most nineteenth-century texts, recovery from illness is associated with the rejection rather than the requital of heterosexual love. There has been a radical reordering of the usual male–female resolution.

NOTES

1. *The Complete Poems of Christina Rossetti*, Vol. 1, ed. R. W. Crump (Baton Rouge and London: Louisiana State University Press, 1979), p. 234. All references are to this edition unless otherwise stated.
2. Cora Kaplan, 'The indefinite disclosed: Christina Rossetti and Emily Dickinson', in Mary Jacobus (ed.) *Women Writing and Writing about Women* (London: Croom Helm, 1979), p. 65.
3. *Playboy* 20 (1973), pp. 115–19.
4. There is a useful discussion of recent writing on the poem in Allen R. Life's summary, 'The Pre-Raphaelites', in 'Guide to the year's work in Victorian poetry: 1980', *Victorian Poetry* 19.
5. Jerome J. McGann, 'Christina Rossetti's poems: a new edition and a revaluation', *Victorian Studies*, Winter, 1980.
6. W. M. Rossetti's 'Prefatory note' to his edition of *Maude* is included as an appendix in the only modern edition of the work: R. W. Crump (ed.) *Maude: Prose and Verse* (Connecticut: Archon Books, 1976). All references are to this edition.
7. ibid., p. 80.
8. Lona Mosk Packer, *Christina Rossetti* (Berkeley: University of California Press, 1963), pp. 58 and passim.
9. Ray Strachey, *'The Cause': A Short History of the Women's Movement in Great Britain* (London: G. Bell & Sons, 1928), p. 399.
10. H. P. Liddon, *The Life of Edward Bouverie Pusey*, 4 vols. (1893-7), Vol. 3, pp. 13-18, quoted in Packer, p. 55.
11. 'The Anti-Marriage League', *Blackwoods*, January 1896, pp. 139–40.

12. Hopkins is a parallel example. A later convent poem of Rossetti's, 'Convent Threshold' (1858) prompted Hopkins's 'A voice from the world: fragments of an answer to Miss Rossetti's Convent Threshold'.
13. Kaplan, pp. 61–2, 70–1.
14. McGann, p. 241. Elizabeth Barrett Browning's poem on the death of Felicia Hemans was also dedicated to L.E.L.
15. Austen's *Sense and Sensibility* is an interesting one in relation to *Goblin Market*. The pairing of Lizzie and Laura, one self-controlled and incorruptible, the other wilful and tempted, is similar to that of Elinor and Marianne Dashwood. The Dashwood family, a mother and three daughters, is entirely female and subject to the attention of a number of men. Willoughby takes a lock of Marianne's hair just as Laura pays for the fruit with a lock of hers. Like Laura, Marianne pines, falls ill and almost dies, nursed by her sister. In both cases recovery is followed by a recognition scene. Marianne realizes that Elinor has also suffered from disappointed love, and Laura learns the strength of a sister's love. There is even a Jeanie figure in *Sense and Sensibility*, Brandon's niece Eliza who has been ruined by Willoughby, the novel's goblin man. Of course there are many differences in emphasis. Not all the men in *Sense and Sensibility* are goblins, and the importance of sisterhood recedes as the marriages which conclude the novel are contracted.
16. These lines are from W. M. Rossetti's edition, *The Poetical Works of Christina Georgina Rossetti* (London: Macmillan, 1904), pp. 192–3. The poem was never published as such by Christina Rossetti, although parts of it appeared in 'Whatsoever is right, that shall ye receive'; see Vol. 2 of Crump's *Complete Poems of Christina Rossetti*, pp. 267–8, 435. 'The heart knoweth its own bitterness', will appear in its own right in Vol. 3 of Crump's edition.
17. Kendrick Smithyman, 'A reading of *Goblin Market*', *Landfall* 8 (4). Smithyman's essay deserves to be better known. It anticipates a good deal of the recent work on *Goblin Market*.
18. William T. Going, '*Goblin Market* and the Pre-Raphaelite Brotherhood', *Pre-Raphaelite Review* 3.
19. Smithyman, p. 282.
20. Moers, p. 105.
21. Steven Connor, ' "Speaking likenesses": language and repetition in Christina Rossetti's *Goblin Market*', *Victorian Poetry* 22 (4).
22. Dorothy Mermin, 'Heroic Sisterhood in *Goblin Market*', *Victorian Poetry* 21(2): 112.
23. Moers, pp. 101–2.
24. Smithyman, p. 283.
25. Jeffrey Weeks, *Sex, Politics and Society*. (London and New York: Longman, 1981), p. 112.

26. Moers, p. 102.
27. Carroll Smith-Rosenberg, 'The female world of love and ritual: relations between women in nineteenth-century America', *Signs* 1 (1).
28. ibid., p. 9.
29. ibid., p. 7.
30. Apart from D. G. Rossetti's illustrations for the first edition, other prominent illustrators include Arthur Rackham (Harrap, 1933) and most recently Martin Ware (Gollancz, 1980). *Playboy's* illustrations are gross parodies of Rackham's.
31. The last sixty lines of this poem were written first, in 1861, and published separately in 1863. The poem was completed in 1865 and published in 1866.
32. I am indebted to an undergraduate essay by Alice Glover for several of the ideas and examples in the following section.
33. Kaplan, p. 67.
34. Sheila MacLeod, 'The way of all flesh', *The Guardian*, 21 June 1983.
35. Lorna Duffin, 'The conspicuous consumptive: woman as an invalid', in Sarah Delamont and Lorna Duffin (eds) *The Nineteenth-Century Woman: Her Cultural and Physical World* (London: Croom Helm, 1978), pp. 26–32.
36. Duffin, pp. 32, 38.
37. ibid., pp. 34–40.
38. Carroll Smith-Rosenberg, 'The hysterical woman: sex roles and role conflict in 19th-century America', *Social Research* 39 (4): 660–3, 667–9.
39. ibid., pp. 653, 678.
40. Duffin, p. 51.
41. Smith-Rosenberg, pp. 655, 663, 672–3.
42. ibid., p. 671.
43. ibid., p. 678.
44. Alethea Hayter, *Mrs Browning: A Poet's Work and its Setting* (London: Faber, 1962), p. 58; also Gardner B. Taplin, *The Life of Elizabeth Barrett Browning* (New Haven, Conn: Yale University Press, 1957), p. 15.
45. Hayter, p. 19.
46. 'Prefatory note', Crump, p. 79.
47. Packer, pp. 21–2.
48. ibid., p. 21.
49. Mary-Kay Wilmers, 'Death and the maiden', *London Review of Books*, 6–19 August 1981. Wilmers is reviewing Jean Strouse's *Alice James* and Ruth Bernard Yeazell's edition *The Death and Letters of Alice James*.

6
'Turbid pictures': George Meredith's *Modern Love*

I

George Meredith's *Modern Love* is a sequence of fifty 'sonnets' (sixteen-line poems of four quatrains) about a disintegrating marriage. The husband and wife are intensely unhappy, able neither to live with nor without each other. At the beginning of the sequence the wife, often referred to as 'Madam' or 'the woman', is involved with another man. Later the husband becomes involved with another woman, referred to as 'the Lady'. Most of the sonnets are organized around a particular scene representing a moment of emotional crisis, revelation, or self-recognition. There are two main kinds of scene. The first of these is private and domestic, in which anger, bitterness, pain, and jealousy are often mixed with sorrow, pity, even tenderness in a Lawrentian flux of conflicting emotions. The other is concerned with the public face of married life in which husband and wife maintain the appearance of a harmonious marriage in bitterly ironic situations. The wife is tortured by her new passion and the husband finds little consolation in his Lady. They are drawn back together in their unhappiness, but bitterness and jealousy are too strong for the attempted reconciliation. Their marriage is dead. In despair the wife kills herself, the husband at her bedside when she dies.

The narrative summaries in earlier chapters have been an unfortunate necessity. In the case of *Modern Love*, narrative summary is almost an impossibility. Although the sequence implies a narrative, much of it remains submerged, and the sonnets themselves are often elusive, ambiguous, and sometimes obscure. The poem has a particularly complex narrative structure which makes it, of all those I've discussed, the most difficult in which to separate what is told from how it is told. Compared with *Aurora Leigh*, or even *The Princess*, its form anticipates a number of modernist 'innovations' by half a century. Alethea Hayter remarked of *Aurora Leigh* that its appropriate form had not been developed at the time it was written. It should have been, she went on, like *The Waste Land*, 'a modern human situation held together not by a plot but by a web of imagery and association'.[1] This criticism is too bald. Imagery and association are the cement of *Aurora Leigh* and plot merely the scaffolding, but the clash between its novelistic and poetic aspects is sometimes damaging; too much scaffolding remains in view. *Modern Love* is much closer to what Hayter had in mind; all the scaffolding is down.

Both works nevertheless occupy the same borderland between poetry and fiction, and were responses to the territorial expansion of the novel in the mid-nineteenth century. Meredith experienced this at first hand. An aspiring poet, he was forced to turn to prose to earn a living as a writer. The *Modern Love* volume (1862) was the last poetry he published for more than twenty years, and until 1896 all his poetry was published at his own expense.[2]

Modern Love therefore marks Meredith's transition from poetry to full-time novel writing. It has, with justice, been described as one of the few Victorian poems to show a formal advantage over the achievements of the Victorian novel.[3] It combines a number of features of the most technically innovative Victorian novels. These include a mixture of first- and third-person narration (e.g. *Bleak House*), an absence of authorial omniscience (*Wuthering Heights*), a dislocated chronology (*Daniel Deronda*), and an intense inward focus (*Villette*). The sonnets work more like chapters in a novel than according to Petrarchan or Shakespearean principles, but with a Modernist compression and ellipsis quite unlike the leisurely unfolding of most Victorian fiction. These and many other features are concentrated into a work of only 800 lines.

Reviews of the poem liked neither its theme nor its form. J.W. Marston in the *Athenaeum* objected to its lack of order, clarity, and connectedness, likening it, rather aptly, to 'scattered leaves from the diary of a stranger'.[4] R.H. Hutton, in a vituperative review in *The Spectator* which provoked a reply in defence of the poem from Swinburne, described the sonnets as 'clever, meretricious, turbid pictures'.[5] This comparison with painting is one that the sequence invites, although hardly in Hutton's terms. Many of the sonnets record a single domestic episode in a manner similar to the narrative-pictorial style of contemporary genre painting. These are often presented as tableaux, 'vivid epitomes' to use Meisel's phrase, providing dramatic summaries which suggest the Victorian stage as well as the genre picture. Meredith's sonnets are, in fact, examples of the dialogue of nineteenth-century literary, pictorial, and dramatic forms outlined in my opening chapter. However, they construct a new language out of this dialogue. Most Victorian narrative paintings insist on being understood in a particular way. The viewer reads the clues, pieces together the evidence, and the picture falls into place. Millais' pen-and-ink drawing *Retribution (The Man with Two Wives)* (1854), allows only a single interpretation. Although I have argued in Chapter 3, above, that Egg's painting *Past and Present* has a subtext which questions the ostensible meaning of the painting, it is clear that contemporary reviewers found its interpretation unproblematic. The problem picture was expected to enclose its own solution, rather in the manner of a crossword. Those that didn't were felt to have broken the rules of the genre. As late as 1903 a review in *The Times* complained about the unanswered questions raised by John Collier's Royal Academy painting 'The Prodigal Daughter': 'The details of the dramatic moment are a little difficult to understand . . . a narrative picture ought to have no ambiguity'. Collier responded with understandable exasperation. 'If I ever again paint a picture of modern life . . . I shall give it a title a yard long, setting forth the life history of the characters, and, if necessary, their names and addresses'.[6] Attitudes like those expressed by *The Times* reviewer help us to understand the bewildered and hostile responses to *Modern Love*. Meredith's sequence refuses to fall into place and resists the kind of reading family narratives were expected to provide. It is, in every sense of the word, 'solutionless'.[7]

The strictures of Marston and Hutton are no longer shared by modern commentators, but revaluation of *Modern Love* has also produced fundamental disagreement about how the poem works.

For example, the concluding sonnet (L) has been described by Denis Donoghue as 'masterly', allowing a full sense of the range of feeling through which the whole poem has passed. John Lucas, however, describes the narrator's generalizations in this concluding sonnet as 'pious inanities', totally inadequate as any kind of judgement on the flow and recoil of the relationship which the poem has explored.[8] There is even disagreement about who speaks the final sonnet. Dorothy Mermin is in no doubt that it is the voice of the narrator, whose wider vision permits an omniscience that the husband cannot achieve. But according to Arline Golden it is the husband who speaks in Sonnet L as an almost omniscient narrator surveying the history and causes of his tragedy. Stephen Watt conflates narrator and husband, seeing the third-person narrative as an attempted but futile strategy of detachment.[9] Who speaks Sonnet L? What is being said? Is it being well or badly said? Critical disagreement of this order is unusual and says much about the complex kind of narrative *Modern Love* offers. The poem's obvious relationship to the Renaissance sonnet sequence, the Victorian novel, and nineteenth-century narrative painting creates particular kinds of narrative expectation which it often leaves unfulfilled.

Meredith would not, I think, have been irritated by these widely divergent readings. He insisted that his poem demanded 'thought and discernment', and that it 'could only be apprehended by the few who would read it many times'.[10] Thirty years after its publication, when asked if the wife had a sexual relationship with the other man, he replied, 'her husband never accurately knew; therefore we ought not to inquire',[11] renouncing the authorial privilege which the poem itself disclaims.

II

Modern Love had its immediate origins in Meredith's own marriage. On one level it is a very personal poem. Meredith married Mary Nicolls, the widowed daughter of Thomas Love Peacock, in 1849.[12] The marriage seems to have been difficult from the start and by 1857 they were more or less separated, Mary now spending most of her time with the painter Henry Wallis. Wallis had been a friend of both the Merediths. His painting *Fireside*

Reverie, exhibited at the Royal Academy in 1855, had used Mary as the model for the woman sitting beside the hearth, and four lines of Meredith's poetry as its epigraph. His best-known painting, *The Death of Chatterton*, exhibited at the Royal Academy in 1856, used George as the model for the dead poet. (This painting was bought by Augustus Egg.) In 1858 Mary and Wallis had a child. George and Mary's separation was now final and bitter. Meredith refused to see her and denied her access to their own son Arthur until she was dying. Mary died in October 1861 and *Modern Love* was written during the winter months which followed. It grew directly out of his wife's death, rather like Hardy's *Poems of 1912–13* written in the months immediately following Emma Hardy's death and after many years of unhappy marriage.

Modern Love, however, like Hardy's sequence, is not simply autobiographical. In the first place, as Dorothy Mermin has shown, fatal or fallen women who defy morality, convention, or their husbands recur frequently in Meredith's early poetry and prose, and are treated seriously, often with sympathy. The experience he lived through with Mary Nicolls was one he had often written about; he found his life imitating his art. Mermin argues that it was impossible for Meredith simply to denounce his wife because some of his own writing had already exculpated such a figure. In *Modern Love*, therefore, he re-examined his earlier treatments of this figure from the point of view of the abandoned husband.[13] Experience recast Meredith's writing but was not its sole progenitor. There is a further irony in that while Egg was painting *Past and Present*, George and Mary were re-enacting its narrative.

There were other examples of failed marriage around Meredith apart from his own. Of particular significance in this respect was that of Elizabeth Siddall and Dante Gabriel Rossetti, who had married in 1860 after a difficult relationship stretching back many years. Meredith first met Rossetti early in 1861 at a time when Rossetti's infatuation with Fanny Cornforth was placing strains on the marriage. The two men admired each other's work and soon became friends. In May 1861 Elizabeth Siddall had a still-birth and her health, never strong, declined. In February 1862 she died from an overdose of laudanum. The verdict at the inquest was accidental death, but there is little doubt she committed suicide. The friendship between the two men had begun at the time of Elizabeth Siddall's still-birth, Meredith had visited the Rossettis frequently in the following months, and he was completing *Modern Love* when Elizabeth killed herself. It is possible that Meredith's startling use of the dead child image in Sonnet XI derives from Elizabeth Siddall's still-birth, although the Merediths had also lost several children either born dead or dying soon after birth.[14] What seems more likely is that the suicide of the wife by drug overdose in the penultimate sonnet of *Modern Love* was prompted by Elizabeth Siddall's death. In mid-January 1862 Meredith had still to write thirteen sonnets to complete the sequence.[15] Elizabeth Siddall died on the night of February 11–12. Meredith had worked hard on the poem since early winter and progress had been steady, but it is difficult to believe he wrote the last thirteen sonnets in less than a month. If the sequence was, in fact, completed before 11 February, it is another, more dreadful, example of life imitating art.

Rossetti and Meredith continued to see each other regularly after the death of Elizabeth Siddall and the completion of *Modern Love*, and in October 1862 when Rossetti, his brother, and Swinburne moved into 16 Cheyne Walk, Meredith became a part-time tenant. This *ménage* lasted less than a year. Meredith never lived there permanently, and domestic friction centring on Rossetti's five-egg breakfasts and Meredith's boots brought it to an end, but it must have been an interesting household while it lasted. Rossetti and Meredith had both 'failed' at married life. Meredith's broken marriage and the recent death of Mary Nicolls had impelled the explorations of *Modern Love*. Rossetti's lost play, *The Wife's Tragedy*, was also probably the product of his marriage experience.[16] It would have made an interesting comparison with *Modern Love*. The new arrangement at Cheyne Walk, short-lived as it was, was an alternative kind of *ménage* to the one both men had recently lost.

More broadly, the marriage in Meredith's poem is presented as symptomatic and exemplary, embodying a larger cultural pattern. *Modern Love* is a pathology of Victorian marriage, a critique of the institution which has come to define and distort love and sexuality. Its ironic use and reversals of the traditional sonnet sequence implies a contrast between the possibilities of love in former centuries and in mid-Victorian England. It is not therefore an example of the eternal tragedy of love but of an historically specific social formation.

Apart from *Amours de Voyage*, the main poems I have examined are about the growth from childhood or adolescence to maturity, culminating in marriage. Marriage closes the text but is the opening of life, a pattern also found in many novels of the 1840s and 1850s. In the 1860s and 1870s, however, there is a shift from marriage as the point of narrative closure to marriage as the subject of narrative investigation. It can be argued that the unhappy marriages we often see in passing in early Victorian novels modify the promise of wedded bliss on which they end. This is perhaps true of Austen's novels as well. But marriage itself remained largely unexplored territory, as the narrator of *Vanity Fair* remarked:

> As his hero and heroine pass the matrimonial barrier, the novelist generally drops the curtain, as if the drama were over then: the doubts and struggles of life ended: as if, once landed in the marriage country, all were green and pleasant there: and wife and husband had nothing to do but to link each other's arms together, and wander gently downwards towards old age in happy and perfect fruition.[17]

The great studies of marriage in Victorian writing came in the decade or so following the publication of *Modern Love*: George Eliot's *Middlemarch* and *Daniel Deronda*, Trollope's *The Way We Live Now*, and the 'middle-brow' novels of Mrs Henry Wood, Mary Bradden, and others. *Modern Love* is an early landmark in the wedlock narrative which was to figure so prominently in later-nineteenth-century writing. In the earlier narratives of courtship, marriage was a reconciling force, an expression of personal or class adjustment and realignment offering new accommodations and possibilities.[18] It was also a guarantee of social stability, the cement of the social order and surety for its future. In *Modern Love*, on the other hand, marriage can offer neither present consolations nor future possibilities. We have a pair of mature protagonists deadlocked in a wretched marriage from which the only escape is the eventual suicide of one of the partners. The family has been reduced to an unhappy couple. The image of the dead child

(Sonnet XI) and the mock pregnancy faint (Sonnet XXI) emphasize the emotional barrenness of the marriage, and there is absolutely nothing in the poem to mitigate this. The heavy, bitter irony of the visit of the love-struck friend in Sonnet XXI, who comes to the couple for their blessing because he 'is convinced/That words of wedded lovers must bring good', illustrates perfectly the sardonic view of modern love and marriage which dominates the poem. Criticism of marriage as an institution did not begin at the end of the century with Hardy, Gissing, Grant Allen, and the other conspirators of Mrs Oliphant's anti-marriage league. The novels cited above were more than simply criticisms of how people behaved within marriage; they involved an examination of the institution itself. And nowhere in nineteenth-century writing is marriage scrutinized more radically and disturbingly than in *Modern Love*.

III

Modern Love opens with the husband and wife lying in bed, awake and estranged.[19] She sobs quietly and her misery wounds him. Neither speaks, and eventually they fall asleep:

> Like sculptured effigies they might be seen
> Upon their marriage-tomb, the sword between.

This is a chilling, petrified image of their dead marriage. Marriage-tomb recalls the 'marriage-hearse' of Blake's 'London'. The sword which separates them is emblematic of the endemic violence of their relationship, but it also sleeps in their hand, leaving the marriage knot uncut. The husband and wife, cast in stone, have become inseparable. This is to be a poem about the hellish closed circle of bourgeois marriage. This *huis clos* atmosphere dominates the sequence, particularly in those sonnets which present vignettes or tableaux of bourgeois marriage and domesticity. These are scattered throughout the sequence, but they cluster thickly between Sonnets XV and XXV sometimes falling into small sequences. One such grouping is Sonnets XV, XVI, and XVII, which forms a kind of triptych within the larger narrative, framing and epitomizing their marriage.

In Sonnet XV the husband stands over his sleeping wife and as she wakes shows her two letters; one she wrote to him when they were lovers, and the other is similarly worded, but written recently and addressed to someone else. Letters figure prominently in many Victorian paintings, those with a black border bringing news of death, and the others often conveying news worse than death. The scene is therefore a familiar one. The wronged husband (wives usually get the death letters) confronts his wife with evidence of her infidelity. Meredith's sonnet, however, although it evokes a painting such as *Past and Present*, offers something more complex than Egg's attempt to win sympathy for the sinner as well as the victim of that sin. In *Modern Love* the categories of sinner and victim are inadequate to the complexities of the relationship, and sympathy is an altogether too conventional and easy response to the emotional realities described. Sonnet XV opens with the husband entering the bedroom:

> I think she sleeps: it must be sleep, when low
> Hangs that abandoned arm towards the floor;

'Abandoned' is nicely poised between given over to abandon, and deserted. As the husband closes the door, he ironically reassures his wife, 'Sleep on: it is your husband, not your foe'. Throughout much of the sequence there is a disturbing blend of passion and violence in the husband's misery. Physical violence has already threatened in Sonnet IX with the husband's eroto-sadistic desire to take his wife's 'shape/To squeeze like an intoxicating grape', and this feeds the worrying irony of his reassurance in Sonnet XV. The implied threat swells, then bursts in the husband's identification with Othello which follows:

> The Poet's black stage-lion of wronged love
> Frights not our modern dames: – well if he did!

Othello's passion is ridiculously inappropriate for modern love, and the wish that this were not so ('well if he did!') is bombast. Othello's revenge was terrible; the husband's will be petty and modern:

> Now will I pour new light upon that lid,
> Full-sloping like the breasts beneath

He simply turns up a light to wake her. But as his eye moves from lid to breast, her beauty and his desire half-salvage the idea of the husband as a modern Othello – passionately jealous, hating while still loving his wife, and, of course, quite possibly wrong about her infidelity. This possibility is lost on the husband, who has come to confront his wife with the Victorian equivalent of Desdemona's scarf – a letter. The picture freezes as the sonnet ends with the wife waking and the husband standing over her with the evidence.

Sonnet XVI moves from bedroom to library, and from the present back into the past. The husband and wife are sitting round a glowing fire in their 'library-bower'. It is a domestic tableau that recalls Wallis's *Fireside Reverie*, for which Mary Nicolls had sat. It also recalls an earlier hearth-side scene in Sonnet VI, where the husband's inner feelings of pain, anger, and confusion are contrasted with the apparently peaceful domestic surface of their life. In Sonnet XVI the couple are sitting within earshot of company elsewhere in the house but are happy to be on their own, complete and self-sufficient with each other. But even in these early days happiness was fragile. A chance remark by the husband; ' "Ah yes!/Love dies!" I said: I never thought it less', blackens the fire and provokes tears from the wife. Her 'sharp scale of sobs' takes us back, via the fireside scene in Sonnet VI where the husband broods on his wife's tears as the sounds of 'Love's ghost', to the opening sonnet where she lay sobbing in bed. The history of their marriage is an echo-chamber of such moments. There never have been halcyon days, or at least there can be no certainty of this because the miseries of the present undermine any such assurance. Memory is tainted by the present and therefore the language of recollection subverts even the peace of the library-bower. From the beginning of this sonnet dissonant notes have disturbed the apparent harmony of the domestic scene. Their 'old shipwrecked days' of the opening line refers to their contented withdrawal from the world, but the image is also a disturbing one. In the opening chapter I showed how shipwreck was commonly used in the Victorian period as an image of domestic disaster. Lines 3 and 4, 'Joined slackly, we beheld the red chasm grow/Among the clicking coals', are ominous. 'Joined slackly' seems portentous as well as being an image of relaxation, and fault-lines are developing at the heart of the domestic scene in the 'red chasm' opening up in the fire. 'Time is whispering' (l. 6) even as they sit contentedly. The idyll is full of hints and warnings of future miseries. Love, even then, was precarious. The husband's glib, unmeant ' "Ah, yes!/Love dies!" ' destroys the moment, and with it the certainty there had ever been a time of love and sympathy. Comfort in the past, like every strategy for relief in this sequence, proves impossible.

Sonnet XVII, the last in this triptych of bourgeois domestic life, returns to the present and shifts to the dining-room. The husband and wife are having a dinner party at which they successfully act out their roles as host and hostess and enjoy doing so:

> Enamoured of an acting nought can tire,
> Each other, like true hypocrites, admire;
> Warm-lighted looks, Love's ephemerioe,
> Shoot gaily o'er the dishes and the wine.

In an ironic elaboration of the theatre imagery of Sonnet XV we are here presented with the stage of domestic life. Delighting in their roles, and easy with each other for the first time in the sequence, among their guests they 'waken envy of our happy lot' (l. 14). The contrast between public image and private reality is intensified by this echo of Keats's 'Ode to a Nightingale'. The 'full-throated ease' of the nightingale's song has become the clever conversation of the dinner table, not the expression of supreme happiness but the mask of pain and despair. The brilliance of the performance dazzles the guests, who, like those at Macbeth's table, 'see no ghost'. Recurring images of reflected light ('With sparkling surface-eyes we ply the ball'), like stage-lighting turned against the audience, blinds the guests to the true situation. What they have really seen is 'Love's corpse-light shine'.

A number of other sonnets exploit the gap between public image and private reality. There is the country house Christmas party in Sonnet XXIII, and another winter party in Sonnet XXXV, where the husband and wife must kiss each other during a game of Forfeits, 'To act this wedded lie!'. Sonnet XLI summarizes this particular emphasis:

> We two have taken up a lifeless vow
> To rob a living passion: dust for fire!

When private feelings are translated into public forms they wither. As *Jude the Obscure* has it, 'The letter killeth'. The substitution of 'lifeless' for 'lifelong' in the lines quoted above would have particularly pleased Hardy. In this collision between the public and private the former is almost always too strong:

> This truth is little known to human shades,
> How rare from their own instinct 'tis to feel!

We base our emotional life on false social values rather than relying on the more truthful promptings of our inner feelings. This is a typically Victorian opposition. Confronted by an inauthentic social world, the individual is forced back into a surer, less treacherous private realm. This however, does not always solve the problem, because the shadow of the public world continues to fall across that of the private. Hence we find that tension between the social and the personal which is characteristic of most major Victorian writers.

Modern Love, however, goes beyond this typical Victorian dualism and subjects the inner world itself to intense scrutiny. Sonnet XVII is more than just an exposure of the sham of the public face of domestic life. At the heart of this sonnet is a deep wonder that acting can be so easy when living is so difficult, and underlying this wonder, an existential uncertainty about the status and authenticity of feeling itself. Feeling and the prompting of our instincts are also troublesome and suspect. The husband's dead love for his wife refuses to stay buried and seizes his 'nursling new love by the throat' (Sonn. XL). 'Can I love one,/And yet be jealous of another?', he asks bewilderedly. Sexuality is a disturbing force throughout the sequence, refusing to come into line with the husband's other feelings. We see this particularly in Sonnets XLI and XLII, which are further domestic scenes but of an intensity unparalleled in other Victorian domestic narratives. In Sonnet XLI the husband and wife are downstairs preparing to go to their bedrooms:

> We have struck despair
> Into two hearts. O, look we like a pair
> Who for fresh nuptials joyfully yield all else?

Sonnet XLII moves upstairs. He follows her, catches her wrists, anguished, potentially violent. She half resists and the sonnet finishes with her unanswered, perhaps unanswerable question:

'You love. . .? love. . .? love. . .?' all on an indrawn breath.

Sonnet XLIII is set next morning, and is a sonnet of bitter disgust.

Nuptials of a kind, though hardly fresh, seem to have taken place:

> If I the death of Love had deeply planned,
> I never could have made it half so sure,
> As by the unblest kisses which upbraid
> The full-waked sense; or failing that, degrade!

Sexual attraction survives the death of love and heaps more earth on its grave. Instinct, too, has proved treacherous, the sonnet concludes: 'We are betrayed by what is false within'. The inner life is no more reliable than the social world. The husband discovers that inner and outer worlds are equally undependable and the retreat into a private realm often taken by Victorian writers is discovered to be a blind alley.

The sequence finishes with the suicide of the wife depicted in a death-bed scene in Sonnet XLIX. Late at night she calls the husband and he comes 'wondering to the bed':

> 'Now kiss me, dear! it may be, now!' she said.
> Lethe had passed those lips, and he knew all.

She has taken an overdose. Here, as in earlier domestic scenes, Victorian genre painting is both summoned up and reread. Death-bed scenes were a favourite subject for Victorian painters. Dying children watched over by grieving parents, and the bereaved wife with her children, were common tableaux. The mid-nineteenth-century cult of widowhood, most prominently exemplified by Queen Victoria, whose own widowhood in 1861 was celebrated in paintings, lithographs, and even cut-outs, perhaps explains why it was so often the husband's death which was represented.[20] Another prominent role played by women in Victorian paintings of death in the family was that of supporting others through their loss, as the title of George Elgar Hicks', 'Woman's Mission – Companion of Manhood' (1863) well illustrates. Common to most of these paintings is the representation of the family as united in the death of one of its members. Loss is balanced by this assurance. This, of course, is noticeably absent in *Modern Love*, where the death of the wife is the culmination of the couple's separateness in life.

Suicide in Victorian painting is usually reserved for social outcasts, female pariahs such as the fallen woman in G.F. Watts' *Found Drowned* (1850) or the homeless and destitute girl in the final print of Cruikshank's temperance series *The Drunkard's Children* (1848). Suicide within the respectable bourgeois household and as a response to the misery of marriage rather than to a fall from purity was outside the lexicon of Victorian painting. There are, of course, Victorian paintings depicting unhappy marriages, but pre-marital tension and discord was a more commonly treated subject. Calderon's 'Broken Vows' (1856) is a well-known example and there are many others. Incompatibilities were to be eliminated before marriage. As with literature, courtship rather than wedlock narratives were more frequent around mid-century. The obvious exceptions to this, such as *Past and Present* and Martineau's *The Last Day in the Old Home* (1861) make unhappy marriage secondary to their main subject; infidelity in Egg's painting, and gambling in Martineau's.[21]

Modern Love therefore ends with a death-bed scene which distorts rather than echoes apparently similar scenes in Victorian painting and writing. There is nothing reassuringly cultic about the death of the wife, and nor is there a family united in loss. Instead, there is a woman dying of an overdose and a solitary husband complicit in her suicide. The final sonnet begins, 'Thus piteously love closed what he begat'. In Meredith's poem modern love is not tragically terminated by death but is itself directly responsible for death. As elsewhere in the poem, conventions are used only to be subverted.

Another set of conventions the poem both uses and undermines is that of female stereotypes. These are mainly applied to the wife and cover a wide range of traditional and contemporary images of women: adulteress, angel, emasculator, murderess, nun, temptress, and witch. However, the attempts of both narrator and husband to apply these images and types to the wife are consistently thwarted by the poem's deeper recognition of a complexity which refutes all such categorization. The transition from one sonnet to another is one of the means whereby the inadequacy of stereotypes to the situation they are intended to summarize is exposed. For example, the label of murderess attached to his wife in the concluding line of Sonnet XI is cancelled by the husband's recognition of complexity ('the whole of life is mixed') in the following sonnet. A similar process often occurs in the very act of using a traditional image or stereotype. In the opening sonnet the wife's strangled sobs are likened to 'little gaping snakes,/Dreadfully venemous to him', and the hinted Medusa image becomes stronger as the sonnet goes on to describe her lying there 'stone-still'. But the conventional associations of this image have been reversed; it is Medusa herself who is turned to stone and becomes her own victim. This reversal complicates our response by intercepting the predictable stereotypes and judgements which the image had first raised.

The association of serpents and hair recurs in Sonnet VII when the wife 'issues radiant from her dressing-room', her hair dressed by a cupid barber:

> The gold-eyed serpent dwelling in rich hair
> Awakes beneath his magic whisks and twirls.
> His art can take the eyes from out my head,
> Until I see with eyes of other men

The Medusa image returns and becomes associated with an implied image of Eve, his wife as temptress and seducer, responsible for man's fall. This in turn feeds the current of sexual disgust which troubles the poem. The conflation of Medusa and Eve survives the sonnet intact, and indeed is pinned by its chilling concluding image – 'the steel-mirror of her smile' – but is immediately challenged by the opening lines of the following sonnet which discard stereotyping for complexity:

> Yet it was plain she struggled, and that salt
> Of righteous feeling made her pitiful.
> Poor twisting woman, so queenly beautiful.

The Medusa/Eve image does not allow for ambivalence or inner conflict, and these opening lines break down the confident assertions of the preceding sonnet. 'Pitiful' is finely balanced between 'deserving of pity' and 'pathetic'. 'The gold-eyed serpent' of Sonnet VII is reduced to 'Poor twisting worm', but this is then contradicted by 'so queenly beautiful'. The hesitant sympathy of the opening two lines is too intricate for either of the images which follow. The whole sonnet twists uncertainly from assertion to question, unable to settle, cancelling the bitter confidence of judgement and categorization expressed in Sonnet VII.

The lovesick friend in Sonnet XXI ('He who at love once laughed/Is in the weak rib by a fatal shaft/Struck through') is cynically presented as another victim of Eve. Again however, the glibness of this stereotyping is exposed as the focus shifts from the friend to the husband and wife, and the sonnet modulates from cynicism to deep sympathy in its concluding image of husband and wife: 'Her lost moist hand clings mortally to mine'. 'Lost' and 'mortally' are perfect, with a cadence reminiscent of one of the finest twentieth-century love lyrics, Auden's 'Lay your sleeping head, my love,/Human on my faithless arm'. They capture the intricacy of the relationship and refute the simplifications embodied in mythic images of women.

Both narrator and husband draw on traditional and contemporary images of women to tell their story, but none of these is adequate. Conventional male wisdom about women never becomes more than a defensive posture which the poem then quickly disturbs. Stereotypes clash with experience, and emblems (the violet for the wife, the rose for the lady) do not fit; attempts at generalization repeatedly break down.

The impossibility of generalization is not confined to the poem's failure to sustain its stereotypes of women. With the inner world of feeling and instinct as treacherous as the social world, indeed inseparable from it, there can be no basis for truth or certainty. In the absence of certainty, then, how are we to read the husband's claim at the end of Sonnet XLVIII, 'I feel the truth; so let the world surmise'? Do we accept this typically Victorian opposition between an authentic private realm and an uncomprehending world? And what do we make of the narrator's conclusion in Sonnet XLIX, 'Lethe had passed those lips, and he knew all'? Does the poem arrive at some kind of resolution in the manner of most Victorian narratives? I don't think so.

From the beginning of the poem both the narrator and the husband have a tendency to make gnomic and sententious pronouncements about life, love, and women, and for these then to be exposed as naïve or trite by the actual experience they are intended to reflect upon. The narrator is more prone to generalization but this is partly a function of the third-person narrative. When the husband imitates the narrator's tendency to abstraction and generalization, his voice is at its least convincing. In Sonnet XXII, for example, the husband watches his wife moving about the room, restless and unhappy, picking up household objects, staring into the mirror, then turning hastily away, and finally approaching him:

> and wavering pale before me there,
> Her tears fall still as oak-leaves after frost.
> She will not speak. I will not ask. We are
> League-sundered by the silent gulf between.

These fine lines, with their desolate and beautiful image of her tears, lead into a conclusion of the utmost banality:

> You burly lovers on the village green,
> Yours is a lower, and a happier star!

This is the *husband's* conclusion, not the poem's. He meets the impasse of their situation by looking out to a pastoral world which has been considered and rejected only four sonnets earlier, in Sonnet XVIII, where the husband's observation of dancing on a village green and memories of his own youthful 'rustic revels' ends in a wry mocking of pastoral solace:

> Heaven keep them happy! Nature they seem near.
> They must, I think, be wiser than I am;
> They have the secret of the bull and lamb.
> 'Tis true that when we trace its source,' tis beer.

This conclusion is forgotten by the husband, but not by the poem or the reader, in the trite sentimentality of the last two lines of Sonnet XXII.

Sonnet XLI opens with these lines:

> How many a thing which we cast to the ground,
> When others pick it up becomes a gem!
> We grasp at all the wealth it is to them;
> And by reflected light its worth is found.

Here again the husband's generalizing voice is distorting. Neither husband nor wife has cast the other to the ground. Their marriage is slowly and painfully disintegrating but they remain clinging to each other amid its wreckage. In the previous sonnet (XL) the husband has asked whether he can love the Lady and yet be jealous of his wife, and expressed the dread that his old love for his wife is killing his new love for the Lady. This question and this fear involves something more complex than the proverbial wisdom of the opening lines of Sonnet XLI can accommodate. Again the husband turns to simplifying generalization to escape from deadlock. As we have already seen, 'wisdom' of this kind provides no help in the upstairs scene which follows this sonnet.

I want to quote the whole of Sonnet XLVIII. It is the husband's final sonnet; in Sonnets XLIX and L the story is handed back to the narrator to conclude and summarize. It is also the most slippery, full of those evasive generalizations and half-truths I have noted in earlier sonnets:

> Their sense is with their senses all mixed in,
> Destroyed by subtleties these women are!
> More brain, O Lord, more brain! or we shall mar
> Utterly this fair garden we might win.
> Behold! I looked for peace, and thought it near.
> Our inmost hearts had opened, each to each.
> We drank the pure daylight of honest speech.
> Alas! that was the fatal draught, I fear.
> For when of my lost Lady came the word,
> This woman, O this agony of flesh!
> Jealous devotion bade her break the mesh,
> That I might seek that other like a bird.
> I do adore the nobleness! despise
> The act! She has gone forth, I know not where.
> Will the hard world my sentience of her share?
> I feel the truth; so let the world surmise.

This opens with another example of the husband taking refuge in gender-typing of a kind which the poem has persistently rejected. It also clashes with the quiet, elegiac scene at dusk of the preceding sonnet. There is nothing gender-specific in this poem about the mixing of sense and senses; the husband has been caught in this throughout the sequence. This opening should make us wary of what follows. Where is 'this fair garden we might win'? There is not a sign of it in the poem, nor of the evolutionary optimism which lines 3 and 4 express. In fact Sonnet XXX has used evolutionary ideas and images ironically to undercut the sonnet convention of love as durable and transcendent. And at this late stage in the poem the husband's claim to have 'looked for peace, and thought it near?' is hollow. Peace and fair gardens are no more than nostalgic yearnings in the world of modern love.

None of these lines can be taken at face value. Each is deceptive and self-deceiving. The sonnet is more than usually full of rhetoric, exclamation, and cliché, whereas the poem as a whole is suspicious of these registers and illustrates the disparity between the conventional poetic vocabulary of love and love's modern reality. 'Fatal draught' is one such cliché. In retrospect it becomes an anticipation of the wife's suicide, but its primary reference is to the opening of hearts and honest speech which the husband and wife have finally managed. Or have they? There is nothing in this sonnet, or elsewhere, which encourages me to accept the husband's account as authoritative. I'm not satisfied with his claim that what he tells his wife about his Lady is ultimately responsible for the end of their marriage and the wife's death. The poem has shown the causes of this to be much deeper. It is surely sentimental for the husband to suggest the wife kills herself in despair at his having a lover. 'Jealous devotion' is the *husband's* explanation of the wife's reaction; the *poem* has raised other possibilities. She has, after all, repeatedly shown signs of wishing to be free of him. 'Jealous devotion' is not her only reason for 'breaking the mesh'. All this makes it impossible for me to accept the husband's final claim to 'feel the truth', and to see *Modern Love* as another Victorian narrative which ends in recognition and self-knowledge. The sharp opposition of the last two lines between world and self, one hard and obtuse, the other tender and unerring, is not, as we have seen, one that the poem has been able to sustain. And what is the 'truth' that he feels? That they love each other? That they don't? That he has discovered some essential verity about human relationships? The world is indeed left to surmise.

The last two sonnets are spoken by the third-person narrator who recounts the death scene in Sonnet XLIX and sums up in Sonnet L. Sonnet XLIX seems to endorse the husband's claim to 'feel the truth': 'Lethe had passed those lips, and he knew all'. It is necessary here to look more closely at the relation between the two voices of the poem. The sequence begins in the third person, but from the opening sonnet the narrator is obviously much closer to the husband than the wife. This intimacy between narrator and husband is strengthened by the dual narrative structure of Sonnets III and VI to IX, in which the narrator opens the sonnet but gives way to the husband. Sometimes, as in Sonnet VI, the narrator's voice takes over again in the concluding lines, providing a third-person frame within which the husband's consciousness is dramatized. From Sonnet X onwards the husband's voice carries the narrative, relinquishing it when the wife's death is described in Sonnet XLIX and the sequence summarized in Sonnet L.

The complicity between narrator and husband works against third-person omniscience. I have already discussed the shared generalizing and simplifying tendencies of both voices. The narrator gives us a whole sonnet in this manner in Sonnet IV, which ends as tritely as the husband's own conclusion to Sonnet XXII:

> Oh, wisdom never comes when it is gold,
> And the great price we pay for it full worth:
> We have it only when we are half earth.
> Little avails that coinage to the old!

The husband's simplifications are usually revised by experience, but in these early sonnets the narrator's truisms remain uncorrected. By the end of the poem, however, the narrator's voice is quieter, subtler, and more authoritative, although this is not to say that it has become all-seeing. Omniscience is impossible in a poem in which all truth is relative. The husband doesn't 'know all'; he can't, because no one can. The narrator remains too close to the husband to claim omniscience. For example, the lines in Sonnet XLIX, 'That night he learned how silence best can speak/The awful things when Pity pleads for Sin', are still from the husband's perspective. 'Sin' is unsatisfactory because it is uncomprehending; it translates the complexity of experience into allegory. The narrator's concluding generalizations in Sonnet L remain inadequate, but they are perhaps as adequate as generalizations can be. At least they are no longer manifestly wrong or misleading. Sonnet L seems to accept that there could be no final point of settlement or accommodation for 'this ever-diverse pair', and the summary which follows this crucial recognition is less flawed than earlier narrative generalizations. The picture of the husband and wife becomes almost mythic:

> Lovers beneath the singing sky of May,
> They wandered once; clear as the dew on flowers

The husband has never felt certain of this Edenic past but does know that they once shared happier times before being caught in the 'snare' of marriage. The institutionalization of love in marriage as a fall from grace, the loss of paradise, has been an important emphasis in the poem, and the couple's wish to regain their prelapsarian state has helped sour their marriage:

> But they fed not on the advancing hours:
> Their hearts held cravings for the buried day

Lines such as these do not deserve John Lucas's dismissal as 'pious inanities'. They are not the definitive judgement on this 'ever-diverse pair' (such judgements are impossible) but they are subtler and more flexible than the narrator's earlier ones. Denis Donoghue puts it well when he says that Sonnet L allows a final sense of the range of feeling through which the poem has passed. Platitude in this concluding sonnet is amended by an ironic self-consciousness (as in 'hot for certainties'), but it is right that it should still be present. Platitude has had an important function in the poem, both dramatizing the deficiencies of conventional wisdom and exposing the difficulties of constructing alternative explanations which remain true to the texture of experience. There is no definitive moral pattern in Sonnet L, as the formulations 'ever-diverse' and 'tragic hints' acknowledge; the pattern offered is provisional, qualified, and finally half-obscured in the poem's concluding lines:

> In tragic hints here see what evermore
> Moves dark as yonder midnight ocean's force,
> Thundering like ramping hosts of warrior horse,
> To throw that faint thin line upon the shore!

The narrator has moved well beyond the glib certainties of the early sonnets and his voice has become more or less consonant with the poem.

IV

In the second section of this chapter I claimed that the treatment of marriage in *Modern Love* exemplified a larger cultural pattern. I now want to look more closely at how *Modern Love*, in its highly distinctive way, was shaped by changes in nineteenth-century bourgeois marriage practice and explored some effects of these changes.

The poem dramatizes the exclusivity of bourgeois marriage as it developed in nineteenth-century England. The shift in marriage choice away from parents and towards the couple getting married, and the separation of work from home, contributed to the process whereby the middle-class family became increasingly closed to outsiders and all but its nuclear members. Mrs Beeton was wary of emotional attachments which might distract a wife and mother from her primary duties:

> Friendships should not be hastily formed, nor the heart given, at once, to every new-comer . . . With respect to the continuance of friendship . . . it may be found necessary, in some cases, for a mistress to relinquish, on assuming the responsibility of a household, many of those commenced in the earlier part of her life[22]

In *Modern Love* there is a complete absence of parents or family supervision of the kind we saw in *The Princess* or *The Bothie*. Only in Sonnet XVI, the sonnet which looks back to their 'old shipwrecked days', do we glimpse such a presence; several rooms away from where the couple sit, 'The nodding elders mixed good wine with chat'. The surrounding family has all but gone. *Modern Love* illustrates the tendency towards exclusive, companionate marriage in a domestic setting emptied of relatives and friends, at its most extreme. A husband and a wife are left facing each other, unsupported except for the false estimate of the social world. And while illustrating this tendency, *Modern Love* also demystifies the idea of the home as a protected and ordered space in a hostile and competitive world. The home itself has become intense and hostile, analogous to rather than distinct from the outside world of economic and social competition. By refusing to sentimentalize domestic life as an ideal against which to measure the fallen state of the world, *Modern Love* avoids the characteristic Victorian antithesis between public and private spheres.

The privatization of marriage was accompanied by rising expectations of the emotional pleasures, comfort, and solace it was meant to provide. In *Middlemarch* it is not only the ardent and idealistic Dorothea but also her mildewed husband Casaubon who is affected by these expectations and disappointed when they are not fulfilled. As it became widely accepted that marriage should be based on conjugal friendship and decorated with romantic love, the sweet icing on the domestic cake, expectations were bound to be disappointed. Meredith's poem explores some of the consequences of this union of romantic love and marriage. Disappointed expectations and the failure of pre-marital bliss to survive the translation of love into marriage are recurring ideas in *Modern Love*. Love is paramount, marriage kills love, but love outside marriage seems impossible. 'Wedded lovers' (Sonn. XXI) becomes a kind of oxymoron, and marriage a life-sentence rather than life's fulfilment. The marriage in *Modern Love* is beyond the reach of legal remedies. Although the divorce legislation of 1857 had made it relatively cheap and easy for a husband to divorce his wife on the grounds of her adultery, in *Modern Love* it is never clear whether the wife has committed adultery. The poem focuses relentlessly on those pressures within marriage which legislation had not touched but which were nevertheless the product of changing social definitions and practices. The intimacy and durability of nineteenth-century marriage became a miserable combination when intimacy failed.

Marriage also became increasingly important during the nineteenth century as *the* means of ordering and regulating sexual relations. This involved different moral codes for men and women. In particular, it stressed sexual exclusivity for women, and a common, though not universal, characterization of women as sexless. Acton spoke for a widely held belief:

> I am ready to maintain that there are many females who never feel any sexual excitement whatever. Others, again, immediately after each period, do become to a limited degree, capable of experiencing it; but this capacity is temporary, and may entirely cease until the next menstrual period. Many of the best mothers, wives, and managers of households, know little of or are careless about sexual indulgences. Love of home, of children, and of domestic duties are the only passions they feel.[23]

Sexual feeling in women, therefore, was widely regarded as pathological. *Modern Love* interrogated and challenged these norms. The marriage of its protagonists has ceased to order and regulate their sexual relations, or at least this is their mutual fear. The expectation of monogamy and its high valuation provokes deep fear of its transgression. The strict merging of the sexual and the familial is shown to be a cause of great strain within their marriage. The wife certainly isn't sexless, but nor is she the polar opposite of the sexless stereotype – whore, seductress, or nymphomaniac. We have seen how the poem resists the conventional pure–impure antithesis, just as it deconstructs other antitheses (e.g. public–private) which helped structure the dominant bourgeois consciousness in the Victorian period. This acknowledgement of female sexuality and refusal to treat it as pathological helps undermine the idea of separate moral codes for men and women. The poem does this quite explicitly in Sonnet XX, when the husband discovers a memento, 'a wanton-scented tress', which forces a recognition and a question:

> If for those times I must ask charity,
> Have I not any charity to give?

His wife's suspected infidelity is confronted by evidence of his own, and the double standard of conventional moral judgement is exposed. The poem shows husband and wife to be similarly placed. Each is unable fully to accept that sexuality must be contained within marriage, yet is guilty at being unable to do so. The strict merging of the sexual and the familial, with the double standard offering an escape route for husbands, is shown to be oppressive and damaging. But the attempt to find alternative practices and establish less rigid and sexist codes results in impasse and misery. Both husband and wife remain deeply embedded in the society whose values they have internalized but transgressed, unable to accept each other's transgressions but also unable to condemn.

This account of some of the changes in nineteenth-century marriage would be disputed by Alan Macfarlane who has rejected the idea that companionate marriage and its accompanying domestic ideology emerged during the eighteenth and nineteenth centuries. In his work on the diary of Ralph Josselin, Macfarlane claimed to find 'modern' customs and attitudes operating in the seventeenth century, and his most recent work, *Marriage and Love in England 1300–1840 (1986)*, argues for the continuity of English marriage and many family practices from as far back as the later medieval period.[24] Macfarlane's starting point is the second edition of Malthus's *Essay on Population* (1803), from which he abstracts certain assumptions about the nature and purposes of marriage which would have been self-evident and 'natural' to anyone living at the end of the eighteenth century. These include independent residence after marriage, a fairly egalitarian relationship between husband and wife, monogamy, unbreakable marriage, permissive remarriage, and centrally, personal choice in marriage: 'Both as to when one married and whether one married at all, it was confidently assumed that the matter was open to choice'. This 'Malthusian marriage system', compared with most prevailing in the world at this time, was highly distinctive.[25] Macfarlane then asks for how long the central features of this system had existed. In particular, he looks at marriage choice, attitudes to childbearing, companionate marriage, and the romantic idea of marriage. Each of these features is traced back at least as far as the time of Chaucer, perhaps even into the Anglo-Saxon period. All the main features of the system Malthus took for granted had existed for more or less as long as records allow us to confirm. This system had sometimes produced different results in changed economic circumstances, as for example in the eighteenth century, when a larger proportion of the population married and the age at which people had children dropped, but the framework of decision-making about marriage and its rules and customs remained the same.[26] Macfarlane's general argument is similar to that of Linda Pollock's on attitudes to childhood discussed in my opening chapter. Family practices, particularly those of marriage, have persisted fundamentally unchanged for many centuries.

Macfarlane establishes this continuity by concentrating on a limited number of basic features treated at a high level of generality. A similar method of argument could be used to establish that the game of cricket has remained essentially the same since Beldham and others in the Hambledon club established basic techniques of batting and bowling in the 1760s. Wickets, a bat, and a ball are still necessary. The bowler still tries to hit the wicket with the ball; the batsman still tries to prevent him from doing so, and also to score runs. Nevertheless, Beldham and a modern international cricketer would have difficulty in recognizing that they played the same game. In Macfarlane's book this method of argument is reinforced by frequent comparisons between the English marriage system and patently non-Malthusian ones of non-European peasant or tribal societies. Contrasts on this scale mask shifts, developments, and distinctions within the history of English marriage practice, and reinforce the picture of an essentially unchanging system between Chaucer and Malthus. It is as if I were to support my case for the unchanging nature of cricket by constantly comparing it with football, pointing out that cricket in the eighteenth century didn't have goal posts either.

I want to look more closely at several of Macfarlane's arguments. The issue of marriage choice is crucial because unless Macfarlane can demonstrate 'that marriage was a matter of individual contract rather than a result of relations of social status'[27] his arguments about companionate and romantic-love marriage become very difficult to sustain. I looked at this question in my opening chapter and found that the literary evidence supported the arguments of Stone, Anderson, and others that the balance of power in marriage choice was shifting away from parents and towards children during the eighteenth and nineteenth centuries. (This refers primarily to those social classes in which marriage involved substantial property transactions. Although Macfarlane has criticized Stone for being primarily concerned with the upper social strata, his own sources are predominantly from these social groups.)

Take *Tom Jones,* for example, in which Mrs Weston tries to break her niece Sophia's attachment to Tom, arguing that in polite society, 'women consider matrimony, as men do offices of public trust, only as the means of making their fortunes, and of advancing themselves in the world'.[28] Later she returns to the same theme, telling Sophia that marriage should be considered 'as a fund in which prudent women deposit their fortunes to the best advantage, in order to receive a larger interest for them than they could have elsewhere'. Dislike of one's spouse, she argues, is no impediment to marriage: 'I have known many couples, who have entirely disliked each other, lead very comfortable, genteel lives'. Sophia's response that she will never marry contrary to her father's inclinations if he won't force her to marry against her own, cuts no ice with her aunt: 'The alliance between the families is the principal matter. You ought to have a greater regard for the honour of your family than for your own person' (Bk 7, Ch. 3, pp. 304–6). Squire Weston, Sophia's father, and his sister Mrs Weston, agree about very little. He is Tory, anti-city, and anti-Hanoverian; she is Whig, metropolitan, and pro-court. Mrs Weston's attitudes to marriage are considerably more sophisticated than her brother's, who we learn had treated his wife as 'a faithful upper servant'. She only saw her husband at meals, from which 'she retired about five minutes after the other servants, having only stayed to drink the King over the Water'. Even so, they had heartily disliked each other, and since her death Weston's favourite invective had become, 'If my wife was alive now, she would be glad of this' (Bk 7, Ch. 4, pp. 309–10). His response to Sophia's refusal to marry Blifil is to lock her up until she changes her mind. Mrs Weston favours persuasion by family pressure. Both, however, for all their differences, are in complete agreement that Sophia should marry the man chosen for her. Of course, there is satiric exaggeration in these scenes, but this does not make the attitudes expressed unrepresentative. Rather it is because they are representative that Fielding is concerned to satirize them. The novel as a whole endorses love marriage, but the dominant attitudes of the society in which Tom and Sophia struggle to translate their love into marriage are manifestly those of the Westons.

The conflict between parents and children over marriage choice is a recurring narrative in eighteenth and nineteenth-century writing. It is not one which has survived with any significance or vigour into the twentieth century. It just won't do for Macfarlane to claim, 'Just as today parents may attempt to introduce their children to suitable partners, and dissuade them from unsuitable ones, so too it was in the past'.[29] That neat construction, 'Just as . . . so too', elides all that has changed.

This raises the question of the use of literature as historical evidence. My own position is that literature has more or less the same status as other kinds of historical evidence. It can tell us a great deal about attitudes and values, about how the world was mentally constructed in any given period. Like any historical source, it represents a particular point of view, shaped by factors such as class, gender, and region, and also by literary traditions and genre. It must therefore be used critically, with full consideration given to other conflicting points of view. Nevertheless, there is a sense in which all history is stories, and all stories are history, with the teller always as important as the tale. This isn't a particularly startling or idiosyncratic position and it is quite likely that Macfarlane would find it acceptable. Certainly, he uses literary evidence to support his own case, and I want to look at how he does so, particularly in relation to his arguments about companionate and romantic-love marriage.

In support of his claim for the longevity and uniqueness of love marriage in English culture, Macfarlane cites C.S. Lewis's *The Allegory of Love*. I cannot find the lines Macfarlane attributes to Lewis,[30] but it is true that Lewis's arguments, particularly in relation to Spenser, are congenial to Macfarlane's position. Spenser, Lewis claimed, was 'the greatest among the founders of that romantic conception of marriage which is the basis of all our love literature from Shakespeare to Meredith'.[31] Lewis, however, is not the last word on the subject. The dominant tradition of love poetry in English literature before the nineteenth century had little to do with marriage. Macfarlane, in his use of literary evidence, conflates the two. For example, *The Princess*, described as the apotheosis of love-marriage poetry, is grouped together with Donne's 'Extasie'. *The Princess*, as we have seen, is indeed a love-marriage poem, although hardly one in which freedom of marriage choice and companionate or romantic marriage is regarded as axiomatic. Like Tennyson's other 'arranged marriage' poems I discussed in Chapter 3, *The Princess* suggests that parental control over marriage choice and lineage marriage were still significant in the nineteenth century. Tennyson, of course, had experienced this himself. 'The Extasie', on the other hand, is a great love poem which has nothing to do with marriage. In fact, Macfarlane's summary half-recognizes this:

> The Metaphysical poets – Donne, Herbert, Marvell, King and others – celebrated love with an intensity and seriousness which it would be difficult to believe could be surpassed. Here, surely, was a passionate outpouring on love within *and outside* marriage that could not be rivalled [emphasis added].[32]

Again this won't do. The existence of love is not in question, although arguably it has meant different things at different times. The issue is the relationship between romantic love and marriage. 'Passionate outpourings on love outside marriage', by far the most common form of Metaphysical love poetry, do nothing for Macfarlane's argument. Of the poets he mentions, King is one he could perhaps have used. Henry King's 'Exequuy' is a deeply felt poem on the death of his young wife. Here would seem to be literary evidence for the existence of companionate and romantic marriage. King's poem, however, is most unusual. There are very few love elegies on the death of one's spouse before the nineteenth century and a great many since. I have argued elsewhere that poetry of this kind constituted a new sub-genre, the domestic elegy, which emerged during the nineteenth century. There are one or two examples of this kind of poem in earlier centuries, notably Milton's sonnet 'Methought I saw my late espoused saint'. These, however, lack the overtly biographical and domestic basis of, for example, Patmore's bereavement odes, Hardy's *Poems of 1912–13*, or most recently Douglas Dunn's *Elegies*. It was most unusual to write a poem mourning the death of one's spouse before the nineteenth century.[33]

Examples of marriages in earlier centuries where the couple liked or loved each other do not prove that romantic love was the primary motive for marriage. Companionship or love, when it existed, must have been very welcome. Even Mrs Weston might have acknowledged this. But affection or love were not essential preconditions of marriage, nor were their absence or disappearance sufficient reason for ending a marriage. Literary as well as other evidence suggests there has been a significant shift in both these areas over the last couple of centuries.

Another important criticism of Macfarlane's arguments about the nature and purpose of marriage has been made by Rosalind Mitchison.[34] She points out that Macfarlane takes almost no account of how women viewed marriage and assumes that once the marital decision was taken by the male, the grateful female would acquiesce. Macfarlane's idea of companionate marriage ignores the possibility that what was companionship for the male might well be simply hard work for the female. Mitchison argues that marriage was the only way for women to achieve or retain status and often the only means of ensuring economic security. In these circumstances personal feelings were likely to be subdued by material pressures. Finally, her point that Macfarlane ignores the changing position of women over time is not difficult to explain. Macfarlane's whole case rests on the absence of change.

All history is contemporary history. Stone's *The Family, Sex and Marriage* is clearly influenced by the liberalism of the late 1960s and early 1970s. Macfarlane's *Marriage and Love in England* is unmistakably a product of the more conservative 1980s. On the one hand, it is proudly insular. Macfarlane's insistence that the Malthusian marriage system was peculiar to the Anglo-Saxon world becomes distinctly ideological. His fascination with the peculiarities of the English, whether compared with West African societies or neighbouring European ones, becomes at times a kind of Podsnappery. Other systems do as they do; this island has been peculiarly blest. Podsnap, however, would have been less pitying of the rest of the world if he could have seen the future as described by Macfarlane. The Malthusian revolution 'is sweeping the world today'.[35] Podsnap's isolationist pride in a providentially bestowed British Constitution has become a neo-colonialist satisfaction at the spread of English marriage and family practices around the world. Although Britain is no longer a significant imperial power, the extension of its influence continues.

The tenacity of the marriage system Macfarlane describes rests on, and is a particular version of, his larger view of English society from the late Middle Ages to the present day as uniquely peaceful, stable, and prosperous. It was not just marriage which persisted more or less unchanged, but the whole nation. Macfarlane argues that at least as early as the fourteenth century, England had moved away from what he terms 'the political and economic cliff-hanging situation':

> the English population ... was relatively affluent in clothing, in diet, in housing .... All the evidence suggests a prosperous society, particularly in that very large middling rank for which England was famed. ... Alongside this relative economic affluence went political security. England was seldom marched over by warring armies, nor subject to a particularly extortionate state. Taxation was light, and the lords kept in check. Yet the state was powerful enough to reduce physical insecurity by providing the 'insurance' of a well organized and effective system of self-policing, courts and law. Relative to other peasantries in both Europe and the rest of the world, it would seem that the English peoples were indeed fortunate through many centuries.[36]

This carefully landscaped picture of English history allows no more than the occasional and gentle undulation. A uniquely privileged past ensured the early development and durability of the Malthusian marriage system. Macfarlane later seems to reverse cause and effect, suggesting that this marriage system was itself a necessary if not sufficient cause of market capitalism, which as readers of *The Origins of English Individualism* will be aware, he thinks had developed several centuries earlier than is commonly thought. He argues that by the thirteenth and fourteenth centuries:

> the central acquisitive ethic, the desire for profit, was widespread.... This acquisitiveness fits with a system of widespread individual property, guaranteed by a developed system of law and powerful government which supported such an ethic. It also fits with a social structure in which there were many grades of status and wealth and in which it was relatively easy to move up and down.... Finally, all this was set against a background of considerable and widely distributed affluence. ... Thus those economic, social and political preconditions for the Malthusian family system, that set of interrelated features which we label 'individualism' or 'capitalism', were already strongly developed. They had probably generated, and continued to maintain, that peculiar marital and demographic structure that was then 'exported' to North America and is now spreading to much of the world. Money, profit, contract, mobility, individualism, competition, had all asserted themselves. Behind the antique modes of speech and the different technology, there existed a recognizably 'modern' world.[37]

This reads more like science fiction than history. Some time-warp has allowed the recreation of Thatcher's England back in the Middle Ages. Stone has pointed to a hidden ideological agenda lurking behind Macfarlane's account of English history as recurring proof of the merits of individual economic behaviour over collective social control.[38] There is, however, nothing hidden in a passage such as the one above.

For all Macfarlane's strictures on Whig history[39] there is a Whiggish inevitability, albeit static rather than evolving, about the kind of history he writes. *Marriage and Love in England* reads like a variant on an historical myth closely associated with nineteenth-century Whig historians, that of Anglo-Saxon freedom and the Norman yoke.[40] Stubbs, Kemble, and Freeman looked back to an idealized Anglo-Saxon past in order to develop a theory of the continuity of the English Constitution, interrupted by Norman conquest and the loss of original freedoms, but latterly recovered. In Macfarlane's hands the continuity of the Constitution is replaced by a theory of the continuity of the family originating from a medieval though not specifically Anglo-Saxon past. In this case, however, there is no Norman yoke or other impediment to the enduring character of the English marriage and family system. Freedom of marriage choice, companionate marriage, and romantic love as the basis for marriage become part of the freeborn Englishman's birthright, and the abiding nature of this system testimony to its contemporary significance.

V

It should be clear from my discussion of Macfarlane's arguments, if not before, that family matters of the kind discussed in this book have been, and still are, of deep social and political importance. It has been my contention that this became particularly so during the nineteenth century, although I am not suggesting that these issues had never previously been discussed. There must always have been conflicting attitudes to family and marriage practices, both between and within classes and genders, and these have affected how people lived. To deny this, as Macfarlane does, is to bleach history of the variety of its patterns and colours. I have no wish to do likewise by suggesting that before the middle of the eighteenth century the central issues this book has been concerned with were entirely unproblematic. Nevertheless, they did take on new urgency and significance in the rapidly changing context of the years after 1750.

By the middle of the nineteenth century the marriage relationship had become a highly contradictory one. The sentimentalization and idealization of marriage conflicted with its legal reality as a contract involving the subordination of women. This reality, in its turn, conflicted with the slow but discernible movement towards equality between the sexes. A wide gap was opening up between cultural norms and the actual experience of marriage.

One way of dramatizing this gap is to point out that *Modern Love* was published one year after *Mrs Beeton's Book of Household Management*. While Mrs Beeton was codifying Victorian domestic ideology, Meredith was performing an autopsy in the bedroom. This is not meant as a frivolous comparison. As well as being produced within and against several specific literary traditions, *Modern Love* was also part of a broader mid-nineteenth-century discourse on marriage, gender roles, domestic life and family codes and practices.

Janet Horowitz Murray's collection *Strong-Minded Women* gives a sample of the different points of view and experiences of women on these matters. Mrs Beeton and Sarah Stickney Ellis speak for only one position, even though their voices are still commonly thought to be the last word on these matters for the Victorians. Florence Nightingale writes bitterly of the young middle-class woman as a household prisoner.[41] Annie Besant describes the ignorance and inexperience with which young women enter marriage.[42] Caroline Norton give her classic account of Victorian middle-class domestic violence.[43] Harriet Martineau and Frances Power Cobbe speak of the advantages and pleasures of remaining single.[44] Most representative perhaps are the voices of Elizabeth Gaskell and Charlotte Brontë, torn between womanly duties as wives and daughters and the development of their own talents.[45] Even in those voices which speak for the dominant ideology shrewd notes of self-interest and survival can be heard. There were practical as well as heaven-sent reasons for fulfilling one's expected role. Life for most middle-class women would become more difficult if they didn't; keeping your husband content could be a way of winning some space for yourself. There are subtexts to be found even in Mrs Beeton.

This discourse was even more various than Murray's collection reveals. Barbara Taylor's *Eve and the New Jerusalem* has rediscovered the world of Owenite socialism of the 1830s and 1840s and its radical ideas on marriage and the family. Robert Owen's *Lectures on the Marriages of the Priesthood in the Old Immoral World*, published as a tract in 1835, was an attack on Christian morality and patriarchal power. It went through five editions in six years and brought the marriage issue back into radical politics and the public sphere.[46] From the late 1830s to the mid-1840s Owenite feminists took the Woman Question out to the country through lectures and writing. Emma Martin was one of these. Unhappily married to a Bristol businessman, she left her husband and joined the Owenites, forfeiting her property to her husband as a result. Her lectures as she toured the country in the early 1840s often attracted crowds of between 2,000 and 3,000, and even more when her subject was marriage and divorce.[47] Owenite marriage doctrine argued for voluntary sexual liaisons and the equality of both partners within them. These ideas were little heard in the years following the collapse of the Owenite movement in the late 1840s, but they must figure nevertheless in any full account of the mid-nineteenth-century discourse on marriage and the family. They had a negative influence on the pragmatic reformism and suspicion of radical sexual politics which characterized feminism in the 1850s, 1860s and 1870s. They were also, however, in their attack on marriage and single family arrangements, a radical version of the dissatisfaction with contemporary domestic existence we have heard among Janet Horowitz Murray's voices and in *Modern Love*. Taylor has argued that Owen's communalist ideas were in part a response to the increased isolation of domestic life and an attempt to recoup a wider context for domestic existence.[48] We have already seen how *Modern Love* explores the consequences of the radically narrowed domestic base of nineteenth-century marriage.

Modern Love is a sophisticated literary text whose focus is private and psychological rather than social, legal, or polemical, but it was within this wider discourse I have outlined that it was ·produced, and its formal literary qualities put to work. The narrowed base of nineteenth-century domestic life could render marriage intensely claustrophobic. *Modern Love*, like many Victorian paintings, depicts those oppressive domestic interiors, unpopulated rooms full of household objects, which were both cause and expression of the maximum insecurity prison of marriage. It is a report from within, which explores the subjective consequences of changes and stresses in domestic life, and the effects of these on the psycho-sexual experience of marriage.

NOTES

1. Alethea Hayter, *Mrs Browning: A Poet's Work and Its Setting* (London: Faber, 1962), p. 163.

2. Ioan Williams (ed.) *Meredith: The Critical Heritage* (London: Routledge & Kegan Paul, 1971), p. 18.
3. John Lucas, 'Meredith as poet', in Ian Fletcher (ed.) *Meredith Now* (London: Routledge & Kegan Paul, 1971), p. 28.
4. Willams, p. 100.
5. ibid., p. 92.
6. *Great Victorian Pictures* (London: Arts Council – Exhibition Catalogue, 1978), p. 27.
7. The term is John Bayley's; see 'The puppet of a dream', *Times Literary Supplement*, October 27, 1978.
8. Denis Donoghue, 'From the country of the blue', *New York Review of Books*, 22 February 1979. Lucas, p. 23.
9. Dorothy M. Mermin, 'Poetry as fiction: Meredith's *Modern Love*', *English Literary History* 43: 115–16. Arline Golden, ' "The Game of Sentiment": tradition and innovation in Meredith's *Modern Love*', *ELH* 40. Stephen Watt, 'Neurotic responses to a failed marriage: George Meredith's *Modern Love*', *Mosaic*, Winter 1984.
10. C.L. Cline (ed.) *The Letters of George Meredith* (Oxford: Claredon Press, 1970), Vol. 1, pp. 148, 160.
11. ibid., Vol. 2, p. 1065.
12. Biographical details in this section come from Jack Lindsay, *George Meredith* (London: Bodley Head, 1956); Lionel Stevenson, *The Ordeal of George Meredith* (New York: Russell & Russell, 1967); Diane Johnson, *The True History of the First Mrs Meredith and Other Lesser Lives* (New York: Alfred Knopf, 1972).
13. Mermin, pp. 101–4.
14. Diane Johnson, pp. 84, 94. It certainly influenced Rossetti. Doughty has pointed out that Rossetti's frequent imaging of death as a little child dates from this period, as does his intensified association of love with death. Oswald Doughty, *A Victorian Romantic* (London: Oxford University Press, 1963), p. 280.
15. Cline, Vol. 1, p. 128.
16. Doughty, p. 301.
17. Thackeray, *Vanity Fair* (Harmondsworth: Penguin, 1976), Ch. 26, p. 310.
18. Courtship, seduction, and wedlock are the three main narrative structures described by Joseph Allen Boone, 'Wedlock as deadlock and beyond: closure and the Victorian marriage ideal', *Mosaic*, Winter 1984.
19. The text used is from Phyllis B. Bartlett's edition, *The Poems of George Meredith* (New Haven & London: Yale University Press, 1978), Vol 1.
20. John Morley, *Death, Heaven and the Victorians* (London: Studio Vista, 1971), plates 25, 30.
21. T.J. Edelstein has argued, however, that close attention to the words and images in Egg's painting shows it to be the representation of an

unhappy marriage rather than a marriage ending in unhappiness because of the wife's infidelity. This reading brings it closer to *Modern Love* than any other Victorian painting I know. See Eldelstein, 'Augustus Egg's Triptych: a narrative of Victorian adultery', *The Burlington Magazine*, April 1983.
22. Isabella Beeton, *Beeton's Book of Household Management* (1861), in Janet Horowitz Murray (ed.) *Strong-Minded Women* (Harmondsworth: Penguin, 1984), p. 151.
23. Murray, pp. 127–8.
24. Alan Macfarlane, *Marriage and Love in England: Modes of Reproduction 1300–1840* (Oxford: Basil Blackwell, 1986). Also, Macfarlane, *The Family Life of Ralph Josselin* (London: Cambridge University Press, 1970), and Macfarlane (ed.) *The Diary of Ralph Josselin 1616–1683* (London: Oxford University Press, 1976).
25. Macfarlane, *Marriage and Love in England*, pp. 35–6.
26. ibid., pp. 25–30, and passim.
27. ibid., p. 291.
28. Fielding, *Tom Jones* (Harmondsworth: Penguin, 1982), Bk 6, Ch. 13, p. 292.
29. Macfarlane, *Marriage and Love in England*, p. 132.
30. ibid., p. 121.
31. C.S. Lewis, *The Allegory of Love* (New York: Oxford University Press, 1958), p. 360.
32. Macfarlane, *Marriage and Love in England*, pp. 184–5.
33. Edmond, as in note 66, p. 41.
34. Rosalind Mitchison, 'Man and wife', *London Review of Books*, 22 May 1986.
35. Macfarlane, *Marriage and Love in England*, p. 322.
36. ibid., pp. 103–4.
37. ibid., pp. 336–7.
38. Lawrence Stone, 'Illusions of a changeless family', *TLS*, 16 May 1986.
39. Macfarlane, *Marriage and Love in England*, p. 333.
40. See Christopher Hill, 'The Norman yoke', in *Puritanism and Revolution* (London: Mercury Books, 1965).
41. Murray, pp. 90–2.
42. ibid., pp. 112–14.
43. ibid., pp. 133–8.
44. ibid., pp. 161–4.
45. ibid., pp. 89–90, 95–6, 160.
46. Barbara Taylor, *Eve and the New Jerusalem* (London: Virago, 1983), pp. 183–5.
47. ibid., pp. 140–1.
48. ibid., pp. 230, 245.

7
Conclusion

One of the problems I encountered in writing this book was the lack of a comprehensive account of the reformation of the middle-class family in the nineteenth century. Large studies of the family, such as Stone and Macfarlane's are based in earlier periods. Stone's concluding section on post-1800 family types is the weakest in his book, and Macfarlane too is essentially an early-modern historian who extrapolates his knowledge of earlier periods forward into the nineteenth century. Detailed studies of particular aspects of the Victorian family abound, and I am indebted to many of them, but throughout the writing of this book I felt the need of a synthesizing account based on the detailed study of source material. Just as I was finishing the book, such a study appeared. Davidoff and Hall's *Family Fortunes: Men and Women of the English Middle Class 1780–1850* can in many ways be seen as a companion volume to E.P.Thompson's *The Making of the English Working Class*. Although very different in approach from Thompson's work, it could well have been subtitled 'The Making of the Victorian Middle Class'. The book's subject is the construction of a new middle-class identity in the last decades of the eighteenth and first half of the nineteenth centuries. It is concerned with how new patterns of social life were formulated and codified, and with what brought these changes about. In this concluding section I want to summarize many of their main arguments, and in doing so step back from the material I have been dealing with and try to place my main texts within the new

Conclusion 241

social formation Davidoff and Hall describe.[1]

From the second half of the eighteenth century middle-class manufacturers, merchants, and professionals sought to convert their economic strength into cultural and moral authority by developing new values and patterns of social life. These were defined partly in opposition to what was seen as, on the one hand, aristocratic licence, and, on the other, proletarian coarseness. Central to this process was the heavily gendered character of the new class formation. Men and women occupied radically different positions within this newly mapped social world. Middle-class identity was 'refracted through a gendered lens' (p. 30). A new model of masculinity was formulated eschewing extravagance and display and based on piety, responsibility, work, and domesticity (pp. 110–13). Middle-class manhood was now legitimated by the ability to secure the needs of its dependants. Business and domesticity therefore became the central elements in this refashioned idea of masculinity (pp. 15–18). Middle-class femininity was its natural complement, confined to the domestic sphere and removed to the suburbs as the physical separation of workplace and home became increasingly prevalent. Its ideal type was the Christian wife and mother, spiritually equal but socially subordinate to her husband. Davidoff and Hall show how closely these ideas were allied to the evangelical revival of the late eighteenth century (pp. 90ff), but also how quickly they became secularized so that by the 1830s and 1840s the idea of separate male and female spheres had become simple common sense for most middle-class people. (p. 149). The middle-class family had been reorganized around a rigidly defined idea of sexual difference.

Of course, these ideas were not entirely new, but between 1780 and 1850 they came to represent the dominant values of a newly ascendant class, and began to influence family life and social behaviour in upper and lower classes as well. In the early part of this period writers on domestic matters had developed their ideas on sexual difference and offered advice on middle-class family life in the knowledge that their views were not widely shared. (p. 176). By mid-century, however, the plethora of middle-class domestic magazines gave advice without urgency, confident that the definition, boundaries and categories by which the middle class shaped and understood itself, and the world, were axiomatic (p. 187).

There were many reasons for this hegemony. New middle-class forms of capitalist enterprise required consumers as well as producers. The creation of a private sphere was central to consumer demand and indispensable to accumulation and expansion (p. 29). There were also political as well as economic imperatives. The period from 1780 to 1850 was one of revolution, war, urbanization, and industrial expansion which threatened social and political order. Maintaining firm boundaries between masculinity and femininity not only upheld men's position of dominance but was also an important element in the struggle against this endemic disorder (p. 415). The ideology of the family and the centrality of domestic values in this increasingly dominant middle-class culture helped unite a class and mask its political, denominational, and gender differences (p. 179). Davidoff and Hall conclude that the first half of the nineteenth century seems to have been a period of close co-operation between middle-class men and women involved in building up the material, social, and religious base of their identity, battling for dominance and for the rightness of their world-view. Only when this view became a reality did women find their sphere isolated, trivialized, and unable to give the support it had promised (p. 454).

However, as Davidoff and Hall recognize, the history they describe was less neat than this, and a particular interest of their study is its amendment of the commonly received view of separate spheres for men and women. They show that this doctrine expressed an ideological divide rather than an actual separation. Social reproduction depended on the family and on women's labour. The family mediated between public and private spheres, connecting the market and the domestic in an elaborate set of relations. Indeed, the family remained the basis for much economic activity well into the nineteenth century (pp. 29–32). This interpenetration of family and production worked both ways. Not only was the family itself part of the market, but its religious and moral values framed and limited economic activity (p. 195). Nor was the middle-class home simply a haven for family withdrawal. It was a primary unit of consumption, a stage for social ritual and a manifestation of status (p. 362): 'Public was not really public and private not really private despite the potent imagery of "separate spheres".' Both were ideological constructs with historically specific meanings (p. 33).

Conclusion 243

As this would suggest, the stricter definition of gender roles which accompanied the division of public and private worlds was full of ambiguities. Women were dependent and fragile but, as mothers, were the keystone of the family. They were also household managers and often continued to contribute directly to the family enterprise (pp. 450–1). England was ruled by a queen who was mother to her people, and Davidoff and Hall argue that Victoria became an important model for the middle-classes. Tennyson's concern in *The Princess* with reconciling hereditary power and domesticated femininity was a contemporary preoccupation. Between women's subordination and their influence lay contested ground; roles were a matter of negotiation as well as acceptance (p. 117). As I have argued throughout this book, the discourse on family was never a closed one, and dominant ideas were frequently contested. On the evidence of the texts I have considered this would seem particularly true on the question of what constituted manliness and femininity.

The development of the market in fact opened new opportunites for women, and the insistence on separate spheres can be understood partly in relation to fears about these opportunities for independent economic activity (p. 275). In a way which illustrates just how complex these processes were, the same forces which defined femininity as antithetical to the market also opened up the public sphere and allowed middle-class feminists later in the century to press for admission to the new world created by their fathers and grandfathers (pp. 416,453). Although separate spheres for men and women became common sense in the social world of Victorian Britain, this common sense was riven with contradictions and the boundaries of female social action were never universally and passively accepted.

What was the role of literature in this process? Davidoff and Hall offer fascinating evidence of how literature mediated between private and public spheres, defining new modes of feeling and relationship, assisting in the social production of domestic ideology. Cowper and Hannah More are seen as important formative influences in the early-nineteenth century codification of middle-class beliefs and practices, but more interesting perhaps are their run-of-the-mill successors. These include John Player, some-time Mayor of Saffron Walden, whose book-length poem 'Home: or the Months, a Poem for Domestic Life' (1838) drew directly on Cowper's *The Task*, and his contemporary Bernard Barton, a Suffolk bank clerk, known nationally as the poet of domesticity (p. 178). My favourite is the Birmingham jeweller James Luckcock, who when he thought he was dying, wrote a poem entitled 'My Husband', which catalogued his own thoughtful and caring qualities in the voice of his wife:

> Whose manly conduct and good sense,
> From fickleness my sure defence,
> Encourag'd boundless confidence?
>   My Husband's.
>   (p. 328)[2]

Could Dickens have had this example in mind when in *Edwin Drood* he had Mr Sapsea inscribe his own virtues on his wife's gravestone?

In concentrating on the construction of a distinctive middle-class identity in the first of the nineteenth century, Davidoff and Hall are mainly interested in 'representative' literary texts which obviously reflected and helped constitute a dominant bourgeois domestic ideology. Their emphasis elsewhere, however, on the strains, contradictions, and contests within this whole discourse on family, makes clear how the texts I have discussed can be understood in relation to a poem such as 'My Husband', and more generally to the dominant values and practices of Victorian middle-class domestic life. As I argued in the opening chapter, no hegemony, however adaptive, can be total or exclusive, least of all in a rapidly changing society experiencing sharp class and gender division. If there was an unusual degree of consensus within the middle class and between its men and women in the early part of the nineteenth century, this was clearly coming under pressure by mid-century. As Davidoff and Hall show, even in these early decades there were struggles within definitions of gender roles and family practices. Although a dominant set of values developed and was codified, it was nevertheless constantly impelled to remake itself. One of the ways in which it did so was through what Foucault termed the incitement to discourse. Both Luckcock's 'My Husband' and Rossetti's *Goblin Market* (in one, the husband speaking for his wife; in the other, the husbands silent and invisible) are examples of this discursive explosion around family practices. One fits comfortably, not to say complacently, within

Conclusion

the dominant values of this discourse; the other has a contradictory relation to these, registering some of the ambiguities and tensions, even subverting what it seems to ratify. There was, in other words, nothing uniform or stable about the discourse on family. Nor was there simply an official and an illicit discourse ('Victorians' and 'other Victorians'). *Goblin Market*, which has been read as both nursery classic and pornography, exemplifies the shifting, fluid and overlapping nature of this discourse. What needs to be stressed is that resistance to dominant definitions of gender, love, marriage, and parent–child relations came not only from outside the hegemonic culture, from the feminist, secularist communalism of the Owenites for example, but also from within these dominant definitions themselves. To read these narrative poems and other related texts from within this field of discourse is to realize the complex and contradictory nature of their insertion.

The Bothie, like most of the poems discussed in this book, is a narrative of growing up. There was a newly urgent sense in the nineteenth century that growing up did not just happen of its own accord. Children and adolescents were tender plants requiring care and nurture if they were to grow up strong and tall. The middle-class family extended and problematized the growth to adulthood. This is why parenting and guardianship is such an important subject in several of these poems. *The Bothie* seems to reject conventional parenthood in favour of a more liberalized, attentive but unintrusive model of guardianship. Unlike the parent, the guardian stands off at a distance, ready to be called upon but reluctant to interfere. The relationship between Adam and Philip is uncontaminated by any blood tie, and this leaves Philip free to grow while remaining under tutelage which will prevent him from running wild. To Adam's moral direction is added Donald Mackaye's practical tuition. Free of parental authority and sanction, Philip can turn where he will for the guidance he needs without guilt or recrimination.

The problem of sexuality is never far from that of growing up. Like stolen goods it is difficult to handle, particularly when, as in Philip's case, it is necessary to go outside one's class for its transaction. In its treatment of the troubled relation between sexuality and class, and in its rejection of class as a basis for love, *The Bothie* is a radical and challenging poem. Here, as in its treatment of guardianship, it rejects many of the axioms of

Victorian family ideology. As we saw, it does so in terms of an earlier pre-industrial model of the family in which gender roles were overlapping rather than polarized and the family was organized around production rather than consumption. It is this backward-looking model of the family which permits the dominance of pastoral in the concluding books and its use as a mode of closure. There are, however, cross and counter-currents which trouble the text to the very end, and the closure effected by pastoral is incomplete. When in the final book Philip asks bewilderedly, 'where *is* the battle?' (Bk 9, l. 87) the text genuinely doesn't seem to know.

There are strong continuities between *The Bothie* and *The Princess*. Tennyson's poem is also preoccupied with parents, particularly fathers; of the two examples it offers, one is repressive and authoritarian, the other indulgent and feeble. Neither offers a satisfactory model of parenthood. In this poem, however, surrogates are less prominent. Ida creates her own family of sisters, prematurely and mistakenly as the poem would have it. The prince is left free to wander as he will in search of an authentic masculine identity. Although both poems are discourses on masculinity, *The Princess* treats gender as a relational concept and is therefore equally concerned with femininity. Uncertainty about sexuality and gender dominates all but the concluding sections of the poem. As gender roles are eventually clarified, sexuality ceases to be problematic, but the fluidity of gender and its uncertain relation to sexuality which the text has dramatized is at least as resonant as the resolution of gender difference on a reformed basis with which it leaves us. The 'midlands' marriage of northern prince and southern princess (Tennyson's 'North and South') does not entirely silence the wide range of positions on gender and marriage to which the poem has given voice. Marriage closes the inner narrative, but the young protagonists of the frame narrative are left contemplating their own and humanity's future. Although inner and frame narratives both offer models of marriage and family, the implications of Lilia's final disrobing of the statue of Sir Ralph are not entirely fixed. Burlesque and the mock-heroic disappear in the gathering darkness of the poem's peaceful but sombre conclusion, and the young Vivians and their friends are left looking towards an uncertain future. Marriage closes one narrative but not the other.

Conclusion

Aurora Leigh makes epic claims of a kind which *The Bothie* and *The Princess* have either mocked or used only with disabling self-consciousness, but which Lilia has yearned for. For the woman writer there is no problem in discovering where the battle is or which side to take; the field has been staked out for her. In *Aurora Leigh* writing itself becomes the main point of resistance to the pressures of middle-class family ideology. By focusing on writing, the poem challenges the reformed image of womanhood represented in *The Princess* and offers a more radical interrogation of prevailing ideas about femininity. At the same time it scrutinizes and reworks many of the narrative conventions common to *The Bothie*, *The Princess*, and other mid-century texts. Locked into debate with these male-authored texts, it is not surprising that it also has much in common with them. Parenthood is again a major subject. In the case of *Aurora Leigh*, however, the problem is not one of breaking free of parents but of the trauma of losing them. Aurora's fruitfully unorthodox parenting is most uncharacteristic of Victorian writing and is in itself a challenge to prevailing norms. It protects her from conventional middle-class socialization until she is orphaned, and enables her to survive this when she is taken in hand by her aunt, a version of the wicked step-parent. Recovery from the loss of her parents, and resistance to the world she is then exposed to, intersect with the writing theme to provide both the shape and substance of the narrative. But *Aurora Leigh*'s relation to the world it challenged should not be simplified. In speaking for women, it spoke mainly for middle-class women. In representing the need for radical change in gender relations and domestic practice, it rejected the social and political practices best able to bring about such change. And although its feminism challenged patriarchal politics, its individualism allowed it to be partly neutralized by high Victorian culture.

The clash of gender dramatized in both *The Princess* and *Aurora Leigh* is, in different ways, resolved. In *Goblin Market*, on the other hand, there is no reconciliation. Heterosexual marriage, the usual Victorian mode of narrative closure, is overwhelmed in a highly unorthodox poem of transgression in which redemption is won by further transgression. In so doing the poem also deconstructs the separation of home and market. Although it sets these in sharp opposition it also dramatizes their connectedness. Lizzie's triumph over the goblin men may seem to be a victory of domesticity over the market, but like *Modern Love*, the poem also demystifies the idea of the home as a protected and ordered space in a hostile competitive world. There is nothing inviolable about the home in *Goblin Market*. It is invaded by the influence of the goblin men, and far from being emptied of sex, it is actually redeemed by it. The poem in fact reveals the inseparability of public and private spheres.

Marriage is all but absent in *Goblin Market*, but in *Modern Love* it is claustrophobically inescapable. By taking marriage as a subject for narrative investigation rather than using it as a means of closure, *Modern Love* makes the resolution offered by earlier domestic narratives impossible. And, more thoroughly than *Goblin Market*, it dismantles the idea of the home as an isolated and protected enclave. Absent parents are a feature of all the earlier poems, but *Modern Love* is different in being a poem without children. In this poem we have the pared down middle-class family unable to reproduce itself, its barrenness a metaphor of its whole condition. There is nothing timeless about this condition. It represents a developed stage in the evolution of middle-class domesticity in which it no longer seems possible to conceive of alternative ways of living. For all its radical scepticism about nineteenth-century domestic values, *Modern Love* is more remorselessly within the discursive field I have surveyed than any of the other poems. It speaks of the impasse reached when life without marriage is inconceivable yet life within it is intolerable. The inability to conceive of any possibility other than marriage places it as firmly as any work of Victorian domestic economy. The codifications of one have produced the miseries of the other.

What needs finally to be emphasized is that these texts, and others I have discussed in relation to them, were not just *about* gender, marriage, and the family; they helped constitute them. The objects of a discourse and that discourse itself emerge together as part of the same process. Of course, marriage and the family existed before Victorian writers started producing narrative poems about them, but rather differently. The heightened significance of the family and domestic ideology in Victorian culture was inseparable from the discourse which grew up around them and helped constitute them. The texts I have discussed were not so much the products of shifts deep in Victorian society, superstructural expressions of fundamental changes in the social fabric, as a material part of these changes themselves. All literary texts are social practices and forms of material production. This emphasis was developed most strongly in Chapter 4, on *Aurora Leigh*, where I argued that the work was not just a reflection of contemporary debates about the social and legal position of women but a constitutive part of them. It has, however, been an underlying assumption of my readings of the other poems as well. It was also in the *Aurora Leigh* chapter where I argued that the social conditions of production of a text should include not only its originating condition but also those forces which keep the text current and make it contemporary. I have found this easier to demonstrate with poems like *Aurora Leigh* and *Goblin Market*, which have most obviously been reincorporated into various forms of sexual politics, but I believe it to be more generally true. Certainly, it has been a decisive influence on my choice of texts and methods of reading.

The writing and painting I have considered in this book suggest that in the nineteenth century the middle-class family became centrally important yet was also the source and object of deep insecurity and anxiety. Its importance heightened the anxiety, and the anxiety reinforced its importance. It would be possible to develop this more broadly and explore how the discourse around the family spread beyond the institutions and practices to which it specifically referred. 'Condition of England' novels, for example, quickly became family narratives. It is also clear that Victorian secular discourse found in the language of the family a rhetorical substitute for the loss of the Word. I have, by and large, followed a narrower path. The interlocking of discourses is a subject altogether too large for the limited scope of this book.

But my subject nevertheless has been a large one, namely the way in which affairs of the hearth became fundamentally important in the Victorian period. In focusing on how narrative poetry helped constitute this discourse, there was a risk of marginalizing my subject by concentrating on what might seem to have been a short-lived mutation, now a literary fossil. But it has also been my purpose to argue that these 'domestic epics', as Arnold dismissively labelled them, were neither ephemeral, predictable, nor short-lived. Clough and Barrett Browning's determination that poetry should engage with modern life has, in general terms, survived better than Arnold's universalist doctrine. Modernist poetry developed a different language and method to deal with modern existence, but this has too easily obscured the experimental and innovative character of these mixed-form narrative poems. Hybrid works, their mixing of form, modes, and registers shows that narrative self-consciousness, indirection, and uncertainty were not early twentieth-century discoveries. Modernist poetry was as much the development of tendencies already present in Victorian poetry as the repudiation of an outworn and naïve poetics.

Views of literary history necessarily change with time. In the late twentieth century there has been a renewed interest in the possibilities of narrative poetry, and at the time of writing even the verse-novel is making a reappearance.[3] These developments in form, along with the sexual politics of our time, therefore become further elements in the rereading, repossession, and making new of this group of Victorian narrative poems.

NOTES

1. Leonore Davidoff and Catherine Hall, *Family Fortunes: Men and Women of the English Middle Class 1780–1850* (London: Hutchinson, 1987). References to this book in the following pages are included in the text.
2. Davidoff and Hall include the whole poem in the Appendix.
3. Recent examples include Les Murray, *The Boys Who Stole the Funeral*, (Sydney: Angus & Robertson, 1980); Vikram Seth, *The Golden Gate*, (London: Faber, 1986); Marilyn Hacker, *Love, Death and the Changing of the Seasons*, (London: Onlywomen Press, 1987). Seth and Hacker's verse-novels are both written in sonnets.

INDEX

Acton, William, 137, 226; *The Functions of Disorders of the Reproductive Organs*, 12
Adams, Maurianne, 99
adolescence: crisis, 171, 172–5, 196–8, 200; to maturity, 50–62, 141–3, 149, 175, 245–6
adultery, 8, 226, 227
Allen, Grant, 211
Allingham, William, *Laurence Bloomfield in Ireland*, 36
amenorrhoea, 197
Anderson, Michael, 20, 229
androgyny theme, 155; in *The Princess*, 94–5, 100–102, 104, 107–8, 109–10
angel in the house imagery, 7, 36, 37, 68, 69, 139–40
anorexia, 196, 200–201
anti-marriage theme, 73, 201, 211, 218–19
Ariès, Philippe, 15; *Centuries of Childhood*, 26–7, 29
Armstrong, Isobel, 47; *Victorian Scrutinies*, 33, 85(n.7)
Arnold, Matthew, 58; on Clough, 45–7, 249; narrative poetry, 35, 36; *Poems (1853)*, 33–4, 45; *Preface*, 34, 45–7; *On Translating Homer*, 49, 50
Arnold, Thomas, 57–8, 59–60, 61, 62
art: life imitating (*Modern Love*), 208, 209; love and (*Aurora Leigh*), 148, 150–51, 153, 157, 163, 165
Art Journal, 78
Ashley, Lord, 18
Association for the Promotion of the Employment of Women, 137
Athenaeum, 130, 205
Auden, Wystan Hugh, 219
Auerbach, Nina, 103, 128(n.14), 139
Aurora Leigh (Barrett Browning): form, 35, 37, 92, 130–32, 133–5, 205; issues (context), 135–9, 249; issues (treatment), 72, 76, 102, 141–58, 247; literary context, 158–65; narrative summary, 132–3; rediscovery, 165–7; reviews, 134–5, 139–41, 157

Index

Austen, Jane, 21; *Mansfield Park*, 22, 23–4; *Persuasion*, 193, 195; *Sense and Sensibility*, 193, 195, 202(n.15)

Banks, J.A., 41(nn.67, 69), 168(n.21)
Banks, Olive, 41(n.69), 168(n.21)
Baring, Rosa, 124
Barmby, Catherine, 98
Barmby, Goodwyn, 98
Barrett, Edward (Bro), 199
Barrett, Michele, 42(n.74)
Bartlett, Phyllis B., 238(n.19)
Barton, Bernard, 244
Bayley, John, 238(n.7)
bedroom scenes (*Modern Love*), 211–13, 215–17
Beeton, Isabella, 225; *Englishwoman's Domestic Magazine*, 24; *Mrs Beeton's Book of Household Management*, 236
Behrman, Cynthia Fansler, 167(n.19)
Beldham (cricketer), 228
Besant, Annie, 236
bigamy theme, 2, 125
birth rate regulation, 13
Blackwoods

Edinburgh Magazine, 135, 139
Blake, William, 211
blinding motif, 99, 150, 163–4
Blunt, Wilfrid Scawen, *Esther*, 36
Boone, Joseph Allen, 238(n.18)
Bothie, The (Clough), 84, 137, 225; adolescence to maturity, 50–56, 175, 245–6; comparison with *Tom Brown's Schooldays*, 51, 57–62; cross-class marriage, 10, 51, 61, 64–78, 134, 162; form, 35, 48–50, 58–9, 78–83; narrative summary, 47–8; reviews, 44–7, 249; surrogate family, 51, 56, 59–64
Boulton, Ernest, 106
Boumelha, Penny, 102
bourgeoisie, *see* middle class
Bowkett, Jane Maria, 'Preparing Tea', 2, 4
boyhood theme (*The Bothie*), 57–61
Bradden, Mary, 210
Brierley, Ben, 'Go, Tak' thi Ragg'd Childer and Flit', 18, 19
British and Foreign Review, 110
British Quarterly Review, 33, 34

broken vows theme, 8, 217
Bronte, Charlotte, 7, 236; *Jane Eyre*, 22, 34, 60, 72, 99, 101, 133, 162, 163, 187, 195–6; *Shirley*, 34, 87(n.48), 100–102, 163, 193–4, 195; *Villette*, 51, 101
Bronte, Emily, 8; *Wuthering Heights*, 5–6, 7, 34, 195
Brown, Ford Madox: 'The Last of England', 8; *Take Your Son, Sir*, 138
Browning, Elizabeth Barrett, 67; family relationships, 130, 131, 156–7, 198–9; illness, 198–9; 'L.E.L.'s Last Question', 179; 'Lady Geraldine's Courtship', 130–31; narrative poetry, 34, 35, 36, 37; *Poems of 1844*, 130; reviews by, 44, 134; *see also Aurora Leigh* (Barrett Browning)
Browning, Robert, 31, 69; family relationships, 130, 131, 156–7; reviews by, 44; *The Ring and the Book*, 36–7
Browning, Robert Weidemann ('Pen'), 156–7
Burden, Jane, 68
Butler, Samuel, 63

Calderon, 'Broken Vows', 217

Index

capitalism, 11, 20, 34, 64, 75, 234, 242
Carlyle, Thomas, 34; *Chartism*, 79
Carroll, Lewis, *Alice in Wonderland*, 30, 170
Chaucer, Geoffrey, 228, 229
Cherry, Deborah, 87(n.45)
Cheyne Walk, 209
childbearing, 228
children: abuse of, 28, 29; boyhood, 57–61; childhood, concept of, 15, 26–30, 57; custody, 110, 114, 135, 136, 138; death, 208–9, 210, 216; in family tableaux, 1–7; to maturity, *see* adolescence; –parent relationship, 26–31, 245, 246, 247; sexuality, 182–3, 185
chlorosis (green sickness), 197
Christ, Carol, 68–9; *Victorian and Modern Poetics*, 32
Church of England, 173
Clarke, Joseph, 'The Labourer's Welcome', 2, 5–6
Clarke, Mary Cowden, *The Girlhood of Shakespeare's Heroines*, 139
class: adolescence/boyhood and, 57, 245; cross-class marriage, 10, 51, 61, 64–78, 132–3, 134, 162; exploitation, 68, 69, 73, 77, 165; reversal, 104, 105; *see also* middle class; working class
'class body', 13–14
Cline, C.L., 238(n.10)
Clinton, Lord Arthur, 106
clothing: gender roles and, 143, 154–7; restrictive, 72, 98–9, 102–3; transvestism, 94–6, 97–110
Clough, Arthur Hugh: *Amours de Voyage*, 83–5, 176, 210; narrative poetry, 34, 35, 36, 37; 'Natura Naturans', 54, *see also Bothie, The* (Clough)
Cobbe, Frances Power, 236
Coleridge, Samuel Taylor, 'Frost at Midnight', 30
Collier, John, 'The Prodigal Daughter', 206
Collins, Wilkie, *The Woman in White*, 102–4, 187
Comfort, Alex, 29
Communist Church, 98
Connor, Steven, 184
Conrad, Peter, 6, 8
consumption (illness), 191
Cook, E.T., 168(n.28)
Cornforth, Fanny, 67, 208
courtship narratives, 210, 217
Cowper, William, 243; *The Task*, 244
Crabbe, George, 131; *The Parting Hour*, 35
Craig, Hardin, 32
Cranbrook group, 142
cross-class marriage, *see* marriage
Cruikshank, George, *The Drunkard's Children*, 217
Crump, R.W., 170
Cullwick, Hannah, 51, 65–8, 69–78, 79, 105
custody rights, 110, 114, 135, 136, 138
Darwin, Charles, 31
Davidoff, Leonore, 68, 69, 72, 77, 78; *Family Fortunes*, 127(n.4), 240–44
death: child, 208–9, 210, 216; elegiacs, 24, 83, 84, 85, 120; imagery, 146, 147; impulse, 174, 175, 176; of spouse, 30, 232; suicide, 179, 204, 208–9, 210, 216–17, 222–3; unrequited love and, 191, 193, 194; wasting illness, 171, 175, 191–201
de Mause, Lloyd, 15
desire: appetite and, 178, 181; frustration/repression, 171,

172, 180–81, 182; gratification, 184; 190–91
dialect literature, 18
diaries: childhood, 27–9; Josselin's 227; Munby's, 51, 65–8, 69–78, 79, 104–5, 107
Dickens, Charles, 68, 160; *David Copperfield*, 4, 7, 30, 34, 60, 69, 100–102, 137, 151, 164–5; *Dombey and Son*, 4–5, 6, 22, 34; *Great Expectations*, 21–2; *Little Dorrit*, 17–18, 78; *The Mystery of Edwin Drood*, 107, 162, 244; *The Old Curiosity Shop*, 30; *A Tale of Two Cities*, 17
Disraeli, Benjamin, *Sybil*, 76
divorce, 135–6, 137, 138, 226
Divorce Act (1857), 136
Dixie, Lady Florence, *Gloriana*, 108
Dobell, Sydney, *Balder*, 37
domestic: ideology, 5–7, 10, 19, 25, 236, 243–4, 246–8; interiors, 21–3; matters (preoccupation), 16–18, 78–80
domesticity, 24–5, 241, 248; art and, 148, 153; feminism and, 26, 120, 243

Donne, John: 'The Extasie', 231;
Donoghue, Denis, 207, 224
Donzelot, Jacques, 26
Doughty, Oswald, 238(n.14)
dream narratives, 177–9
Duffin, Lorna, 197, 203(n.35)
Du Maurier, George, 109
Dunn, Douglas, *Elegies*, 232

Eagleton, Terry, 126, 138–9, 140, 141
eating, illness and, 195–6, 200–201
Ecclesiastical Commissioners, 75
Edelstein, T.J., 238(n.21)
Edmond, Rod, 24, 239(n.33)
education, 27, 119
Egg, Augustus, *Past and Present*, 17, 114–16, 142, 206, 208, 212, 217
Egley, William Maw: 'Aurora Leigh', 139, 142 *Military Aspirations*, 142; *Omnibus Life in London*, 139
elegies, 232
Eliot, George, 152, 209; *Adam Bede*, 160; comparison with Barrett Browning, 158–61; *Daniel Deronda*, 30, 199, 210; *Middlemarch*, 22, 24, 30, 50,

107–8, 160, 210, 225; *The Mill on the Floss*, 7, 107–8, 163, 176; *Silas Marner*, 99
Eliot, T.S., 31, 42(n.92); *The Waste Land*, 205
Ellis, Sarah Stickney, 25, 236
emigration theme, 8, 79–80, 162
employment of women, 135, 137, 138, 140, 151–2, 154
Englishwoman's Journal, 137
epics: *Aurora Leigh* as, 92, 133–4; mock, 48, 50, 92
epistolary narrative, 83, 85
Eve imagery, 218

fairy tale, 96; *Goblin Market* as, 170, 177–9, 181
fallen woman theme, 8, 53–4, 137, 160–62, 164, 208, 216
family: conflict, 7–8, 123–4, 125–6; disturbance/reconstitution, 110–19; history, 2, 19–21; ideology, 5–7, 10, 19, 25, 236, 243–4, 246–8; middle class, 12–19, 62–4, 240–43; nuclear, 15, 20, 21, 22, 27, 29, 30, 31, 189 pre-industrial, 79–80, 229, 246; reformation, 240–50; rituals, 2,

Index

22, 173, 186; relationships transposed, 4–5, 142; surrogate, 51, 56, 59–64, 245, 246; tableaux, 1–7, 112–13, 114–16, 189–91; working class, 2, 18–19; *see also* home; parents
father-daughter relationships, 4–5, 17–18, 142–3, 144, 146, 148, 247
father returning home, 1–2, 4, 17–18, 125, 153
Faucit, Helen (Mrs Martin), 105
female: relationships, 185–7; sexuality, 13, 196–8, 200–201, 226–7; stereotypes, 108, 153, 217–19, 227; transvestism, 99–101, 104–5, 107; *see also* feminism; femininity; women
feminism, 108, 110, 119, 123, 126, 170; *Aurora Leigh* and, 165–7; as challenge, 93–4, 96–7, 98–9, 100, 108, 111, 124; domesticity and, 26, 120, 243; motherhood and, 114, 115, 117; Owenite, 236–7
femininity: marriage, 94–6, 243; masculinity and (union), 94–5, 98, 100–102, 104, 107–10; redefined, 98, 100–105, 107; social construction, 147–8, 157–8, 241, 243, 247
feudal society, 119 *bis*
Fielding, Henry: *Joseph Andrews*, 49–50; *Tom Jones*, 23, 229–30, 232
Flandrin, Jean-Louis, *Families in Former Times*, 21, 22, 24
food, illness and, 195–6, 200–201
Foucault, Michel, 196, 244; *The History of Sexuality*, 11–14, 19
Fraser's Magazine, 33
Freeman, Edward Augustus, 235
Frewin, Mrs, *The Inheritance of Evil*, 136
Frith, W.P.: 'Many Happy Returns of the Day', 2; 'The Road to Ruin', 8
Furnivall, F.J., 66

Gaskell, Elizabeth, 236; 'Lizzie Leigh', 137; *Mary Barton*, 7, 34, 79–80, 99, 137; *North and South*, 163–4; *Ruth*, 133, 137, 160
Gelpi, Barbara Charlesworth, 157, 158, 168 (n.40)
gender roles: clothing and, *see* clothing;

differentiation, 25, 29, 57, 77, 241–50; genre and, 91, 92; as marriage determinant, 94–7; reversal, 101–2, 104, 105, 109; sexuality and, 94–110, 126, 246; *see also* female; feminism; male; masculine
gender theme (in *Aurora Leigh*), 141, 143, 147–8, 153–7, 162–4
genre paintings, 2–3, 4, 5–6, 112, 206, 216–17; narrative-pictorial style, 16–18, 113–14, 206
Germ, The, 36
Gilbert, Sandra M., 127 (n.3)
Gissing, George, 211; *New Grub Street*, 152
Glover, Alice, 203 (n.32)
Goblin Market (Rossetti): as allegory, 170, 181, 201; dream narratives, 177–9; fairy tale, 170, 177, 178–9, 181; form, 35, 37, 172–3, 176–9; illness theme, 191–201; readings of, 170, 185, 190, 244–5; recurring patterns, 171–81; sexuality theme, 176, 178, 181–91, 196, 247–8; two sisters pattern, 171, 179–81

goblin men, 171, 181–5, 188–91, 200–201, 247–8
Going, William, 43, (n.105), 202(n.18)
Golden, Arline, 207
Goode, John, 84
Goody, Jack, 20
Gramsci, A., 9
Graves, Algernon, 168(n.29)
green sickness, 197
Greenham Common, 141
Grey, Charles, Earl, 108
Grey, Margaretta, 108
Grylls, Rosalie Glynn, 87(n.44)
guilt, 75, 82, 146, 180; about writing, 173–5, 176; sexuality and, 53–4, 56

Hacker, Marilyn, 250(n.3)
Hall, Catherine, *Family Fortunes*, 127(n.4), 240–44
Hardy, Barbara, 167 (n.10)
Hardy, Emma, 208
Hardy, Thomas, 23, 211; *The Hand of Ethelberta*, 152; *Jude the Obscure*, 108, 176, 214; *A Pair of Blue Eyes*, 102, 152; *Poems of 1912–13*, 208, 232; *Tess of the d'Urbevilles*, 108
Haley, Bruce, 57
Hayter, Alethea, 167 (nn.7, 8), 203 (n.44), 205

hegemonic culture, 9–11, 13–14, 16, 26, 242, 244, 245
heroic qualities, 92, 100, 156
heterosexuality, 13, 26, 77, 95, 186, 247
Hewitt, Margaret, 40 (n.43)
hexameters, 83; in *The Bothie*, 49, 66
Hill, Christopher, 239(n.40)
Hogarth, William, 113
home: public/private space, 21–3; survival, 188–9, 190–91
Homer, 180; *Iliad*, 49
homosexuality, 105, 107, 109, 185
Hood, Thomas, 'The Bridge of Sighs', 137
Hopkins, Gerard Manley, 202 (n.12)
Houghton, Walter, *The Victorian Frame of Mind*, 7, 8, 15
Household Words, 137
Hudson, Derek, 76, 77, 86 (n.22), 128 (n.15)
Hughes, Arthur, *Aurora Leigh's Dismissal of Romney*, 139, 142, 144–5, 156
Hughes, Thomas, *Tom Brown's Schooldays*, 51, 57–62, 78–9
Hunt, Holman: 'The Awakened Conscience', 138; 'Claudio and Isabella', 17
Hunt, John Dixon, 112
Hutton, R.H., 206
hysteria, 196, 197, 198–9, 200

ideology, *see* domestic; family
illness, 171, 174–5, 185, 191–201
individualism, 15, 234, 247
industrialization, 34, 64, 75
infidelity, 217; adultery, 8, 226; 227
inheritance theme, 20
Irwin, Michael, 23

James, Alice, 198, 199–200
James, Henry, 37, 200; *What Maisie Knew*, 30, 103
James, William, 199, 200
Jerrold, Douglas, *The Rent Day*, 113
Johnson, Diane, 238 (n.14)

Kaplan, Cora, 133–4, 164, 167(n.8), 178, 196, 201(n.2)
Keats, John, 'Ode to a Nightingale', 214
Kemble, J.M., 110, 117, 235
Kenyon, Frederic G., 167(n.2)
Ker, W.P., 37

Index

Kilham, John, 110, 127 (n.2)
King, Henry, 'Exequuy', 232
Kingsley, Charles: *Alton Locke*, 22, 34; *Yeast*, 34
Kintner, Elvan, 167 (n.6)
Kunzle, David, 98–9, 109

Landon, Letitia Elizabeth, 179
language: clash of, 120–22; of family, 61–2; of *Goblin Market*, 185, 187, 190; of women writers, 140–41, 157–8
Lasch, Christopher, 25; *The Culture of Narcissism*, 26; *Haven in a Heartless World*, 26
Laslett, Peter, 20
Lerner, Laurence, 120, 122
L'Esperance, J., 78
Lewes, G.H., 134, 209
Lewis, C.S., *The Allegory of Love*, 231
Liddon, H.P., 201 (n.10)
Life, Allen R., 201 (n.4)
Lindsay, Jack, 238 (n.12)
Lister, Raymond, 8, 168(n.39)
long engagements, 8
Longfellow, Henry Wadsworth, *Evangeline*, 49
love: art and, 148, 150–51, 153, 157, 163, 165; death of, 209–25, 230; family conflict, 123–4, 125–6; female closeness, 185–7; illness and, 191, 193, 194–5, 200–201; marriage, 162, 230, 231–2, 235; pre-marital, 210, 217, 226; romantic, 177, 178, 226, 235; socialization, 83–5, 123
Lowry, H.F., 85(n.4)
Lucas, John, 207, 224, 238(n.3)
Luckcock, 'My Husband', 244
Lutman, Stephen, 38 (n.4)
Lytton, Edward Bulwer, 36; *Eva, or the Unhappy Marriage*, 35, 131
Lytton, Robert (Owen Meredith), *Lucile*, 36

Macaulay, Thomas Babington, 33
Macfarlane, Alan, 27, 230–32; *Marriage and Love in England*, 227–9, 233–5, 239(n.24) 240; *The Diary of Ralph Josselin*, 239 (n.24) *The Origins of English Individualism*, 234, 239(n.24)
McGann, Jerome J., 172, 179
McIntosh, Mary, 42 (n.74)
MacLeod, Sheila, 203 (n.34)
maiming motif, 99, 163–4
male: absence from *Maude*, 172–3, 182; chauvinism, 94, 96, 114, 126; goblins, *see* goblin men; sexuality, 68–9; *see also* masculinity
Malthus, Robert, 234; *Essay on Population*, 228–9
marriage: anit- (theme), 73, 201, 211, 218–19; arranged, 93, 123–4, 162, 225, 229–30; break-up, *see* divorce; choice, 23–4, 225, 228, 230, 235; companionate, 23–4, 26, 93, 97, 225, 227–8, 231–2, 235; cross-class, 10, 51, 61, 64–78, 132–13, 134, 162; determinants, 94–7; discord, 8; economic, 23, 229–30, 232; failed, 211–37, 248; lineage, 23–4; love, 162, 230, 231–2, 235; as narrative closure, 95–6, 210, 246, 247; relationships, 23–6; socialization of love by, 83–5
Marriage and Divorce Bill (1854), 135, 137, 138

Married Woman's Property Bill, 136, 138
Marsh, Jan, 87(n.45)
Marston, J.W., 205, 206
Martin, Emma, 237
Martineau, Harriet, 236
Martineau, Robert, 8; 'The Last Day in the Old Home', 217
Marxist theory, 9, 39, (n.24)
masculinity, 246; femininity and (union), 94–5, 98, 100–102, 104, 107–10; marriage determinants and, 94–6, 97; problems of, 68–9, 73, 75; social construction of, 157–8, 241
masturbation, 29
maturity, journey to, 50–62, 149
Mayhew, Henry, 138
medicalization of female sexuality, 13, 196–8, 200–201, 226–7
'Medusa image, 218
Meisel, Martin, 8, 35, 113, 114–15, 206; *Realizations*, 16–17, 18
Meredith, George: *Diana of the Crossways*, 151; 'London by Lamplight', 137; *Poems*, 1851, 137; see also *Modern Love* (Meredith)

Meredith, Owen (Robert Lytton), *Lucile*, 36
Mermin, Dorothy, 184, 207, 208
middle class: culture, 13–14, 15, 63–4; deployment of sexuality, 12–14; family history, 2, 19–21; family identity, 240–43; marriage (changes), 224–35; marriage (cross class), see marriage; private/public space, 21–3; relationships, 23–31; values, 9–11, 18–19, 25
Millais, Sir John Everett: 'The Order of Release', 17; *Retribution*, 206; *Virtue and Vice*, 138
Miller, Betty, 167 (n.3)
Milton, John, 33, 100; 'Methought I saw my late espoused saint', 232; *Paradise Lost*, 133
Mitchison, Rosalind, 232
Mitford, Mary Russell, 130, 131, 132, 140–41
mixed-genre writing, 35–7, 250; in *The Bothie*, 48–50; in *Maude*, 172–3, 176–9; 'medley' principle, 119–23; tensions, 80–81, 82–3

mock-epic, 48, 50, 92
Modern Love (Meredith): cultural context, 224–35; form, 35, 36, 204–7; marriage (reality), 235–7; marriage system (change), 224–35; marriage theme, 211–24, 248; origins/context, 207–11; reviews, 205–7; sexuality theme, 207, 209, 215–16, 226–7
Modernism 31, 32, 33, 37, 205, 249–50
Moers, Ellen, 92, 152, 156, 158, 167 (n.8), 182–3, 185
Moi, Toril, 109–10, 128 (n.29)
monogamy, 26, 227, 228
Montagu, Lord Robert, 67
Moore, Tom, 'Come, Rest in this Bosom', 17
More, Hannah, 243
Morley, John, 238 (n.20)
Morning Chronicle, 138
Morris, William, 35
mother-daughter relationship, 173
'mother-want' (*Aurora Leigh*), 146, 147
motherhood, 110, 146–9, 159; feminism and, 114, 115, 117
Mulhauser, F.L., 86 (n.14)

Index

multiple framing, 114
Munby, Arthur: *Benoni*, 75; diaries, 51, 65–79, 104–5, 107
Murray, Janet Horowitz, 237; *Strong-Minded Women*, 128(n.27), 236, 239(n.22)
Murray, Les, 250 (n.3)

narrative: paintings, 7–9, 112, 249; - pictorial style, 16–18, 113–14; poetry, 16–17, 33–7, 123–6, 249–50
narrator: frame, of *The Princess* 90; of *Modern Love*, 207, 217, 219, 221–4
National Magazine, The, 24–5, 138
Nead, Lynda, 86 (n.22)
neurasthenia, 197
Newby, H., 78
Newcastle, Duke of, 106
Nicolls, Mary, 207–8, 209, 213
Nietzsche, Friedrich, 31
Nightingale, Florence, 51, 159, 236; *Cassandra*, 72, 174
North American Review, 43(n.103), 85(n.7)
North British Review, 134, 137, 138, 140
Norton, Caroline, 135–6, 138, 151, 236

novel-poems, 35–7, 130–33
novella, *Maude* as, 172
novels, 34, 35, 250
nursing theme, 93, 162

Oliphant, Margaret, 176, 211
O'Neil, Henry Nelson, 'Home Again', 2, 3, 17
Othello (character), 212–13
Owen, Robert, *Lectures on the Marriage of the Priesthood in the Old Immoral World*, 236
Owenite communities, 165, 236–7

Packer, Lona Mosk, 173, 176, 199
Palgrave, Francis, *Golden Treasury*, 31
parents: -child relationship, 26–31, 245–7; surrogate, 51, 56, 59–64, 245, 246; *see also* father-daughter relationship, mother-daughter relationship; mother-want, motherhood
Park, Frederick, 106
pastoral mode, 246; *Amours de Voyage*, 84–5; *The Bothie*, 48–9, 50, 58–9, 71, 74–5, 78–83;

Modern Love, 220; *The Princess*, 118–19
Patmore, Coventry, 68, 134, 138, 232; *The Angel in the House*, 36, 37, 69, 139–40; *The Victories of Love*, 36
patriarchy, 15, 133–4, 148, 247
Peacock, Thomas Love, 207; *Four Ages of Poetry*, 33
pets (use of), 2, 5–6
Playboy, 170, 185, 191
Player, John, 243
Podsnappery, 233
politics: of marriage, 84, 126; sexual, 165–6, 235, 236–7, 249
Pollock, Griselda, 87(n.45)
Pollock, Linda, 228; *Forgotten Children*, 27–30
pornography, 12, 170, 185
Pound, Ezra, 31, 32
power: exploitation, 68, 69, 73, 77, 165; patriarchal, 16, 26, 165, 236; relations, 25–6; sexuality and, 11–12
Pre-Raphaelites, 67–8, 69, 73, 75, 114, 139, 182
Princess, The (Tennyson): comparisons, 123–6; Elizabeth Barrett Browning on, 132, 134, 140, 162–3; family

Index

disturbance/reconstitution, 110–19; form, 35, 36, 90–94, 205, 231; gender roles, 94–7, 134, 243, 246–7; 'medley' principle, 119–23; readings, 126–7; transvestism motif, 97–110
private/public spheres, 211–12; divison of, 21–3, 242–3, 248; private reality and, 204, 213–16, 225
property rights, 15, 25, 135–6, 137, 138
prostitution, 8, 53–4, 135, 137–8
public sphere, *see* private/public sphere
Punch, 109

Rackham, Arthur, 203(n.30)
relationships: father-daughter, 4–5, 17–18, 142–3, 144, 146, 148, 247; marriage, 23–6; mother-daughter, 173; parent-child, 26–31, 245, 246, 247; sister-brother, 182–3, 184; sisters, 171, 179–80, 181
religion, 8, 9, 181
religious vocation, 173, 175–6, 178–80, 182
repression-liberation model, 14–16
'repressive hypothesis', 11–12, 14
Richardson, Samuel, 141; *Clarissa*, 23, 139, 140
Ricks, Christopher, 119, 120, 124, 127 (n.1)
Roberts, Helene E., 38(n.1), 89(n.75)
Romanticism, 31
Rosenblum, Dolores, 157, 168(n.40)
Rossetti, Christina, 37; 'The Convent Threshold', 178; 'Cousin Kate', 180; 'From House to Home', 178; illness, 198, 199; 'L.E.L.', 179; 'The Lowest Room', 179–80; *Maude*, 152, 172–7, 179, 182, 191, 197, 199; 'My Dream', 177–8; 'Noble Sisters', 180; *The Prince's Progress*, 178, 191; recurring patterns, 171–7; 'Sister Maude', 180; 'A Triad' 194; 'The World', 181; *see also* Goblin Market (Rossetti)
Rossetti, Dante Gabriel, 76, 179, 203(n.30); 'Found', 138; 'Jenny', 137; Meredith and, 208–9; Pre-Raphaelites, 67–8, 69, 73, 75, 114, 139, 182; *The Wife's Tragedy*, 209
Rossetti, W.M., 167 (n.16), 172, 173, 199, 202(n.16)
Royal Academy, 139, 206, 208
Ruskin, John, 8, 68, 69, 74, 107; *The Elements of Drawing*, 139; 'Of Queens' Gardens', 7; *Sesame and Lilies*, 7

Sand, George, 135, 155–6, 161; *Consuelo*, 133
Sandford, Mrs John, 25
Scott, Patrick, 38(n.3), 61, 83, 85
Scott, William Bell, 135, 173
seduction, 8, 11, 53–4, 181, 218, 238(n.18)
self-role conflict, 107–8, 111–12, 222
Seth, Vikram, 250(n.3)
sexual politics, 165–6, 235–7, 249
sexuality, 29, 147, 245; awakening, 51–6, 61; child, 182–3, 185; deployment of, 12–14, 196–7; female, 13, 196–8, 200–201, 226–7; gender roles and, 94–6, 97–110, 126, 246; In *Goblin Market*, 176, 178, 181–91, 196, 247–8; male, 68–9; in *Modern Love*, 207, 209, 215–16,

226–7; power and, 11–12; *see also* androgyny theme; heterosexuality; homosexuality; transvestism
Shakespeare, William, 105, 139
Shanley, Mary Lyndon, 167(n.18)
Shaw, David, 120
Sheridan, Alan, 12, 39(n.25)
Shorter, Edward, *The Making of the Modern Family*, 15, 27, 41(n.55)
Showalter, Elaine, 163
Siddall, Elizabeth, 67, 68, 174, 208–9
sister-brother relationship, 182–3, 184
sisters, 184–5, 187–90, 201; religious sisterhood, 173, 175–6, 178–80, 182; two (pattern), 171, 179–80, 181
Smith, Alexander, 47; *A Life Drama*, 36, 45
Smith, Barbara Leigh, 136; 'Women and Work', 137
Smith-Rosenberg, Carroll, 185–6, 187–8, 197–8
Smithyman, Kendrick, 181, 182
social class, *see* class
social order, 78, 117–19, 123–5, 210
socialism, 165, 236

Solomon, 'Waiting for the Verdict', 17
sonnets (*Modern Love*), 204–37
Spasmodic poets, 36
Spectator, The, 206
Spenser, Edmund, 231
spousal unity doctrine, 136, 137
Staël, Madame de, *Corinne*, 133, 148
Stanfield, Clarkson, 'The Abandoned', 17
Stanhope, Spenser, 'Thoughts of the Past', 138
Stanley, Liz, 69, 87(n.42)
Steinmetz, Virginia V., 157, 168(n.40)
Sterling, John, 34
Stevenson, Lionel, 238(n.12)
Stone, Lawrence, 229, 240; *The Family, Sex and Marriage in England, 1500–1800*, 14–16, 21, 22
Stowe, Harriet Beecher, 159
Strachey, Lytton, 32
Strachey, Ray, 25, 86(n.18), 168(n.22), 201(n.9)
Stubbs, William, 235
suicide, 179, 204, 208–9, 210, 216–17, 222–3
Super, R.H., 86(n.16)
Swinburne, Algernon Charles, 105, 165, 206, 209

Taplin, Gardner B., 167(n.1), 203(n.44)
Taylor, Barbara, *Eve and the New Jerusalem*, 127(n.5), 169(n.59), 236–7
Tennyson, Alfred, Lord, 68, 159; 'Aylmer's Field', 123, 124–5; 'Edwin Morris', 94, 122, 123; 'Enoch Arden', 1–2, 4, 6, 35, 125–6; 'The Flight', 124; *Idylls of the King*, 35; 'Locksley Hall', 94, 123, 124, 131; *Maud*, 47, 123, 124; 'The Miller's Daughter', 52; narrative poems, 31, 34, 35, 37; 'The Wreck', 124; *see also Princess, The* (Tennyson)
Thackeray, William Makepeace, 69; on *The Bothie*, 44–5; *Pendennis*, 34, 60, 151; *Vanity Fair*, 34, 51, 210
Thompson, E.P., 168(n.24); *The Making of the English Working Class*, 240
Thomson, Patricia, 155, 167(n.8)
Thorpe, Michael, 82(n.2)
tight-lacing, 98–9, 102–3

Tillotson, Geoffrey, 37, 42(n.96), 48, 86(n.15)
Tillotson, Kathleen, 85(n.12), 86(n.15), 168(n.20)
Time Out, 167
Times, The, 206
Tinker, C.B., 85(n.9)
transvestism, 94–6, 97–110
triptychs: Egg's, 114–16, 142, 206, 208, 212, 217; Tennyson's, 112–14, 115
Trollope, Anthony, 34; *The Way We Live Now*, 103, 151, 210
Turgenev, Ivan, 36

unisex clothing, 98

verse-novel, 35, 250
Vicinus, Martha, 18
Victoria, 216, 243
Victorians: normative values, 9–11; poetry (role), 31–7
village life, 58–9, 78, 79; *see also* pastoral mode
Virgil, *Eclogues*, 80
'vivid epitomes', 113, 115, 206

Waldfogel, Melvin, 8
Walker, Thomas, 104–5
Wallis, Henry: 'The Death of Chatterton', 208;
'Fireside Reverie', 207–8, 213
Walsh, J.H., *A Manual of Domestic Economy*, 24
'Walter', *My Secret Life*, 12
Wandor, Michelene, 164, 166–7
Ware, Martin, 203(n.30)
Watt, Stephen, 207
Watts, G.F., 'Found Drowned', 138, 216
Waugh, Edwin, 'Come Whoam to thy Childer and Me', 18–19
Webster, Thomas, 142
Wedderburn, Alexander, 168(n.28)
wedlock narrative, 210, 217
Weeks, Jeffrey, 19, 25, 26, 39(n.25), 40(n.33), 61, 105, 202(n.25)
Westminster Review, 135
Whitman, Walt, 105
widowhood, 216
Wilkie, David: 'Distraining for Rent', 8, 113; 'The Rent Day', 113
Williams, Ioan, 238(n.2)
Williams, Raymond, 9–11, 16, 19, 166
Wilmers, Mary-Kay, 203(n.49)
Windus, W.L., 'Too Late', 191, 192

Wolfe, Humbert, 122
women: as artists, 158–9; creation of, 67–8, 69, 72–3, 76–7, 78; female relationships, 185–7; rights, 15–16, 25–6, 110, 135–6; status, 15–16, 138; work, 135, 137, 138, 140, 151–2, 154; writers, 133–5, 140–41, 166–7, 247
Women's Press, 166
Wood, Christopher, *Victorian Panorama*, 2, 8, 168(n.39)
Woolf, Virginia, 165, 166; *Orlando*, 108
Woolner, Thomas, *My Beautiful Lady*, 36
Wordsworth, William, 35, 130; *Lyrical Ballads*, 30; *The Prelude*, 30
working class, 165; family, 2, 18–19; marriage (cross-class), *see* marriage
Working Women's College, 66 *bis*
Wrightson, Keith, 27
writing theme, 141–2, 149–54, 173–5, 247; illness and, 197, 199, 200

Yeo, Eileen, 168(n.24)

Zaretsky, Eli, 64